Playing with Theory in Theatre Practice

Playing with Theory in Theatre Practice

Edited by

Megan Alrutz
Julia Listengarten

and

M. Van Duyn Wood

Introductions, selection, and editorial matter © Megan Alrutz,
Julia Listengarten, and M. Van Duyn Wood 2012
Individual chapters © Sarah Bay-Cheng, John Bell, Herbert Blau,
Carol Brown, Lenora Inez Brown, Stephen Di Benedetto, Laura R. Dougherty,
Harry Feiner, Mark Fortier, Dorita Hannah, Brook Hanemann, Michal Kobialka,
Julia Listengarten, John Lutterbie, Donald C. McManus, Bruce McConachie,
Alissa Mello, Christopher Niess, Michael Rohd, Shannon Scrofano,
Manon van de Water, S. E. Wilmer, Stephani Etheridge Woodson © 2012.

First published 2012 by
PALGRAVE MACMILLAN

Palgrave Macmillan in the UK is an imprint of Macmillan Publishers Limited,
registered in England, company number 785998, of Houndmills, Basingstoke,
Hampshire RG21 6XS.

Palgrave Macmillan in the US is a division of St Martin's Press LLC,
175 Fifth Avenue, New York, NY 10010.

Palgrave Macmillan is the global academic imprint of the above companies
and has companies and representatives throughout the world.

Palgrave® and Macmillan® are registered trademarks in the United States,
the United Kingdom, Europe, and other countries.

ISBN 978–0–230–57779–4   hardback
ISBN 978–0–230–57780–0   paperback

This book is printed on paper suitable for recycling and made from fully
managed and sustained forest sources. Logging, pulping, and manufacturing
processes are expected to conform to the environmental regulations of the
country of origin.

A catalogue record for this book is available from the British Library.

A catalog record for this book is available from the Library of Congress.

10   9   8   7   6   5   4   3   2   1
21 20 19 18 17 16 15 14 13 12

Printed in China

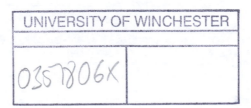

To our mothers, whose balance of intuition and intellect inspires our every day

Contents

List of Illustrations

Acknowledgments

The editors and publisher wish to thank the following for permission to reproduce copyrighted material:

- The University of Minnesota Press for permission to include excerpts from "Elsinore: An Analytic Scenario" by Herbert Blau, originally published in 2002 in *The Dubious Spectacle: Extremities of Theater, 1976–2000.*
- Herbert Blau for his photograph and poster image from *Elsinore.*
- Matthew Brandt for his photographs of *Marisol.*
- Sarah Burrell for her photographs of *Tongues of Stone.*
- Robert Catto for his photograph of *Aarero Stone.*
- Harry Feiner for his photograph of *Waiting for Godot.*
- Fotis Traganoudakis for his photographs of *Her Topia.*
- Tim Trumble Photography, Inc. and Tim Trumble for his photograph of *Venus.*

The editors would also like to acknowledge the support of the University of Central Florida and the University of Texas at Austin. We thank these institutions for supporting our research and creative endeavors and providing us with the necessary resources to complete this project. Our graduate assistant Elizabeth Brendel Horn offered us invaluable assistance during multiple stages of the book's development and her perspective proved essential to our work on this collection. Our graduate students from Research Methods, Theory and Criticism, Contemporary Theatre Practice, and Design Seminar inspired the idea for this book; their questions, concerns, and ideas influenced the shape of this collection and we appreciate their willingness to play with multiple possibilities around converging theory and practice. Our artistic collaborators at the University of Central Florida, the Orlando Repertory Theatre, and the Eugene O'Neill Theatre Center further encouraged us to experiment with theory in production, and we are grateful for their creative input.

We would like to thank Kate Haines, Felicity Noble, and Jenni Burnell from Palgrave Macmillan for their generous guidance and insight throughout every stage of this process. Our sincere thanks go to our readers whose feedback and constructive criticism encouraged us to think "outside the box" and to move forward with this book project. We also thank ATHE,

SETC, and PSi participants from our roundtable sessions and workshops for challenging our ideas and sharing personal experiences with theory in their own theatre-making processes. Our special appreciation also goes to our contributors who agreed to tackle this elusive topic and expanded our understanding of theory in practice through their theoretical discussions and case studies.

Finally, we would like to express our heartfelt gratitude to our families and friends who contributed much needed space and time to our writing and editing.

Notes on Contributors

Sarah Bay-Cheng is Associate Professor of Theatre at the University at Buffalo and an affiliated faculty member in the Departments of Media Study and English. Her research interests include avant-garde theatre and film, modernism and theatre, and digital media and theatre. Publications include *Mama Dada: Gertrude Stein's Avant-Garde Theater* (Routledge, 2005), *Poets at Play: An Anthology of Modernist Drama* (Susquehanna University Press, 2010), and articles in the journals *Theatre Journal, Theater Topics, International Journal of Art and Technology*, among others. Her current book projects focus on the intersections of digital media and theatre performance.

John Bell is Chair of the Performing and Fine Arts Department at DeSales University. Prior academic appointments include Musical Theatre Coordinator at the University of Central Florida, Director of Music Theatre and Opera at James Madison University and Assistant Professor of Voice and Movement at the University of Michigan-Flint. He holds an MFA in Musical Theatre from San Diego State University and a BM in Music from Ohio Wesleyan University.

Herbert Blau is Byron W. and Alice L. Lockwood Professor of the Humanities at the University of Washington. He has also had a parallel career in the theatre, as Co-Founder and Co-Director of the Actor's Workshop of San Francisco, then Co-Director of the Repertory Theater of Lincoln Center in New York, and as Artistic Director of the experimental group KRAKEN, the groundwork for which was prepared at California Institute of the Arts, of which he was founding Provost, and Dean of the School of Theater and Dance. His most recent books are *The Dubious Spectacle: Extremities of Theater, 1976–2000* (University of Minnesota Press, 2002), *Nothing in Itself: Complexions of Fashion* (Indiana University Press, 1999), and *Sails of the Herring Fleet: Essays on Beckett* (University of Michigan Press, 2000). He is currently working on *As If: An Autobiography* and *Reality Principles: From the Absurd to the Virtual*.

Carol Brown is a performer, choreographer, and Senior Lecturer in Dance Studies at NICAI, University of Auckland. Her work is practice-led and evolves through collaborative research with artists and scholars from other disciplines, in particular architecture, music, and media design. Her creative works include theatre performances, site-responsive interventions, performance installations, interactive dances and dance-architectures. Formerly Choreographer in Residence at the Place Theatre, London, Brown's works have toured throughout the world and she has received numerous awards including a Jerwood Award for Choreography, the Ludwig Forum Prize for Innovation and a NESTA Dream Time.

Lenora Inez Brown has served as Head of Dramaturgy and Dramatic Criticism at the Theatre School, DePaul University, and as President of Theatre for Young Audiences/USA Board. Her book *The Art of Active Dramaturgy: Transforming Critical Thinking into Dramatic Action* (Focus, 2010) defines and explores the philosophical approach dramaturgs often adopt. She has worked as a dramaturg for adult and youth theatre at: Sundance Theatre Lab 2000 and 2001, the Goodman Theatre, and the Kennedy Center's New Vision/New Voices. She has an MFA in Dramaturgy and Dramatic Criticism from the Yale School of Drama and a BA from Dartmouth College.

Stephen Di Benedetto is Assistant Professor of Theatre History & Theory at the University of Miami. Current research and publications explore scenographic design in various cultural contexts, and examine the ways in which the five senses are harnessed by artists in performance from a phenomenological perspective. His *The Provocation of the Senses in Contemporary Theatre* (Routledge, 2010) considers theatrical practice through the lens of contemporary neuroscientific discoveries and lays the foundation for considering the physiological basis of the power of theatre practice to affect human behavior. Selected essays and reviews have been published in *Theatre Research International, Performance Research, New Theatre Quarterly, Journal of Dramatic Theory and Criticism, and Scenography International.*

Laura R. Dougherty is a voice and speech practitioner and pedagogue. She has twice completed study with the Lessac Training and Research Institute, studying under Arthur Lessac. A professor at Winthrop University, she has also worked as a voice and speech coach and instructor at Arizona State and Drew Universities. A graduate of the doctoral program in Theatre and Performance of the Americas program at Arizona State University, her research interests include the interstices of post-coloniality and performance in the production of the Americas, focusing on using theatre—specifically Suzan-Lori Parks' *The America Play*—as a methodology for mapping linguistic and spatial borders of America, as well as investigations of race, gender, nostalgia and complicity in neo-burlesque performance.

Her work has been published in *The Humanities Review*, *Theatre Journal*, and in the forthcoming *Festive Performance: Staging Identity, Politics and Utopia in the Americas*.

Harry Feiner has designed for many theatre stages including the Pearl Theatre Company, the Pittsburgh Public Theatre, the Philadelphia Drama Guild, the McCarter Theatre, Syracuse Stage, Actors' Studio, and the North Carolina, New Jersey and Colorado Shakespeare Festivals. He designed opera for Central City Opera, the Philadelphia Opera Theatre, Syracuse Opera, Opera Theatre of Rochester, and Boston Lyric Opera, among others. His dance designs were seen on the stages of North Carolina Dance Theatre and the Pascal Rioult Dance Theatre. Feiner's past positions include Resident Designer for the Missouri Repertory Theatre (1980–4) and Principal Designer for the Lake George Opera Festival (1995–7). Feiner has taught at the North Carolina School of the Arts, University of Missouri at Kansas City, and Queens College, where he is currently a professor of theatre.

Mark Fortier is Director of the School of English and Theatre Studies at the University of Guelph. He is the author of *Theory/Theatre* (2nd edn, 2002) and co-editor of *Adaptations of Shakespeare: An Anthology of Plays from the Seventeenth Century to the Present* (Routledge, 2000). He also works on early-modern culture and law and literature, especially on theories of equity.

Dorita Hannah is an architect, scenographer and Professor of Spatial Design at Massey University's College of Creative Arts, where her research focuses on the intersection between space and performance. She has published on trans-disciplinary creative practices, including co-editing *Performance Design* and a themed issue on Performance/Architecture for the *Journal of Architectural Education*. Dr Hannah is actively aligned with Performance Studies International, OISTAT (International Organisation for Scenographers, Theatre Architects & Technicians) and the Prague Quadrennial. Her projects have gained awards and citations, including a UNESCO Laureate (1999), NZIA and DINZ Awards (1993–2007), the selection of her work for the International Archive of Women in Architecture (2003) and silver/gold medals at World Stage Design (2009).

Brook Hanemann taught theatre for five years at the Mississippi University for Women in Columbus where she was appointed the first Head of the Columbus Tennessee Williams Foundation. She formerly served as Executive Producer/Artistic Director for the Orlando International Fringe Festival and acted as VIP Coordinator and Filmmaker Liaison for the

Florida Film Festival. She has performed, produced, and directed across the south-eastern United States with companies such as Redmoon Theatre Joint, Mad Cow, the Vine, and Soulfire Traveling Medicine Show. She is currently working toward her PhD in theatre literature, history, criticism, and theory at the Louisiana State University in Baton Rouge.

Michal Kobialka is Professor of Theatre in the Department of Theatre Arts & Dance at the University of Minnesota. He is the author of two books on Tadeusz Kantor's theatre, *A Journey Through Other Spaces: Essays and Manifestos, 1944–1990* (University of California Press, 1993) and *Further on, Nothing: Tadeusz Kantor's Theatre* (University of Minnesota Press, 2009). He is the editor of *Of Borders and Thresholds: Theatre History, Practice, and Theory* (University of Minnesota Press, 1999) and a co-editor (with Barbara Hanawalt) of *Medieval Practices of Space* (University of Minnesota Press, 2000). His book on the early medieval drama and theatre, *This is My Body: Representational Practices in the Early Middle Ages* (University of Michigan Press, 1999) received the 2000 ATHE Annual Research Award for Outstanding Book in Theatre Practice and Pedagogy.

Julia Listengarten is Associate Professor and Director of Graduate Studies at the University of Central Florida. Her research interests include avant-garde theory and performance, translation theory, and nationalism. Her translation of *Christmas at the Ivanovs'* premiered Off-Broadway at Classic Stage Company and was included in *Theater of the Avant-Garde, 1890–1950*. She is the author of *Russian Tragifarce: Its Cultural and Political Roots* (Susquehanna University Press, 2000) and co-editor of *Theater of the Avant-Garde: 1950–2000* (Yale University Press, 2011). She has contributed to various books and theatre periodicals including *Theatre Research International*, *Slavic and Eastern European Performance*, and *Scenography International*.

John Lutterbie is Professor at Stony Brook University where he teaches the history of performance art and performance theory. He is the author of *Hearing Voices: Modern Drama and the Problem of Subjectivity* (University of Michigan Press, 1997) and numerous articles in such journals as *Theatre Journal*, *Journal of Dramatic Theory and Criticism*, *Theatre Topics*, *Modern Drama*, and others. His current project is *The Embodied Mind in Acting: Cognitive Studies and Performance*, where he explores the language used to talk about acting from the perspective of the cognitive sciences and dynamics systems theory.

Donald C. McManus is Assistant Professor and Resident Artist at Emory University. He has worked professionally as an actor, director, musician, and clown in Canada, the US, Asia, and Europe. His research and teaching interests include: popular entertainment, twentieth-century theatre, foreign plays in translation, dramaturgy, physical theatre, intercultural and multimedia performance. His book *No Kidding! Clown as Protagonist in Twentieth-Century Theater* (University of Delaware Press, 2003) was a Choice Award, winning Outstanding Academic Title in 2004. *The World-Fixer*, his English version of Thomas Bernhard's German-language play *Der Weltverbesserer*, was published by Ariadne Press in 2005.

Bruce McConachie is Chair of Theatre Arts at the University of Pittsburgh. As a scholar, he has published widely in the areas of American theatre history, performance historiography, and cognitive studies and theatre. His major books include *Interpreting the Theatrical Past* (University of Iowa Press, 1989, with Thomas Postlewait), *Melodramatic Formations* (University of Iowa Press, 1992), *American Theatre in the Culture of the Cold War* (University of Iowa Press, 2003), *Theatre Histories: An Introduction* (Routledge, 2006, with Phillip Zarrilli and Carol Fischer Sorgenfrei), and *Performance and Cognition* (Routledge, 2006, with F. Elizabeth Hart). A past president of ASTR, McConachie is a co-editor of *Cognitive Studies in Literature and Performance*, a book series with Palgrave Macmillan.

Alissa Mello is a theatre maker and performer based in New York City, a founding member of Inkfish, and a doctoral candidate at Royal Holloway, University of London. She is currently developing a new production in London and teaching. Her research focuses on contemporary puppet-theatre practices. Her work has been published by *Animations Online*, *The Puppet Notebook*, and *Platform*.

Christopher Niess is Chair and Artistic Director for the University of Central Florida Conservatory Theatre. His career spans classical and contemporary theatre and dance. Niess' work as an actor, director, dancer, choreographer, movement and fight coach has taken him throughout the US, and to Canada, Germany, and Scotland. Most recently, he co-presented a paper with Julia Listengarten at the International Federation for Theatre Research in Lisbon.

Michael Rohd is Founding Artistic Director of Sojourn Theatre in Portland, Oregon, a 2005 recipient of Americans for the Arts' Animating Democracy Exemplar Award. In addition to his 22 original shows with Sojourn, his work as a creator/director includes projects with Ping Chong & Company, Cornerstone Theater Company, Woolly Mammoth Theater Company, Oregon Shakespeare Festival, the House Theatre & Alliance Theater. He has been supported by TCG, Ford Foundation, the NEA, Rockefeller's MAP Fund, Doris Duke Foundation, Americans for the Arts and Arts Councils in states around the nation. He is Assistant Professor at Northwestern University's School of Communication with a focus on Devising Performance, Directing & Civic Engagement. He is author of the book *Theatre for Community, Conflict, and Dialogue* (Heinemann, 1998).

Shannon Scrofano is a scenic and multimedia artist based in Los Angeles. Working to create original devised work with a focus on site-specificity, integrated media, civic engagement, and participation strategies, her collaborations include live performance, installation, and film projects throughout the US and internationally. She teaches at California Institute of the Arts.

Manon van de Water is Professor of Theatre Research and Director of the Theatre for Youth program at the University of Wisconsin-Madison. Her research interests include the interdependence of meaning and material conditions in theatre for adults and youth, Russian theatre, and Dutch theatre for youth, and she has published widely on theatre, drama education, and theatre for young audiences in national and international journals. Her book publications include *Moscow Theatres for Young People: A Cultural History of Ideological Coercion and Artistic Innovation, 1917–2000* (Palgrave Macmillan, 2006) and *Dutch Theatre for Children: Three Plays* (New Plays Inc./Dramatic Publishers, 2008).

S. E. Wilmer is Head of the School of Drama, Film and Music at Trinity College Dublin and author of *Theatre, Society and the Nation: Staging American Identities* (Cambridge University Press, 2002) and (with Pirkko Koski) *The Dynamic World of Finnish Theatre* (Like Publishing, 2006). Other recent publications include *Native American Performance and Representation* (University of Arizona Press, 2009); (with Anna McMullan) *Reflections on Beckett* (University of Michigan Press, 2009); *National Theatres in a Changing Europe* (2008); (with Pirkko Koski) *Humour and Humanity* (2006); and (with John Dillon) *Rebel Women: Staging Ancient Greek Drama Today* (Methuen Drama, 2005). He is also a playwright and a member of the executive committee of the International Federation for Theatre Research, and has been Visiting Professor at Stanford University and the University of California at Berkeley.

Stephani Etheridge Woodson is Associate Professor of theatre at Arizona State University, where she teaches in the Theatre for Youth MFA and PhD programs. Dr Woodson took her BFA and MA degrees from the University of Texas at Austin and her PhD from Arizona State

University. Her research and creative interests focus on the social construction of childhood through performance, representational ethics, children's media environments, and the group creation and performance of original work. She is the author of several book chapters, and articles for such journals as *Youth Theatre Journal, Journal of American Culture, Stage of the Art, Research in Drama Education,* and *Bad Subjects.*

Introduction

Megan Alrutz and Julia Listengarten

Playing with Theory in Theatre Practice aims to present and interrogate theory as an accessible, although complex, tool for theatre students and early-career practitioners interested in critically engaged theatre making. This collection of original chapters, written by theatre practitioners and scholars alike, suggests a necessity for new, productive ways of understanding the relationship between theory and practice, one which is fraught with contestations that are "particularly pernicious in the arts, because of historical frictions between artists and critics."[1] By approaching theory from different perspectives and remaining mindful of its complicated connections to theatre practice, these chapters invite readers to (re)imagine theory as a site of possibility or framework that can shape theatre making, emerge from practice, and foster new ways of seeing, creating, and reflecting. The contributing authors consider the role of theory in theatre practice within historical and contemporary contexts, interrogating the "romantic presumption that thought ruins creativity."[2] By reflecting on how theory is at play within different parts of the theatre-making process, the authors work to close the perceived gap between scholars and practitioners, theorists and theatre makers. As practicing artists and scholars grapple with questions surrounding the function, form, and value of theory in their practice, *Playing with Theory* offers possibilities for engaging theoretical constructs toward, from, and within dynamic and intentional production work.

For several years, the three editors of this book have worked together on scholarly and artistic projects ranging from academic papers and workshops to professional, university, and community-based theatre productions, all of which involved various negotiations between theory and theatre making, and ultimately prompted us to consider the role of theory in our own practices. Specifically, the idea for this book grew out of our collective experiences working with graduate and undergraduate students in various theatre spaces and university training programs in the US with a strong emphasis on conservatory training. Our students often express skepticism toward intellectual ideas and demonstrate far more confidence around, and connection to, practical theatre work than theoretical discourse. As we talked with colleagues across the country about our individual experiences of working with student performers, designers, directors, playwrights, and dramaturgs, we realized that many of us in higher education face similar challenges in our efforts to help pre-professional artists bridge the gap between theory and practice in their theatre making, as well as in their writing and reflecting. In classes such as Research Methods and Theory/Criticism, as well as more practice-based courses like Design Studio and Digital Storytelling, students expressed the desire for concrete answers about the relationship(s) between theory and their own practice—what does theory do? Why is theory relevant to me? How is theory useful to my work in the theatre? While we continue to engage students around these questions and concerns, we became increasingly interested in how other practitioners positioned their own relationship(s) to theoretical paradigms and theatre practice. We began to imagine a collection of chapters that would acknowledge the real tensions and disconnects that exist between theory and practice while also articulating possibilities and offering concrete examples of how theory and practice can dance with, for, and in response to each other. We hoped to acknowledge various definitions of, and approaches to, theory within different disciplines of theatre, as well as to provide conscious reflections on the often unconscious process of engaging with theory in/through creative practice. The resulting book is a collective effort to further discourse around theory/practice; it invites consideration of how theory can and does operate in the life of an artist while forwarding a multifaceted and contemplative, albeit partial, picture of the relationship(s) between theory and practice.

The process of assembling this book revealed some important through lines around the dynamics of theory and theatre practice that ultimately helped to contextualize who and what is included and emphasized within this collection. In exploratory conversations for this book, we found that many of our colleagues expressed a lack of interest or confidence in, and/or perceived value around, writing about theory, even in relation to one's own practice. In *Geographies of Learning*, Jill Dolan writes that "The split between research and practice often draws the fault lines in theater departments in research institutions, as various sets of faculty are positioned against one another in the struggle for resources such as graduate assistantships and other student aid and faculty assistance."[3] While research and theory certainly are not equivalent, Dolan's recognition of this split speaks to an important tension that tends to be perpetuated in/by the academy. Contrary to the above observation, however, several readers for this book project questioned whether the theory/ practice gap as we discuss it even exists within the UK and elsewhere outside of the US, and subsequent conversations with several artists currently working in the UK revealed a widely held belief that theory and practice are so interwoven that pinpointing the relationship(s) would be difficult, if not unproductive altogether. These differing viewpoints cross cultural and geographic borders, and the debate between them becomes an indication that scholars and practitioners continue to grapple with articulating this contentious and elusive, if not intuitive, set of relationships between theory and theatre practice.

Examples of this continuing dialogue can be seen in recent publications on practice-as-research (PaR), performance as research (PAR), and practice as research in performance (PARIP),[4] pointing to current interests in bridging practical and scholarly engagements in the arts and legitimizing creative production as a site for producing new knowledge. Shannon Rose Riley and Lynette Hunter suggest that "Perhaps the most singular contribution of [these] developing areas . . . is the claim that creative production can constitute intellectual inquiry."[5] These developing research methods, or modes of inquiry, indicate one of the ways that theory functions, specifically, in a dialogue with practice that can emerge from the creative process, and ultimately works to privilege arts practice in spaces where written scholarship and theory are traditionally given more weight. While publications on PaR and its related areas of inquiry contribute to the development of new knowledge, in some ways situating PaR within traditional research paradigms, this book expands the dialogue to consider not only how practice functions as research but how theory can function in relation to theatre production and performance/research paradigms.

Just as PaR and its related areas continue to be met with suspicion from both academics (with their often traditional ideas about research, scholarship, and knowledge making) and artists (with historically justified skepticism about privileging scholarship over creative activity), this book sits in a space of dual-pronged anxiety. The process of developing a theoretically minded book project, one that does not intend to speak directly to scholars or theorists but works to engage their efforts in very practical ways, revealed challenges related to a target audience. As editors, we worked to assemble a book aimed at theatre artists newly considering the role of theory in their work. The resulting collection articulates and explores practical ideas for engaging theory but does not attempt to offer in-depth theoretical foundations or altogether new theoretical paradigms. In doing so, this book both assumes some exposure to theory and also invites practitioners to seek out further reading and details on theories themselves.

Furthermore, given the range of contributors for this book, all of whom are practicing artists and/or academics, we also faced challenges around unifying vocabulary, writing style, and even our expectations about the assumed or base knowledge of our readers. While we intentionally brought the writing of scholars and practitioners together into one collection to explore a variety of practices, the process of doing so reminds us that discussions of theory by and for scholars and theorists are often quite different from discussions by and for practitioners—in tone, vocabulary, purpose, and application. Various chapters run the risk of disappointing those who are already deeply engaged in theory and/or theorized practice, or baffling practitioners who do not yet possess some inclination toward theoretical discourse. For these reasons, this book may best target Master of Fine Arts students and early-career professionals who are working collaboratively across theatre disciplines (such as directing, performance, devising, design, and dramaturgy), as well as undergraduate Theatre Studies students being introduced to theory/practice dialogue. Finally, depending on one's background, experiences, and inclinations, readers may wish to approach this text as a linear whole to be read in its entirety, or by specific groupings of chapters that speak more directly to one's discipline or interest areas within theatre. Either way, provocative dialogues emerge when considering these chapters in relation to one another.

While a significant body of publications exists that trace specific theories in the context of theatre/performance, most often foregrounding the use of theory as a tool for play and production analysis, this book explores theory/practice in a different way. Specifically, we encouraged authors to examine their relationship to theory from the inside out, rather than as an external tool for analyzing a written or performed text upon its completion. Foregrounding productive tensions and issues between and around creative practice, as well as creative intellectual processes, the resulting essays and case studies raise critical questions and ultimately offer ideas, models, and inspiration for approaching and framing theoretical paradigms in our artistic lives, particularly as we engage in the production process. In recognizing the long tradition of theoretical discourse among theatre makers, this book does not attempt to address all aspects of theory and/or the totality of its implications for theatre practice. Rather, it aims to examine theory's potential for offering theatre artists new ways of imagining their work.

We approached this book project with the premise that the relationship between theory and practice is constantly evolving and inherently fluid, and that these sometimes-artificial categories prove necessarily interdependent in varying degrees. In a transcribed conversation with Michel Foucault, Gilles Deleuze considers how theory and practice rely on one another: "Practice is a set of relays from one theoretical point to another, and theory is a relay from one practice to another. No theory can develop without eventually encountering a wall, and practice is necessary for piercing this wall."[6] Mark Fortier, a contributor to this collection and author of *Theory/Theatre: An Introduction*, further describes the nature of some of these interdependencies: "Theatre can sometimes be analogous or equivalent to theoretical reflection. . . . Closely related – sometimes interchangeable – are cases in which theatre enacts a theoretical position. . . . Moreover, theory can be used to explain and elucidate theatre in general or particular works of theatre. . . . Finally, theatre can answer back to theory, calling presuppositions into question and exposing limitations and blindness."[7] Theory and practice, then, work in tandem—in, of, through, and for the other; and *Playing with Theory* offers some articulations of, and reflections on, these very intersections.

Within the scope of this book, we refer to theatre theory in broad contexts, working from the premise that, particularly in the field(s) of theatre, the borders between theory and methodology, as well as philosophy, remain fluid in many respects. Indeed, distinctions between theory and philosophy have often blurred in the theatre, as reflected in seminal theoretical texts on theatre written by philosophers such as Aristotle, G. W. F. Hegel, and Friedrich Nietzsche. In addition, theatre and performance have broadened in scope as traditional boundaries have become less distinct between various fields of study and practice, and hence the vocabulary of theatre/performance has come to include theoretical and methodological discourse from a myriad of disciplines, such as visual arts, architecture, anthropology, linguistics, cognitive science, and sociology. Our understanding of theory has also expanded and evolved over time to include (and exclude) various forms and functions within theatre practice. David Saltz questions whether Theory-with-a-capital-T has entered an era of "conceptual blending" (in Bruce McConachie's expression),[8] "bringing together practitioners of hard science and biology with those of social sciences such as psychology and anthropology and humanities disciplines such as literary studies and philosophy – and now, performance and theatre studies."[9] At the same time, social, literary, political, and critical theories (such as feminist theory, cognitive theory, semiotics, border theory, and media theory to name only a few) have continued to encourage new ways of seeing and analyzing theatrical text and performance.

While the interplay between theory and practice is not necessarily a new phenomenon, Jane Milling and Graham Ley point out in *Modern Theories of Performance* that the theoretically minded practitioner has emerged as a modern phenomenon and that the twentieth century is marked by many influential theoretical practitioners such as Constantin Stanislavski, Antonin Artaud, Bertolt Brecht, Jerzy Grotowski, and Anne Bogart. These artists' written and performance work exemplifies praxis, or a process of making active choices that reflect an intentional engagement with the dialectic between theory and practice, reflecting some parallels with the aforementioned practices in areas such as PaR. Many of these artists developed theoretical or practical systems that eventually evolved into theorized methodologies, thus offering new models of theoretically engaged practice. Often, for instance, the artists' innovative goals in practice/performance present a need for theory, inviting practitioners to employ theory in service of their theatre making and frequently moving theory/practice into the realm of methodology. Theory can present a similar need for experimentation, or practice, inviting scholars and artists to interrogate theory within or through practical work. In these examples, theory and practice are therefore in constant dialogue, informing a kind of theorized methodology that, in turn, affects practical developments in theatre and propels the emergence of new theories. In their examination of the notion of a theoretically minded practitioner, Milling and Ley assert that "part of the attraction of these select figures was undoubtedly that they produced ideas as well as performances, and when juxtaposed they might be thought to present a methodology of theatre practice for modern times."[10] These methodologies and resulting theatre practices remind us of the multiple ways that theory and knowledge are embodied, produced, and challenged.

Despite the celebration of these theoretically minded practitioners and their widely recognized examples of praxis, tensions around the relevance of theory in theatre continue to exist. Recent critical discourse in the field suggests that "theory has been discredited," "grown outdated," or "vanished into new and better critical practice."[11] *Playing with Theory* comes on the heels of *After Theory*,[12] *life.after.theory*,[13] the collection of essays in *Post-Theory: New Directions and Criticisms*,[14] and the entire issue of *Theatre Journal*[15] dedicated to new paradigms for scholarship in theatre and performance studies, and works to offer clear examples of how moving theory to the forefront of our consciousness/conscience can help forward critically engaged and dynamic representations. Contextualized by criticisms lobbied against theory and its relevance to theatre and practice in general, the chapters in this book invite the reader to reconsider the contemplative and applied components of both theory and practice. These implied "deaths" and consequent rebirths, or revisions, reinforce the evolving nature of theory and its relationship to theatre practice. For Deleuze, "A theory does not totalize; it is an instrument for multiplication and it also multiplies itself."[16] As we continue to interrogate the relationship between theory and practice, the very act of its negotiation will shape, influence, and ultimately re-make the ways we understand, value, and use theoretical frameworks in theatre practice.

Applied theatre scholar Helen Nicholson argues that theory offers us "a way of looking at the world differently, a focus for asking risky questions."[17] In a similar vein, this collection invites readers to consider how theory helps us see the world and our work anew, while also providing specific examples of how various scholars and artists define and use theory in ways that suit their discipline or focus within theatre/performance making. While many of the chapters point to theory as an external stimulus or inspiration for new ways of seeing or knowing, others push us to consider theory as an internal muscle, or an intuition, that unconsciously guides us through familiar processes, gaining strength through its very use. For several contributors, theory functions as a mirror, helping artists to see themselves—their values and perspectives—and to articulate their ideas and questions around a production, or to understand the concrete and hypothetical consequences and possibilities of their artistic choices. Other chapters suggest that theory operates as a tool for challenging the status quo or unifying an approach to developing character, devising new work, or staging a play. Several authors consider theory as a political strategy for debunking systems of power and value, while others suggest that theory can offer a vocabulary for knowing, understanding, or articulating something beyond our own experience. Additional contributors argue that theory provides angles for investigation by focusing our attention to various aspects of meaning, story, and representation. Furthermore, the included chapters invite an examination of the descriptive, prescriptive, and probing nature of theory, encouraging us to (re)consider our own decision making as we engage in theatre production.

In almost every one of these examples, the word theory can be replaced with the word theatre, pointing again to parallels between the function of theory and theatre, as well as the sometimes-complicated and indistinguishable borders between theory and practice. The chapters also reflect a multifaceted and ongoing conversation between theory and practice in theatre making; theory often comes from practice, practice often results from theory, performance can be theory in practice. And as these various dialogues or interactions between theory and practice become intentionally activated through praxis, new knowledge and creative forms develop. Ultimately, this book demonstrates a range of possible theoretical engagements and applications, stimulating interest in theory and conscious reflection on, and action toward, artistic choices.

In many ways, this collection points to a disruption of categorical absolutes for theory and practice, inviting us to continually reassess and expand definitions of our work. As contributors from various disciplines in the field write about theatre, theory, practice, and praxis from multiple perspectives, this book reiterates that theory plays with, in, and through theatre in endless ways. Rather than providing a set of stable definitions, this collection focuses on ways of thinking about and intentionally engaging with theory; and it is our hope that these chapters inspire complex questions, understandings, and actions within the theatre-making process.

Playing with Theory in Theatre Practice is organized into three parts consisting of essays and case studies. While we provide a brief overview of the three parts of the book in this main introduction, more detailed introductions to each part and analyses of the relationships between individual chapters can be found in focused introductions that immediately precede Parts I, II, and III.

Part I, "Contextualizing Theory and Practice," explores and contextualizes the historically complicated dynamic between theory and theatre practice. For this section, three scholars reflect on some of the historical, social, political, and practical contexts that shape ensuing discussions in the text. These chapters remind us that theoretical and practical knowledge and skills have been alternately privileged throughout history and in various contexts, raising questions about the cultural and use value of both theory and theatre to society at large. Examining several possible functions of theory, this part invites consideration of how theory can both "thwart us" and "allows us to carry on" in theatre.[18] The authors in Part I offer us contexts for considering representational practices and accepted forms of knowledge, posing several ways to think about the role of theory in our creative/intellectual practices, and asking provocative questions about the complex marriage between scholars and practitioners. Furthermore, the chapters in this part introduce definitions of theory and practice, offering contexts for thinking about the future of theory and ultimately the theoretical implications of theatre practice.

The chapters in Part II, "Interrogating Theory in Theatre Practice: Productive Tensions, Questions, and Implications," tease out theorized and un-theorized practice, offering fruitful questions around the integration of theory and practice and exploring theory's potential for fostering intentional, responsible, and reflective theatre making. The authors in this part direct our attention to the ideological and performative implications of theory for, within, and from artists' work, encouraging us to imagine how theoretical discourse can literally be performed on stage, grow out of performance/production, and ultimately shape who and what gets valued or privileged in our theatre making. Engaging cultural and media theory, history and criticism, and new developments in cognitive theory and neuroscience, these chapters invite us to reflect on how theory and practice inform one another and how both can simultaneously function in/as practice. Furthermore, the authors remind us of how theoretical paradigms and new developments in the sciences can help us better shape the audience's experience in the theatre. In addition, a few chapters in Part II suggest that theory, coupled with criticism, historical data, and other research, can complicate creative and intuitive processes and contribute to dynamic choices for the stage. Together, the chapters work to acknowledge, if not reconcile, tensions—between thought and emotion, intuition and intellect, power and responsibility, science and culture, and theory and practice, to name a few. Interestingly, the contributors are not all in agreement about the possible conflicts, questions, and implications surrounding theory in theatre practice; more than anything, the authors offer a starting place for considering our own beliefs and practices, and hopefully, the productive, although not always easy to navigate, anxieties around theory and theatre making.

Finally, Part III, "Case Studies: Activating Theory within and through the Production Process," provides a series of reflective studies on artists' praxis, illuminating possibilities for playing with theory in theatre practice, as well as questions and tensions raised by theoretically engaged theatre making. This section brings together a diverse group of practicing artists that work across many disciplines in theatre and represent a wide range of perspectives on how theory is at play in the artistic process. Several of the chapters encourage us to consider how theatre/performance itself can function as a theoretical framework for creating embodied knowledge/practice and new methodologies for approaching character, song, story, collaborative devising, and audience engagement. Furthermore, Part III suggests that theory operates as a dramaturgical tool, offering clarity around story structure, content, and purpose. Several case studies also invite us to consider whether a production itself is, or can be, a theoretical idea or if it helps us negotiate theoretical ideas. The chapters in this part suggest that theory is at play in multiple ways within our practice, widening creative possibilities, inspiring new ways of seeing and creating, while operating as a process of making meaning.

In conversation with one another, the chapters in all three parts invite us to consider where and how theory and practice converge, as well as what possibilities exist for playing with theory in our own practice. In what ways does theory have the potential to help construct common ground and unify artistic vision? What does the dialectic relationship between theory and theatre making offer our production processes? And how does theory help us "make the familiar strange," or illuminate systems of value and power that lie at the core of our personal beliefs and intentions, as well as our artistic processes and products? As you move through the chapters that follow, we hope you will find elements of inspiration, new questions, and exploratory maps for building your own theoretically minded practice.

Notes

1. Jill Dolan, *Geographies of Learning* (Middletown, CT: Wesleyan University Press, 2001), 4.
2. Ibid.
3. Ibid., 50.
4. See Shannon Rose Riley and Lynette Hunter, eds, *Mapping Landscapes for Performance as Research* (Basingstoke: Palgrave Macmillan, 2009); Estelle Barrett and Barbara Bolt, eds, *Practice as Research: Approaches to Creative Arts Enquiry* (London: IB Tauris, 2007); and Ludivine Allegue, et al., eds, *Practice-as-Research in Performance and Screen* (Basingstoke: Palgrave Macmillan, 2009).
5. Shannon Rose Riley and Lynette Hunter, eds, *Mapping Landscapes for Performance as Research*, xv.
6. See "Intellectuals and Power: A Conversation between Michel Foucault and Gilles Deleuze," in D. F. Bouchard, ed., *Language, Counter-Memory, Practice: Selected Essays and Interviews by Michel Foucault* (New York: Cornell University Press, 1977), 205–6.
7. Mark Fortier, *Theory/Theatre: An Introduction*, 2nd edn (London: Routledge, 2002), 10.
8. See Bruce McConachie and Amy Cook's essays in *Theatre Journal*, 59.4 (December 2007).
9. David Saltz, "Editorial Comment: Performance and Cognition," *Theatre Journal*, 59.4 (December 2007), ix–xiii.
10. Jane Milling and Graham Ley, *Modern Theories of Performance: From Stanislavski to Boal* (Basingstoke: Palgrave Macmillan, 2001), vi.

11. Michael Payne and John Schad, eds, *life.after.theory* (London: Continuum, 2003), ix–xi.
12. See Terry Eagleton, *After Theory* (New York: Basic Books, 2003).
13. See Payne and Schad in *life.after.theory*.
14. See Martin McQuillan, Robin Purves, Graeme MacDonald, and Stephen Thomson, eds, *Post-Theory: New Directions in Criticism* (Edinburgh: Edinburgh University Press, 1999).
15. See *Theatre Journal*, 59.4 (December 2007).
16. See Deleuze in *Language, Counter-Memory, Practice: Selected Essays and Interviews*, Michel Foucault, 208.
17. See Helen Nicholson's reference to bell hooks' ideas on theory as social production. Helen Nicholson, *Applied Drama: The Gift of Theatre* (Basingstoke: Palgrave Macmillan, 2005), 14.
18. See Mark Fortier's chapter "The Function of Theory at the Present Time?" which is included in Part I of this book.

Part I
Contextualizing Theory and Practice

Introduction: Part I

Megan Alrutz and Julia Listengarten

The chapters in Part I, "Contextualizing Theory and Practice," explore various definitions of theory, the use value of theory (and theatre) for scholars and practitioners, and the complex historical relationship(s) between theory and theatre production. Setting the stage for the ensuing dialogue in Parts II and III about the practical application of theoretical paradigms, these opening chapters contemplate the current status of theory, suggest the impossibility of clear-cut definition(s), and present a multi-layered theoretical landscape with a range of possibilities for its further integration with theatre making. Situating theoretical paradigms in the field of theatre practice, this section also encourages us to imagine and participate in a productive contemporary theatre praxis, where theory and theatre making exist in a dialogic relationship. While offering examples of how practitioners historically have come to theory, incorporated, developed, embodied, and performed it, the chapters in Part I inspire us to explore new approaches and chart new frameworks for an interplay between theory and our own practice.

Mark Fortier, author of the seminal text *Theory/Theatre*, opens Part I with a discussion of the contemporary landscape of theory in relation to theatre, reflecting on critical lenses traditionally applied in theatre, as well as new theoretical fields that are shaping theatre practice. Questioning whether theory should "be the handmaid of theatre" or rather "a thorn in the side of practitioners," he engages in a debate about the use value of theory, urging readers to reconsider the very concept of "usefulness" in relation to theory and, ultimately, theatre itself. Fortier goes on to suggest that "to cause thinking, . . . to provoke somewhat impious questioning, is the most important function of theory in its relation to theatre as in its relation to anything else." While implicating himself in the perpetuation of the sometimes problematic

15

nature of current theoretical discourse, he contemplates possibilities (and *impossibilities*) of different approaches to, and functions of, theory. Specifically, Fortier engages in a discussion with Bruce McConachie and Herbert Blau, among others, whose chapters are included in the later sections of this book, debating McConachie's earlier claim that scientific theory will replace cultural theory and questioning Blau's messianic assertion he is "in theatre to save the world" while simultaneously recognizing "its" impossibility.[1] Reminding us that theories come in and out of fashion and suggesting that the nature of theory is both context specific and elusive, Fortier troubles the "presentness" of theatre and invites us to think about "the relation between the present and the past, the living and the dead" in order to (re)imagine a future landscape of theatre/theory.

In Chapter 2, theatre theorist and practitioner Manon van de Water contextualizes historically significant "theoretical practitioners" in theatre, as well as the dialectic relationship between theory and practice, and theorists and practitioners. She raises the notion that theatre practitioners (particularly in the US) often have tenuous relationships to theory, and specifically draws on Jill Dolan's call for more productive collaborations between scholars and practitioners to remind us that "the disdain and distrust in which theorists and practitioners sometimes hold each other is counterproductive, if not destructive." Like Dolan, van de Water believes that in order to create and sustain culturally relevant theatre, theory and practice need each other. Looking at theory as "a system of ideas" and practice as "the application of ideas," she further suggests that ideology can be seen as a conduit between theory and practice. Pointing to examples from her own directing practice, van de Water contemplates a dialogic praxis, considering the ways practice can challenge one's own theory, and theory, in turn, can challenge and lead to new practice.

In the final chapter of Part I, theatre scholar Michal Kobialka reminds us of how grand theoretical discourses of the 1970s and 1980s gave way to widespread skepticism about the radical claims of cultural theory, and later, public announcements that, in fact, theory was dead. While acknowledging current discourse that condemns theory's lack of political activism and moral purpose, due in large part to postmodern cultural relativism, Kobialka proposes that theory and practice are modes of thinking that "acquire material shapes in a space where theatre is viewed not in terms of Aristotelian poetics, utopian performative, or scientific desire for certitude, but in terms of an autonomous practice which betrays the established reality or the ordinary realm of approved knowledge." His discussion of an autonomous practice is thus grounded in the notion that works of art must operate independently from unstable cultural contexts such as time and space in order to disrupt dominant representational practices and escape the criticisms lobbied at the cultural relativism of most theatre. Defining theory as "the way one critically and dialectically thinks about things" and practice as "the way one does things," Kobialka complicates their interplay through examples of the practitioner as theorist and the theorist as practitioner, offering his definition of praxis as an "endgame of theory and practice." Drawing on Antonin Artaud and Tadeusz Kantor, he contends that an autonomous practice has the potential to foreground that which is marginalized and explode "normative representational theatrical categories or structures" to provide our response to reality rather than a simple reflection of it.

Each chapter in this section is unique in its approach to theory in relation to practice: Fortier provides a provocative assessment of the field; van de Water discusses various relationships that practitioners have to theory; while Kobialka offers specific examples of praxis that touch on the political potential and relevance of theory/theatre. All three writers, however, in their distinct ways remind us of the intangible and evolving nature of theory and encourage us look ahead to the role that theory will play in the future.

Offering various perspectives on how theory and practice can relate to representation and reality, these chapters raise questions about context specific (both Fortier and van de Water) versus autonomous (Kobialka) practice as well as the role of various ideologies at play in our theoretical/practical work. The chapters also encourage us to think about different functions of theory in relation to practical versus intellectual exploration, contemplate theory's potential to envision and/or create new realities, question our own engagement in theoretical activity, and prompt a series of basic questions about playing with theory in our practice. When and where might theory offer an immediate practical application in our creative work and/or how might it become a tool for theatre practitioners to question critically their assumptions and approaches to production? In our own practices, how do we determine the value of theory? When and how might the value of theory extend beyond its practical applicability? The authors in Part I offer multiple possibilities surrounding the relationship between theory and practice and their writings inspire us to define our own approaches to theory, explore its cultural relevance in today's theatre making, and analyze the impact—both present and potential—of theory on our own creative process.

Note

1. See Mark Fortier's essay, included in this collection, in which he quotes from Herbert Blau, *Take Up the Bodies: Theater at the Vanishing Point* (Urbana: University of Illinois Press, 1982), 32.

1
The Function of Theory at the Present Time?

Mark Fortier

> I'm an academic person, a man of books, and I've always been out of my depth in practical matters.

> No, not knowing is better. At least there's still hope.

> Besides, she knows I have no use for the theatre. She adores the stage. Serving humanity in the sacred cause of art, that's how she thinks of it. But the theatre's in a rut nowadays, if you ask me.[1]

Anton Chekhov's theatre, as instanced in the citations above, is strewn more with problems and conundrums, with self-reflection on inadequacy, than it is with answers and solutions, with performative self-confidence. It is, therefore, in a rather Chekhovian spirit that I write this chapter, which revisits the relations between cultural theory and theatre, which I treated previously in my book *Theory/Theatre: An Introduction*, first published in 1996 and in a revised edition in 2002. What, in the intervening years, is new, what has developed, and what abides? The patchwork discussion I provide here (and the questions it raises) is brief and impressionistic and not meant to complete or arrest thought but rather, in Antonin Artaud's phrase, to cause (a bit of) thinking. To cause thinking, I continue to believe, to provoke thinking, to provoke somewhat impious questioning, is the most important function of theory in its relation to theatre as in its relation to anything else. What abides most compellingly for me is a deep and insistent skepticism.[2]

But the singular importance of skepticism is not, I dare say, a truth universally acknowledged. There are tensions around theory, theatre, and their functions and interrelationship that continue to be vexing at the present time. What good is theory? What use is theory? What can theory do for the practice of theatre? People want answers! So let me begin by exploring recent discussions around these questions.

The use of theory

The title of my essay is adapted from Matthew Arnold's "The Function of Criticism at the Present Time." In that work, Arnold opposes his own view to what he takes to be the commonplace (English) position, which arises from "a practical view of things." Arnold, in opposition to this practical view, is more interested in "a free play of the mind on all subjects which it touches."[3] I confess that I myself am of the free play of mind school, but for present purposes It is more important to explore how the tension that Arnold notes between thinking and practice continues to be a pressing one.

One corollary, according to Arnold, of the practical view of things is the belief in "the inherent superiority of the creative effort of the human spirit over its critical effort."[4] Practice is more important than theory, and in our specific area of concern, actually doing theatre is more important than thinking about it. Theory should have a practical function, aiding in the making of theatre. If it doesn't do that, it can do nothing good.

To tease out this train of thought further: there is a long history of theatre scholars and practitioners questioning the usefulness of theory for the understanding or practice of theatre. This history continues in recent articles by Julian Meyrick and Bruce McConachie. Meyrick argues that theoretical and academic understanding is less relevant than professional understanding in solving theatre problems. Moreover, Meyrick argues, theory, with its jargon and hermetic prose and systematizing, has come to dominate and displace more useful practical understanding.[5] McConachie argues that the present age of theory will inevitably wane (*sic transit gloria mundi*) and that those who follow us will be more interested in theories, especially those from cognitive psychology, that are scientific and subject to the test of falsifiability, and that are able to tell us more accurately how an audience experiences a performance, for instance.[6]

Meyrick's argument is that if theory actually assisted theatre practitioners and was useful to them, that would be one thing, but in reality it is more obstructive than useful. Theory is less than helpful. Meyrick argues, in effect, that interfering and wrongheaded theory has usurped authority over creative art. My response, as someone who is more of a theoretician than a theatre practitioner, is that the usefulness of theory always remains to be seen, but even more, that usefulness is not necessarily what we should look for in theory. Meyrick, I think, also implies once again the inherent superiority of creative to critical or theoretical effort. When we engage in theoretical activity are we lesser beings or involved in effort of lesser worth? Those who can put on plays, and those who can't theorize them? Should theory be the handmaid of theatre—pitching in to put on a show, always there to advise and defer—or should it be a thorn in the side of theatre practitioners, questioning them, providing them not with tools but with problems, some of which would question the very foundations of theatrical knowledge and assurances?

Meyrick is also troubled by the *"eclectic use of a broad range of cross-disciplinary interpretive schemata,"* which, he argues, produces analysis that is inconsistent, insufficiently grounded, and the product of intellectual laziness.[7] I share, in part, Meyrick's concerns. Here is a quotation from a recent work by Judith Butler, which I have adapted ever so slightly:

> I make eclectic use of various philosophers and critical theorists in this inquiry. Not all of their positions are compatible with one another, and I do not attempt to synthesize them here. Although synthesis is not my aim, I do want to maintain that each theory suggests something . . . important.[8]

This passage could function as the template for the ascendant *modus operandi* of current theoretically informed scholars, who follow no (single) party line and work from no one theoretical perspective but rather cherry-pick from various theories as needed. In some ways this practice is the continuation of something I noted in my overview some years ago, when I wrote:

> Many theorists . . . have hybrid interests. Gayatri Spivak . . . combines in her work Marxism, deconstruction, feminism and post-colonialism. Julia Kristeva . . . combines feminism, semiotics and psychoanalysis.[9]

A few years later, noting how Butler uses phenomenology in a feminist context, I wrote "most theoretical work now proceeds by combining elements from different theories. Few these days are orthodox Freudians or Marxists or even deconstructionists."[10] Things have continued down this road of eclecticism, with the result that rogue elements of various theories often appear in a single book or essay and Freudians, Marxists, deconstructionists even of the unorthodox sort are hard to find in the multitude of those with a more generalized and ad hoc investment in theory. This development would appear to go hand-in-hand with a current post-structuralist, postmodernist, diasporic episteme favoring hybridity and bricolage.

My own question, at an early moment in this development, was: "Is there really much intellectual integrity and honesty in picking and choosing whatever suits you from whatever theories you like?"[11] Moreover, does this practice foreclose on a certain kind of rigorous and sophisticated thinking that arises from systematically working through a theoretical position? McConachie has rightly noted how I myself have contributed to this dispersed and de-centered (but nonetheless canonized) body of theory.[12] I remain deeply ambivalent about the development of theoretical bricolage, but I think for now it is here to stay. Moreover, as questionable as it is, it runs against an orthodoxy and discipleship that I myself am as incapable of as are many of my contemporaries—I, like many of us, am not a card-carrying anything and never had the temperament to be a true believer of any one school.

McConachie's reminder that our age of theory will not last is a bracing and important one. Certainly we have seen theory change over the last forty years or so—especially those of us old enough to remember New Criticism as alive and dominant. That those in the future—if we surmise like characters in a Chekhov play—will think differently with different authorities seems inevitable. I am not at all certain, however, that more scientific theories will be the way of the future. They may be, they may not be; science might clarify some things, others not so much.

In effect, McConachie suggests that theory as we have known it is largely "bullshit," in the sense analyzed by Harry G. Frankfurt—claims for which the question of truth or falsity is irrelevant.[13] Poetry, as understood by Philip Sidney ("[The Poet] nothing affirms, and therefore never lieth"),[14] is such bullshit. Should theory be more like science or more like poetry? A position based on scientific principle ignores other rationales for theory that recognize theory's deep skepticism about truth claims and empiricism: its function as provocation, heuristic, suspicion, strategy. As a litmus test, falsifiability is most easily applied to a fairly narrow range of theoretical concerns—as in McConachie's text, for instance, how the brain perceives patterns. It can't do much, as McConachie notes, with a very engaging and productive idea such as "there is nothing outside the text."[15] Such a statement is self evident if you accept a certain notion of the text but hardly empirically (dis)provable. Which of these kinds of concern will most interest those in the future? None of us can know.

The use of theatre

Let us return to the relative values of theatre and theory. Turning the tables ever so slightly, we as theorists might ask what is the use of theatre? What is its function? Isn't theatre itself a rather useless thing? Outmoded even? Often, when critics talk about the use of theory or theatre, they mean their political uses. Our present historico-political moment is still often placed in the aftermath of the fall of Eastern bloc communism as an actual alternative to global capitalism—which at the very least has complicated the road map to global social justice—and more recently, in writings by Diana Taylor, in the aftermath of the events of 9/11— which has created an era of fear, paranoia, cynicism, and reaction.[16] The difficulties of political action in the early twenty-first century have been recently and prominently tackled in Michael Hardt and Antonio Negri's *Empire* and its sequel, *Multitude* (works that bring to the fore the theorizing of Gilles Deleuze and Félix Guattari).[17] We find ourselves once again (as always) in Hamlet's position: "The time is out of joint. O cursèd spite / That ever I was born to set it right!"[18] Moreover, *Empire* and *Multitude*, like most studies of the postmodern world not specifically focused on theatrical concerns, give little or no attention to theatre. To those not involved in thinking about or making theatre, theatre seems to offer very little to aid in understanding or changing the complex technological world in which we live.

The continual return to the question of theatre and politics might look to some like the repeated reinvention of the wheel. It can be explained, however: different situations require different strategies; moreover, history does not provide much in the way of examples of politically effective theatre. Wheels work; political theatre mostly not. Certainly there is no end of those who claim they are doing political theatre; but what do they actually accomplish? If your deepest interest is politics, why, in our world, do theatre?

Relatively recent and important books by Baz Kershaw and Jill Dolan continue this line of pursuit.[19] Kershaw argues that with the collapse of communism and the rise of global capitalism "old notions of political theatre are falling into disrepute."[20] Traditional theatre is marginalized, but "Contemporary [radical] live performance, especially outside theatre buildings," "participates in the most vital cultural, social and political tensions of its time."[21] The complex possibilities of radical postmodern performance, therefore, instill in Kershaw, at a time of crisis in political theatre, a "pathology of hope."[22] The notion of a pathology of hope seeks to have it two ways at once: hope is pathological, it is admitted, because there is precious little reason for it; hope, it is affirmed, is nonetheless a necessary political virtue. Hope is a key notion in Dolan's recent work as well:

> *Utopia in Performance* argues that live performance provides a place where people come together, embodied and passionate, to share experiences of meaning making and imagination that can describe or capture fleeting intimations of a better world. *Utopia in Performance* tries to find, at the theater, a way to reinvest our energies in a different future, one full of hope and reanimated by a new, more radical humanism.[23]

By its very nature, utopian performance "can't translate into a program for social action," but it can "resurrect a belief or faith in social change."[24] Utopian theatre, therefore, does preparatory political work, visionary and uplifting for those who make or witness it, sending them out of the theatre with faith, hope, and (unspecified) work to do.

Is hope, however, an illusion? Heiner Müller, the German playwright, declared, "I am neither a dope- nor a hope-dealer,"[25] implying that hope is an opiate for, among others, the disenfranchised intellectual or theatre practitioner. How do utopian faith and hope hold up against what Paul Ricoeur called the "hermeneutics of suspicion," which he located in Karl Marx, Friedrich Nietzsche, and Sigmund Freud,[26] but which includes more contemporary thinkers such as Jacques Derrida? Or, further, against the "kakangelic," the bad news, the anti-evangelic, which some cultural theory has been so adept at delivering?[27] Oscar Wilde sniffed that art is quite useless,[28] but there is a strain of theory that aspires, in a spirit of one-upmanship, to be worse than useless. Lee Edelman, for example, has recently made drastically negative claims for queerness: that it provides a "bad education" and teaches nothing.[29] This somewhat nihilistic strain of theory is in radical tension with the drive to usefulness, which remains dominant and taken for granted in our time (think how those of us in the liberal arts have come to justify what we do in very explicit terms of social utility that underplay the value of the thing itself, let alone its potential for social disruption). Philip Auslander, for instance, writes of his latest book, in a way that seems hardly (but deeply) worth questioning, that it is "designed to be useful."[30]

What in our world isn't?

Not too many years ago I was accused by an anonymous referee of "still" doing "unreconstructed deconstruction"—the implication being that the moment and relevance of (disengaged) deconstruction had certainly passed. Derrida and deconstruction, however, have been given a second wind by a focus on ethics (the so-called ethical turn) and "undeconstructible justice, the undeconstructible condition of any deconstruction"[31]—a transcendent value in deconstruction itself. Recently, Duncan Jamieson argued that "the increased orientation around ethics and politics in deconstructive discourse should provoke us to reassess the place of Derrida's work in performance theory."[32] Derrida's ethical turn, however, troubles political thought and action more than it facilitates them, and Derrida's book on Marx—one of the primary vehicles of the ethical turn—is one of his most harshly criticized works.[33]

What is Derrida's Marxism? Derrida is not interested in "a new theoreticism"[34] (interpreting differently rather than changing the world) that would be the sole or dominant mode of Marxism. Something must be done, but what? Rather than hope and belief in the utopian (or, in his terms, the apocalyptic), he yearns for, he affirms the promise of messianic justice. How might we set hope and belief in relation to/against yearning, affirming, promising? How does the promise of messianic justice differ from mere hope and belief? Justice is undeconstructible because it affirms an inevitable distance between ethics and politics: politics tries to do the right thing but will always come up short. Messianic justice is aligned with radical and endless critique that affirms justice by deferring it, by never settling for the inevitable second best.[35] Messianic justice is *beyond therefore the living present in general.*"[36] It is always to come.

How could theatre, even if it wanted to, serve the cause of undeconstructible justice? By instilling hope and faith or by a vigilant and endless critique of justice's inevitable and necessary simulacra? It would not necessarily be a political theatre but rather an ethical theatre relentlessly questioning politics for the sake of a justice always deferred. It would have a deeply suspicious relationship to hope. Let's say one accepted such an enormously and relentlessly vigilant task: would theatre bring anything special to serving such justice? Would it bring anything specifically its own to the struggle?[37] Perhaps theatre is special because it is such an unpromising place from which to escape illusion or attempt to change the world, and creates a working space in the gap between delusion and failure. Here I am reminded of the "messianic" work of Herbert Blau (work worth revisiting) and his double assertion that he is "in theatre to save the world" and that "it" (changing the world? theatre? the relation between the two?) is impossible.[38] Such a theory/theatre runs the strong risk of being more bracing than uplifting, more impossible than successful. It hardly seems political or activist in any implementable sense.

The (after)life of theory/theatre

Theory or theatre can have a function—in the political sense, for example—but they also function in the same way that we might speak of a functioning heart or a functioning marriage: they exist in an internal and external arrangement that allows them to carry on, or, in the alternative, thwarts their functioning, undermines their existence. Recently, the function of theatre in this sense has been explored through work on the afterlife of theatre.

In Derrida's late work on the archive, *Archive Fever*, he maps two principles at work in the word "archive": an ontological principle and a nomological principle.[39] In other words, on one side (although these principles are not so readily separable) are questions of what an archive is and what an archive archives, and on the other are questions of law, power, control, and violence. Both sets of questions, ontological and political, have recently engaged theatre theorists as they think through the relations between theatre and the archive, especially at a time of rapid technological development.

As to the first set of questions, Constantin Stanislavski wrote many years ago: "A work of art born on the stage lives only for a moment, and no matter how beautiful it may be it cannot be commanded to stay with us," and "the theatre cannot give the beginner such results as the library and the museum give to the writer and the artist."[40] Is theatre, then, essentially unarchiveable in a way not as true of other arts? Questions of liveness and presence are involved here—which, despite the trenchant critiques of Elinor Fuchs and Auslander,[41] remain compelling ideas for theatre studies. In an article on digital archiving, Christie Carson argues that "any move towards reducing the spontaneity of what takes place on stage and the sense of community which takes place in the theatre, thereby creating a more rigid, universalized or solitary experience, seriously threatens the integrity, and also the point, of the live theatre experience."[42] Steve Dixon, on the other hand, argues that watching a theatrical production reproduced on a small screen entails a Brechtian alienation effect that is, in itself, theatrical.[43] The theatrical here, paradoxically, is that which alienates us from liveness. For Matthew Reason, the instability, uncertainty, and incompleteness of the theatrical archive—its status as detritus—is itself a reflection of theatre's liveness.[44] Liveness here denotes a particular kind of transitoriness, a quick susceptibility to oblivion. Ellen MacKay argues that theatre is a self-consuming art, "an event whose occurrence is defined by its loss."[45] Therefore, the liveness of theatre, such as it is, is at least as much death affirming as it is life affirming. Death is the inevitable future, the originating promise of live theatre. Derrida argues that the death drive both enables and undermines the archival project.[46] If things didn't die, there would be no need to archive them; since things are dead, the archive can never preserve life. The afterlife of theatre in the archive, therefore, illuminates the necessary presence of death and the death drive in the "live" theatrical event as it happens.

Such ideas, obviously, run counter to naïve affirmations of the presence of live theatre. But what do they do to the political project of someone like Dolan, quoted earlier: "*Utopia in Performance* argues that live performance provides a place where people come together, embodied and passionate, to share experiences of meaning making and imagination that can describe or capture fleeting intimations of a better world."[47] Where is death in this?

Here we may turn to political questions around theatre and archive. For Derrida, the archive is inherently political and inherently violent (violence as exclusion, distortion, ordering, obliterating), and the most we can shoot for is to do the lesser rather than the greater violence. The most extended study of the politics of theatre and archive is Diana Taylor's *The Archive and the Repertoire*. Taylor argues that the hegemony of Western imperialist theatre practices (and politics) has been carried out in the Americas by traditional archival work, which has oppressed and excluded indigenous practices. These practices have been transmitted, rather, by the repertoire, "a nonarchival system of transfer,"[48] which keeps knowledge alive and passes it on among the people. Thus these performance practices persist rather than disappear. As an historical study, Taylor's work leaves us with some general abstract questions: must the archive always be on the side of oppression, always the greater violence, or could it be harnessed to the project of emancipation or at least the lesser violence? How are the politics of archive and repertoire tied to their relative ontological abilities of preservation and loss? Is the repertoire inherently more resistant and emancipatory or would oppressed theatrical practices benefit from having the power of the archive at their disposal? These questions lead us back to all the questions concerning the political efficacy of theatre raised earlier: the repertoire may have functioned well as a means of preserving, but has the theatre it preserves been itself politically effective?

Questions of the archive are related to questions of the canon—its formation and preservation—relating to both theory and theatre.

How do theories, for instance, come in and out of fashion, or maintain their hold on our interests? As noted above, McConachie foresees a time when our present theories will have been discarded and lay abandoned like Ozymandias in the desert. But within the present theoretical era, some theories remain strikingly current. Derrida often seems to imply a deep consistency in his work from beginning to end, as if it sprang fully formed from his head in 1967 ("Deconstruction has always meant . . ."). But what goes under a name does not necessarily stay the same. One way that a theory can maintain and spread its influence is through the expansion of the purview of its relevance. Such a theory is phenomenology, which has had its strengths and weaknesses play against each other. Its emphasis on the *Dasein* of embodied experience makes it alluring for the study of theatre. On the other hand its affinity with quasi-essentialist notions of truth and the recent questioning of the liveness of live theatre have undermined its authority. Most limiting would appear to be a sense that *Dasein* developed from a European and masculine (and in the case of Martin Heidegger, a Nazi sympathizer's) model of the human subject. This sense has been somewhat allayed, however, by work in feminist phenomenology[49] and even more recently by work in queer phenomenology.[50] There also continues to be important work in phenomenology and theatre—a recent book by Alice Rayner, for instance, or phenomenological work on African diasporic theatre.[51] Phenomenology has moved with the times in order to remain relevant.

Of course, the canon of theatre itself changes with changing concerns, often political concerns. Because it is Canadian and because it deals with the diasporic condition—an interest that has now become a prominent concern in post-colonial studies (the word "diaspora" doesn't even appear in the index to *The Post-Colonial Studies Reader*,[52] published in 1995)—Guillermo Verdecchia's *Fronteras Americanas*[53] is a play that many of my students have encountered repeatedly in their courses. On the other hand, *Cats* is as close as most people now get to the theatre of T. S. Eliot. And yet perhaps more striking is the staying power of much of the traditional canon. Why, for instance, do we still, after well over 2,000 years, turn to *Antigone* as Butler recently has?[54] Few of us except antiquarians are interested in ancient Greek society, and so our interest rarely arises from the specific connections between art, society, and politics that often spur our interest in plays from our own time. Theatre practice is particularly presentist in its outlook—why go through all the trouble of putting on a play if it is merely antiquated and irrelevant? We choose to put on plays because they appear to be alive and to speak to us.

In a long chapter of her book *Athens in Paris*, Miriam Leonard traces the complex western interest in *Antigone* (as well as *Oedipus Rex*) since G. W. F. Hegel.[55] Her view is that it hasn't so much been something in the play itself that has held our interest but rather the cultural capital we still derive from making the Greeks supporters of our own interests and positions that has been at work. *Antigone* is interesting because we can use it to back up our own positions on family and state, gender, law and conscience, or whatever, and for whatever reasons, it is still considered an intellectual *coup* to have the Greeks on one's side. This explanation rings true, as far as it goes, despite that theorists persist in claiming they are drawn by something primal in Sophocles' play. Phillipe Nonet has recently attempted to get past the play's "fame" to listen to the phenomenological truths in the text itself.[56] Even those who see the meaning of the play in the history of its readings find themselves turning to the text—often in its Greek original. The interplay between readings and the text can be seen in this short passage from Butler:

> When I reread Sophocles' play, I was impressed in a perverse way by the blindnesses that afflicted these very interpretations. Indeed, the blindnesses in the text—of the sentry, of Teiresias—seem invariably repeated in the partially blind readings of the text.[57]

Is Butler claiming that there is a way to read the text directly, without any blindness? Is the meaning of the play completely or predominantly a product of its readings or is there something primal and enduring in the play itself?[58] How were the Greeks able to seize on primal matters whose relevance can last millennia? What would such primal matters be? Why have the texts endured long after we have abandoned the theatrical practices that first brought them to light?

In her recent book *Why Shakespeare?*, Catherine Belsey poses a similar question about Shakespeare's plays: what makes his plays so important to us today? Her answer is that our interest in Shakespeare comes from his reliance on traditional folk tales—although he always presents them with an interesting difference.[59] The folk tales deal with abiding issues, which Shakespeare is able to complicate and particularize so as to appeal to a more sophisticated audience. A similar argument could be made about the use of myth in Greek plays, which is also open to difference and variation—in how many different lights (hero, villain, loyal counselor, backstabbing schemer, pitiless murderer) does the character of Odysseus appear? Here we are approaching something like the archetypal criticism of someone like Northrop Frye, a type of criticism that has been out of vogue for some time, never having really found its post-structuralist legs. Archetypal criticism has manifested an ahistoricist indifference to specificity and difference that has kept it on the outside of our theoretical canon. Belsey's book brings difference, if not histori-cal specificity, back into the study of what might be called archetypes. It may be time to revisit archetypal criticism to see if there is a way it can speak to us other than in an ahistorical and essentialist voice. But in doing so we will have to ask ourselves the uncomfortable question ("nothing should be sure here, for essential reasons"[60]) as to whether an ahistorical and essentialist voice (as we have been assuming for some time) must always be a bad thing.

In this brief overview I have focused on a few abiding questions about theory and theatre that have come to the fore once again in recent theo-retical work. One set of questions deals with the use of theory and the use of theatre. Behind these questions are other questions: why should theory be useful? Why should theatre be useful? Another set of ques-tions has to do with the (after)life of theory and theatre: how can we account for the relation between the present and the past, the living and the dead? How can theatre, ephemeral as it is, abide? In theory and in theatre such questions continue to be at play.

Notes

1. Anton Chekhov, *Five Major Plays* (Toronto: Bantam Books, 1982), 76, 164, 170.
2. The opportunity for thinking about the subject of this essay was provided by a graduate course I led in theory and theatre at the University of Guelph in the winter of 2008. I am deeply indebted to the students in that course: their participation, dedication, and perspicacity were all I might have hoped for.
3. Matthew Arnold, "The Function of Criticism at the Present Time," in *Critical Theory since Plato*, ed. Hazard Adams (New York: Harcourt Brace Jovanovich, 1971), 588.
4. Arnold, "The Function of Criticism," 584.
5. Julian Meyrick, "The Limits of Theory: Academic versus Professional Understanding of Theatre Problems," *New Theatre Quarterly*, 19: 3 (August 2003), 230–42.
6. Bruce McConachie, "Falsifiable Theories for Theatre and Performance Studies," *Theatre Journal*, 59 (2007), 553–77.
7. Meyrick, "The Limits of Theory," 236. Emphasis in original.
8. Judith Butler, *Giving an Account of Oneself* (New York: Fordham University Press, 2005), 23.
9. Mark Fortier, *Theory/Theatre: An Introduction* (London: Routledge, 1997), 10.
10. Mark Fortier, *Theory/Theatre: An Introduction*, 2nd edn (London: Routledge, 2002), 45, 221.

11. Ibid., 221.
12. McConachie, "Falsifiable Theories for Theatre and Performance Studies," 553–4.
13. Harry G. Frankfurt, *On Bullshit* (Princeton: Princeton University Press, 2005).
14. Philip Sidney, "An Apology for Poetry," in *Critical Theory Since Plato*, ed. Hazard Adams (New York: Harcourt, Brace, Jovanovich, 1971), 168.
15. McConachie, "Falsifiable Theories for Theatre and Performance Studies," 572.
16. Diana Taylor, *The Archive and the Repertoire: Performing Cultural Memory in the Americas* (Durham: Duke University Press, 2003), 237–67.
17. Michael Hardt and Antonio Negri, *Empire* (Cambridge, Massachusetts: Harvard University Press, 2000); Michael Hardt and Antonio Negri, *Multitude: War and Democracy in the Age of Empire* (New York: The Penguin Press, 2004). In his recent handbook, *Theory for Performance Studies: A Student's Guide* (London: Routledge, 2008), Philip Auslander states, "Arguably, Deleuze and Guattari have had a greater direct impact on both the theory and practice of performance than any of the other theorists discussed in this volume" (89).
18. William Shakespeare, *Hamlet*, in *The Norton Shakespeare*, ed. Stephen Greenblatt, et al. (New York: W. W. Norton, 1997), 1.5.189–90.
19. Baz Kershaw, *The Radical in Performance: Between Brecht and Baudrillard* (London: Routledge, 1999); Jill Dolan, *Utopia in Performance: Finding Hope at the Theatre* (Ann Arbor: University of Michigan Press, 2005). The students in my recent graduate course, I found, were very drawn to thinking about theatre in political terms.
20. Kershaw, *The Radical in Performance*, 5.
21. Ibid., 7.
22. See ibid., 5–26 (especially 8–12).
23. Dolan, *Utopia in Performance*, 2.
24. Ibid., 19, 21.
25. Heiner Müller, *Hamletmachine and Other Texts for the Stage* (New York: Performing Arts Journal Publications, 1984), 140.
26. Paul Ricoeur, *Freud and Philosophy: An Essay on Interpretation* (New Haven: Yale University Press, 1970), 32.
27. Geoffrey Hartman, "The Interpreter's Freud," in *Modern Criticism and Theory: A Reader*, ed. David Lodge, 2nd edn (Harlow, Essex: Pearson Education Limited, 2000), 375–86.
28. Oscar Wilde, "Preface," *The Picture of Dorian Gray* (New York: Airmont Publishing Company, Inc., 1961), 10.
29. Lee Edelman, "Learning Nothing: *Bad Education*" (paper presented at the annual conference of the Association of Canadian College and University Teachers of English, Vancouver, 1 June 2008); also see his *No Future: Queer Theory and the Death Drive* (Durham: Duke University Press, 2004).
30. Auslander, *Theory for Performance Studies*, 4. Jill Dolan's new book has the project of "Using Theater" (*Utopia in Performance*, 13).
31. Jacques Derrida, *Specters of Marx: The State of the Debt, the Work of Mourning, & the New International* (New York: Routledge, 1994), 28.
32. Duncan Jamieson, "Between Derrida and Grotowski," *Contemporary Theatre Review*, 17.1 (2007), 59. This renewal of deconstruction was noted many years

ago, for instance by Jeffrey T. Nealon, but it seems to me that it remained until more recently a wish or a prediction rather than an actuality (Jeffrey T. Nealon, "The Discipline of Deconstruction," *PMLA*, 107, 5 [October 1992], 1266–79).

33. For those with an interest in theatre, it is noteworthy how important a supporting role *Hamlet* plays in Derrida's thinking about Marx.
34. Derrida, *Specters of Marx*, 32.
35. Ibid., 17.
36. Ibid., xx. Emphasis in the original.
37. Such questions are tackled by Sam Stedman in his dissertation, *Always Already Almost Here: Levinas, Derrida, and an Ethico-Political Theatre* (University of Toronto, 2007).
38. Herbert Blau, *Take Up the Bodies: Theater at the Vanishing Point* (Urbana: University of Illinois Press, 1982), 32.
39. Jacques Derrida, *Archive Fever: A Freudian Impression* (Chicago: University of Chicago Press, 1996), 1.
40. Cited in Fortier, *Theory/Theatre*, 2nd edn, 49.
41. Elinor Fuchs, "Presence and the Revenge of Writing: Re-thinking Theatre after Derrida," *Performing Arts Journal*, 26/7, 163–73; Philip Auslander, *Liveness: Performance in a Mediatized Culture* (London: Routledge, 1999).
42. Christie Carson, "Theatre and Technology: Battling with the Box," *Digital Creativity*, 10.3 (September 1999), 129.
43. Steve Dixon, "Remediating Theatre in a Digital Proscenium," *Digital Creativity*, 10.3 (September 1999), 135–42.
44. Matthew Reason, "Archive or Memory? The Detritus of Live Performance," *New Theatre Quarterly*, 19 (2003), 82–9.
45. Ellen MacKay, "The Theatre as a Self-Consuming Art," *Theatre Survey*, 49.1 (May 2008), 96.
46. Derrida, *Archive Fever*.
47. Dolan, *Utopia in Performance*, 2.
48. Taylor, *The Archive and the Repertoire*, xvii.
49. Linda Fisher and Lester Embree, eds, *Feminist Phenomenology* (Dordrecht: Kluwer Academic Publishers, 2000). See also various important works by Judith Butler.
50. Sara Ahmed, *Queer Phenomenology: Orientations, Objects, Others* (Durham: Duke University Press, 2006).
51. Alice Rayner, *Ghosts: Death's Double and the Phenomena of Theatre* (Minneapolis: University of Minnesota Press, 2006); Esiaba Irobi, "What They Came With: Carnival and the Persistence of African Performance Aesthetics in the Diaspora," *Journal of Black Studies*, 37.6 (July 2007), 896–913.
52. Bill Ashcroft, Gareth Griffiths, and Helen Tiffin, eds, *The Post-Colonial Studies Reader* (London: Routledge, 1995).
53. Guillermo Verdecchia, *Fronteras Americanas* (Vancouver: Talonbooks, 1993).
54. Judith Butler, *Antigone's Claim: Kinship Between Life & Death* (New York: Columbia University Press, 2000).
55. Miriam Leonard, *Athens in Paris: Ancient Greece and the Political in Post-War French Thought* (New York: Oxford University Press, 2005), 96–156.
56. Philippe Nonet, "Antigone's Law," *Law, Culture, and the Humanities*, 2 (2006), 314–35.

57. Butler, *Antigone's Claim*, 5.
58. I realize some of the questions I have posed here are in the form of the much maligned binary opposition; I ask my students, however, if binary oppositions are always wrong?
59. Catherine Belsey, *Why Shakespeare?* (Basingstoke: Palgrave Macmillan, 2007).
60. Derrida, *Archive Fever*, 36.

2
Approaching Theory: Scholar and Practitioner

Manon van de Water

The relationship between theory and practice—theorists and practitioners—is a tenuous one, full of contradictions and mistrust, both in the US and in many places beyond.[1] Theory is generally seen as the prerogative of the scholar. Practice, on the other hand, is bound up with the artists and the artistic output. Many scholars feel that they do not necessarily need the practice to theorize or produce scholarly work. Many artists may feel that theory or scholarship is not important for their specific field. Some people contest the mere idea that one person can combine both scholarly and practical/artistic work, questioning whether one can truly activate two halves of the brain at once.

Theory and practice

Nevertheless, the most exciting developments in theatre in the twentieth century came exactly from the interaction of theory with practice, often combined in the same person or group of persons. This interaction of theory and practice—practice theorized, theory practiced—is demonstrated and documented in plays, manifestos, treatises, paintings, eyewitness accounts, histories, case studies, videos, audios, and reviews. These marriages were never easy and filled with challenges and tensions within the theorists/practitioners themselves, as well as their relationship with the outside world. All the same, we find numerous examples that suggest that theory and practice are more inherently connected than is often assumed. Filippo Tommaso Marinetti's futurism was an artistic movement, but also an ideology rebelling against the past and glorifying speed, technical invention, and aggression. Hugo Ball's dada started in a café—the owner of which he promised an increase in the sale of beer, bratwurst, and rolls—as the manifestation of an idea and ultimately an

34

artistic theory. The Russian avant-garde theatre practiced the theories of Constantin Stanislavski's realism, Vsevolod Meyerhold's biomechanics, Kazimir Malevich's cubo-futurism, and Vladimir Mayakovsky's revolutionary art. Adolphe Appia and Edward Gordon Craig's theories changed the world of design, but they also wrote utopic treatises on the total theatre experience. Appia experimented with Emile Jaques-Dalcroze in the factory town Hellerau; Craig wrote *On the Art of Theatre* (1904), worked with Isadora Duncan, and designed the notorious "white" *Hamlet* for the Moscow Art Theatre. The famous painter Vassily Kandinsky put his theories on the future of art—published in a volume *On the Spiritual in Art* (1912) and his essay "On Stage Composition"—into practice in his play *The Yellow Sound*. Bertolt Brecht is just as well known as a theorist of the epic theatre as a director and playwright of epic plays. This by no means exhaustive list illustrates the importance of both theory and practice in experimenting with and advancing the field of theatre, a cause more recently also taken up, for instance, by theorist/practitioner Augusto Boal and developed further in various areas of applied theatre.

This chapter explores the differing relationship(s) that scholars and practitioners have to theory. Although it focuses on the question of what role theory plays for theatre practitioners, and how this role(s) moves away from, and intersects with, that which theory offers the scholar, the above examples, however brief and sketchy, make clear that a separation of theory and practice is oxymoronic at best.[2]

Ideology

Various contemporary dictionaries define theory as "a supposition or a system of ideas, intended to explain something," "a set of principles on which the practice of an activity is based," and "an idea used to account for a situation or justify a course of action" (*Oxford American Dictionary*). While other dictionaries emphasize theory as an analysis of fact (*Merriam Webster*), the notion of an "idea" seems to be ontologically related to "theory." Similarly, practice is, among other definitions, defined as "the actual application or use of an idea, belief, or method as opposed to theories about such applications or use" (*Oxford American Dictionary*). In these definitions, then, "idea" seems to be the conduit between theory—a system of ideas, and practice—the application of ideas.[3] Ideas also underlie the much debated and contested concept of ideology.

Destutt de Tracy, who with his friends coined the term ideology in the eighteenth century, stated that "Nothing exists for us except by the idea we have of it, because our ideas are our whole being, our existence itself."[4] Since then, the meaning ascribed to ideology has undergone significant changes. While the original term is understood to refer literally to the metaphysical world of ideas, twentieth-century philosophers added some interpretative nuances of their own to this general definition, all of which have a bearing on the relationship between practice and theory. Many twentieth-century philosophers (such as Louis Althusser, Claude Lefort, Zygmunt Bauman, Walter Benjamin, and Michel Foucault) refer to classic Marxism as the basis for their theories. Karl Marx (1818–83), perhaps the most influential theorist, philosopher, and revolutionary of the nineteenth and twentieth centuries, articulated a theory based on historical materialism, which argued that not the idea but the material circumstances were the determining factor in the process of thinking, or forming ideas: "The idea is nothing else than the material world reflected by the human mind, and translated into forms of thought."[5] Extrapolating on this, Lefort points out that the current conception of ideology is almost contrary to its original meaning; from "a logic of dominant ideas, concealed from the knowledge of social actors and only revealing itself through interpretation and in the critique of utterances and their manifest sequences, [ideology] has been reduced to a corpus of arguments, to the apparatus of beliefs, which provides the visible framework of a collective practice [liberal, Leninist-Stalinist, fascist]."[6] In these definitions, ideology obtains a political dimension through a tendency by which ideas substitute for reality, in a process that Jean Baudrillard calls "simulation."[7]

Ideology is a slippery concept, often used pejoratively, but also postulated as a way to understand our ideas and our actions—in effect our theories and practices. Ideology can be seen as dominant and coercive, a legitimizing and perpetuating force that affects all areas of life. Or it can be seen as forms of social thoughts by which people set forth, explain, and justify the ends and means of social action, without the specific purpose of uprooting the culture. It can be linked to Marxist "false consciousness," or neo-Marxist "lived relations." Ideologies can be rationally rejected or accepted, but no one can fully escape them. The very function of ideology is to explain and rationalize. As individual subjects, people are always implicit in the functioning of ideology. We live in a transideological society where multiple ideologies function side by side as well as in often complex combinations. Terry Eagleton asserts that ideology is omnipresent because people do not cease to dream, imagine, and hope, even under the direst circumstances.[8] As a field that is invested in imagining and creating, theatre and drama is intrinsically linked to ideological thought in theory and practice, part of what Althusser identifies as the Ideological State Apparatus.[9]

Eagleton sums the various notions of ideology up in the introduction to his seminal work *Ideology* (1991) and concludes, rather philosophically, that "what persuades men and women to mistake each other from time to time for gods or vermin is ideology."[10] While this says a lot about the power of ideas, and the power of persuasion through ideas, the notion that a practice comes out of a theory, or an idea if you will, which in turn is a reaction to a practice, is neither revolutionary nor innovative in and of itself. The manifestation of this dialectical relationship goes back to Aristotle's *Poetics* and the *Natya Shastra* by Bharata Muni. The ideology that underlies both theory and practice permeates our work whether we are engaged in scholarship or creating art. This becomes evident when we compare theatre practice and theory under national or dominant meta-ideologies, such as fascism, communism, and capitalism, as well as those influenced by other belief systems, including local ideas of morals, values, and religions.

Practicing theory—theorizing practice

While scholars could ostensibly argue that they can conduct scholarly research without considering contemporary practice, in historical and historiographical research for example,[11] contemporary theatre research needs the practice in order to validate the theory. As a scholar/artist myself, trained in both academics and practical theatre and engaged in both on a daily basis, it is impossible to delineate between the two. Clearly, there are formal differences between engaging in scholarly research and writing, as I am doing here, and rehearsing a production, or teaching a drama class. Although the peddler in *Caps for Sale*[12] wears many caps at once, only one is his peddler cap, which filters the ideas in his head, and in that sense we change hats according to the task at hand. But a large part of my director's cap is filled with the theories and ideas I acquired through scholarly research, and a large part of my theory cap here is informed by my director's work, translations, and observations. Whether I am a better scholar or a better director or practitioner is irrelevant here, because if I am a better scholar it is because of my work as a director and practitioner and vice versa. For example, years ago I published a scholarly article "Adults Performing Children: Ideology, Representation, and the Construction of 'Real,'" in which I looked at the constructed notion of a child-reality in Theatre for Young

Audiences (TYA), an adult perceived construction that is presented to the child as the reality a child literally or metaphorically experiences.[13] This notion is enforced by the common practice in professional TYA of having children's roles performed by adults. The article used a number of theoretical arguments, illustrated with my own (complicit) practice of prepping college actors to take on the role of children in my own productions. At that time, for me, as a scholar and an artist, the idea of using adults in child roles remained unquestioned; after all, children miss the necessary training to perform themselves believably. When two years later I decided to experiment and directed a production with two ten-year-old protagonists, I discovered that children can actually be very powerful in performing their own age group. My practice had challenged my theory (children should not/cannot act) while my theory led me to practice (let's see if this is true).

I am not implying that every scholar should practice or that every practitioner should actively engage in scholarly research per se, but a certain awareness of how theory informs the practitioner and how practice informs the theorists would behoove both. Jill Dolan, for example, has conducted groundbreaking work as a scholar rooted in practice. In *Geographies of Learning: Theory and Practice, Activism and Performance* (2001) Dolan, who sees herself as a translator and mediator in the theory/practice debate, points out that the disdain and distrust in which theorists and practitioners sometimes hold each other is counterproductive, if not destructive, arguing that "it is vitally important that activists and academics, theorists and critics and more positivist scholars, find ways to interrupt our repetition of these [disparaging] debates and learn to work together productively."[14]

> [T]heory is not antiaesthetic or anticreative, and thinking about theater might actually enhance its value within American culture. . . . My theoretical reading also allowed me to see theater as even more central to the project of culture. . . . Given the right critical and creative tools, active, rather than passive, consumption of theatre and film and dance and performance contributes to a richer conversation about arts and its efficacy.[15]

Here Dolan addresses another important aspect of the dialectic between theory and practice: scholarly research and publication can help make theatre and performance visible by contesting the general notion of performance as mere entertainment and ascribing cultural, social, political, and academic value to it. In other words, theory and practice need

each other to sustain each other and the field of theatre and performance in general.

If I have established the symbiotic relationship of theory and practice for the theorist here, what does and could theory mean for the
practitioner? Tony Kushner writes in his foreword to Tim Miller's 2002
book *Body Blows*: "As a tribute to Tim I'm typing this naked."[16] Miller
draws attention to the body in his writing, in his performances, and
in his activism, and Kushner felt compelled to capitalize on this. Both
Kushner and Miller are intellectuals and artists, theorists and practitioners. They espouse their theories and their activism not through
academic treatises, but through their art as a mode of expression. What
does it mean to direct, design, or perform in Kushner's plays without
having any notion of Kushner's theories and ideologies? How does
a Miller performance impact an audience that has no notion of gay,
lesbian, and queer theory or activism? Would people feel compelled to
try to find out more, starting the dialectical theory-practice cycle, or
would they reject it out of hand? Both, most likely, because a lot of our
pleasure in performance, as well as in research, derives from recognition, however small this may be, and from seeing the familiar in a new
light. Research stems from curiosity, from wanting to know more about
or experience more of what we do not know and are not familiar with.
Benjamin, Brecht, Dolan,[17] and countless others have pointed out that
thinking has its own pleasures and rather than spoil it, critical thinking
may actually enhance the experience to what one of my students (in
tech and design) called "the moment of epiphany."

Which brings this chapter almost full circle. All the artists/theorists
mentioned at the start of this chapter experimented with new ways
of making theatre. Some were more theory oriented, some were more
practice oriented, but all are known for both theory and practice. To
separate the two is indeed "destructive" in Dolan's words, and at the
very least, stagnating for both research and practice.

While these artists/practitioners are directly linked with theatre/
performance arts, cultural theorists have also undeniably impacted
contemporary practice. Eagleton starts his 2003 book *After Theory* as
follows: "The golden age of cultural theory is long past. The pioneering
works of Jacques Lacan, Claude Lévi-Strauss, Louis Althusser, Roland
Barthes and Michel Foucault are several decades behind us," while
simultaneously pointing out that this doesn't mean we can go back to
the age of pre-theory innocence.[18] On the contrary, although new theorists and theories may not be visible on the horizon, we are doomed to
continue to expand and apply the theories of the golden age: "If theory

means a reasonably systematic reflection on our guiding assumptions, it remains as indispensable as ever."[19] Practitioners and artists may not have any direct familiarity with the works of Foucault or Barthes. But it would be a mistake to think that these theorists have not impacted contemporary practice, in part through those who studied these scholars, and translated and applied their work to contemporary practice, which subsequently became an inspiration to other artists. I don't think there is any serious practitioner who doesn't take cultural context into account, which was championed by Barthes in his post-structuralist semiotics.[20] Likewise Foucault's discourse, and the concept of power, has fused mainstream theatre practice, consciously or unconsciously.[21] Feminist criticism has drawn attention to the role and representation of women on stage to the extent that this cannot simply be ignored, in both the generation and perception of females on stage.[22] The male gaze theory, borrowed from media studies, affected both reception theory and directing.[23] Post-colonial theory has made us sensitive to the portrayal of other cultures and "exotic" characters, as well as casting choices.[24] Most theatre directors have at least some concept of (cultural) theatre semiotics—the theory of the signs illuminating how meaning is constructed and understood—a highly theoretical concept with highly practical implications.[25]

Implications and considerations

If contemporary theatre artists are aware of these theories as well as their own ideological positions they can make theatre that is relevant to contemporary society. Theatre artists who choose to stage "period pieces" usually delve into historical and archival research, but at the same time it may be useful to take into account the theoretical question of what "period" means for a contemporary audience and engage with the idea of period itself as a monolithic concept. Theatre artists that are committed to engaged theatre—political, social, cultural—would do well to be informed of the theories and ideologies that drive contemporary society, while considering questions of form and style in the generation and perception of meaning through their artistic choices. The devastating result of a lack of such considerations is, for example, very apparent in many contemporary theatre for children and youth productions, in which an absence of research and theoretical knowledge often leads to substandard and uninteresting productions contributing to the pejorative epithets often assigned to children's theatre, such as "theatre-but-not-theatre," "kids' stuff," or "second class theatre."

Joseph Roach, who writes theoretical, erudite, and witty works about performance, history, and memory by researching cultural phenomena such as Mardi Gras and the appeal of "abnormally interesting people" in his latest work *it*, states that "texts may obscure what performance tends to reveal."[26] Extending this to what has been discussed in this chapter, I paraphrase this as "theory may obscure what performance tends to reveal" while at the same time "performances are the outcome of or lead to theory." Regardless though, as this chapter demonstrates, it is exactly in the vortices of theory and practice where the most exciting developments happen. And unlike the common beliefs stated at the top of this essay, the practice needs its scholars, just as much as scholarship needs its practitioners, if we want theatre and performance, influenced by and expressing our ideologies, knowledge, research, and creativity, to matter in society.

Notes

1. The focus of this chapter is the relationship between product-oriented theatre and theory. The many forms of applied theatre and drama over the last five decades or so show a far less tenuous relationship between theory and practice.
2. Etymologically, the origins of the word theory are directly related to theatre. The word theory derives from the Greek "theorein," which means "to look at." According to some sources, it was used frequently in terms of "looking at" a theatre stage. Scholars in ancient Greece also used the noun "theoria."
3. Idea (1) concept, notion, conception, thought; image, visualization; hypothesis, postulation. (2) Plan, scheme, design, proposal, proposition, suggestion, brainchild, vision; aim, intention, purpose, objective, object, goal, target (first two meanings of idea in *Oxford American Dictionary*).
4. Destutt de Tracy, qtd in Zygmunt Bauman, "Ideology and the *Weltanschauung* of the Intellectuals," in *Ideology and Power in the Age of Lenin in Ruins*, eds Arthur Kroker and Marilouise Kroker (New York: St. Martin's Press, 1991), 114.
5. Karl Marx, *Das Kapital*, vol. 2 (Hamburg: Europaische Verlaganstalt, 1968), 27.
6. Claude Lefort, "On the Genesis of Ideology in Modern Societies," in *Ideology and Power in the Age of Lenin in Ruins*, eds Arthur Kroker and Marilouise Kroker (New York: St. Martin's Press, 1991), 47.
7. Jean Baudrillard, *The Illusion of the End* (Cambridge: Polity, 1994).
8. Terry Eagleton, *Ideology* (London: Verso, 1991), xiv.
9. Louis Althusser, "Ideology and Ideological State Apparatuses [Notes Towards an Investigation]," in *Lenin and Philosophy and Other Essays* (New York: Monthly Review Press, 1971).
10. Eagleton, *Ideology*, xiii.
11. Although this too, of course, is highly contested. See, e.g., one of the latest thought provoking editions *Theorizing Practice: Redefining Theater History*, eds Peter Holland and W. B. Worthen (New York: Palgrave Macmillan, 2003).

12. Esphyr Slobodkina, *Caps for Sale: A Tale of a Peddler, Some Monkeys and Their Monkey Business* (n.p.: 1938) (Republished in 1987 by HarperCollins).
13. Manon van de Water, "Adults Performing Children: Ideology, Representation and the Construction of 'Real,'" *Youth Theatre Journal*, 17 (2003), 109–18.
14. Jill Dolan, *Geographies of Learning: Theory and Practice, Activism and Performance*. (Middletown: Wesleyan University Press, 2001), 1.
15. Ibid., 4–5.
16. Tim Miller, *Body Blows* (Madison: University of Wisconsin Press, 2002). Foreword by Tony Kushner, ix.
17. Walter Benjamin, *Illuminations*, trans. H. Zohn, (London: Fontana, 1973); Bertolt Brecht, *Brecht on Theatre: The Development of an Aesthetic*, trans. and ed. J. Willet (New York: Hill and Wang, 1964); Dolan, *Geographies of Learning*.
18. Terry Eagleton, *After Theory* (New York: Basic Books, 2003), 1.
19. Ibid., 2.
20. See Roland Barthes, *The Semiotic Challenge* (New York: Hill and Wang, 1988).
21. See Michel Foucault, *The Foucault Reader*, ed. Paul Rabinow (New York: Pantheon, 1984).
22. See, for instance, Jill Dolan, *The Feminist Spectator as Critic* (Ann Arbor: University of Michigan Press, 1988).
23. See, for instance, Gay Gibson Cima, "Strategies for Subverting the Canon," in *Upstaging Big Daddy*, eds Ellen Donkin and Susan Clement (Ann Arbor: University of Michigan Press, 1993).
24. Homi K. Bhabha, "Representation and the Colonial Text: A Critical Exploration of Some Forms of Mimeticism," in *The Theory of Reading*, ed. Frank Gloversmith (Brighton: Harvester, 1984), 93–122.
25. See, for instance, Keir Elam, *The Semiotics of Theatre and Drama* (London: Methuen, 1980) and Erika Fischer-Lichte, *The Semiotics of Theater* (Bloomington: Indiana University Press, 1992).
26. Joseph Roach, *Cities of the Dead* (New York: Columbia University Press, 1996), 286. See also Joseph Roach, *it* (Ann Arbor: University of Michigan Press, 2007).

3
"There is a World Elsewhere": The Endgame of Theory and Practice

Michal Kobialka

On October 8, 2004, Jacques Derrida, a French philosopher, died in Paris. Even those who have little to do with the academe and who may know even less about Derrida must have heard a term "deconstruction," which is associated with him. Once perceived as a rigorous method of analysis intending to show that any piece of writing is laden with ambiguities and contradictions, today 'deconstruction' has become an artifact of popular culture, fashion, and daily speak.

At the same time, as Emily Eakin contended in "The Theory of Everything, R.I.P.," published in *The New York Times*, "Derrida is gone, as are grand, revolutionary claims by scholars."[1] This one sentence laid the debates about the use of theory in the humanities and the fine arts into a proverbial grave. The argument goes that, in the 1970s and the 1980s, the decades of the theory boom, there were radical and emancipatory claims made by scholars challenging not just texts or performances, but also the political system, its reified categories, and society at large. Today, since revolutionary claims were pronounced unwise or simply dead and, as Francis Fukuyama argued in his 1989 essay, "The End of History," the triumph of the West was evident in the total exhaustion of the viable systematic alternative to Western liberalism, scholars can devote themselves to writing at its most general and abstract.[2]

After theory?

Thus, we are told that theory is over. The crisis, however, not to say the death of theory, has already been announced a few times: recall Paul Bové's *In the Wake of Theory* (1992), Terry Eagleton's *After Theory* (2003), or Michael Payne and John Schad's *life. after. theory* (2003).[3]

Consider, for example, Eagleton's *After Theory*. It claims the demise of the age of cultural (i.e., postmodern) theory and a return to modernist aesthetics and politics.[4] Theory for Eagleton is a capacious term used to embrace the academic discourses which arose out of the impact of structuralism, and more particularly post-structuralism, on the humanities. Key figures of this transformation were French thinkers—Roland Barthes, Jacques Lacan, Louis Althusser, Derrida, and Michel Foucault—who subjected the methodologies of structuralism of Ferdinand de Saussure and Claude Lévi-Strauss and the ideologies of other modernist thinkers like Karl Marx and Sigmund Freud to a scrutiny that was at once critical of its content and its modes of operation. In due course, this transformation was also made visible in the US by writers such as Paul de Man, J. Hillis Miller, Geoffrey Hartman, Jonathan Culler, Gayatri Spivak, Fredric Jameson, and Edward Said who extended the scope of traditional (late modernist) literary criticism. In their writings, they drew attention to the whole range of cultural production with its non-aesthetic approaches to the material, as evidenced, for example, by the strategies of new historicism, post-colonial studies, subaltern studies, queer theory, feminist studies, and gender studies. No matter how diversified these strategies have been or still are, the effect of theory on academic study was to undermine the authority of the modernist canon and to install in its place a set of alternative sub-canons such as women's writing, gay and lesbian writing, post-colonial writing, and the very texts of theory itself. Not surprisingly, theory met with resistance from those with a vested interest in more traditional modes of scholarship.

Now theory meets with resistance from those who struggled on its behalf, including Eagleton. He begins the book by locating the origins of theory in the 1960s—the decade marked by liberation politics, student revolts, and intellectual risk taking. Initially, new cultural criticism, avant-garde art, and revolutionary politics joined forces against capitalism and abuses of socialist politics in Eastern Europe. By the end of the 1970s, according to Eagleton, this was no longer the case, and in the anti-ideological 1980s, the progressive left had to face the fact of its defeat. Throughout the book, Eagleton seems to admire theory for continuing to question the accepted order of things, but he admonishes it for recent turning away from radical political action. Much of the blame is attributed to postmodernism, which, according to him, denies the validity of universals and fundamentals, and encourages a kind of relativism of ideas and experiences, depriving even ostensibly progressive projects like post-colonialism of practical effect and moral purpose.

Eagleton's is a lesson of theoretical nostalgia. More than that: it suggests that the possibilities embodied in and made feasible by theory have been exhausted or rendered impotent. But this talk is nothing more than a pre-emptive gesture, which encourages that what is now conceived as a failing project be abandoned for the new life ("the life after") of the post-theory condition—for example, the application of neurobiology to the study of audience reception and the practice of theatre; the blurring of genres; the cultural or performative turn; the identitarian politics of recognition—or that we return to the pre-lapserian times of the Aristotelian *Poetics*, the centuries-old blueprint for making works of art, and forget about representational practices which are always time and site specific and, by extension, always delimited by politics and ideology.

This talk can only be counter-balanced with theory's abiding fundamentally critical engagement with what is going on in the space of the now (Walter Benjamin's *Jetztzeit*). Theory, as Timothy Brennan reminds us, "must be seen—positively—as a critique of instrumental reason, a critique of an anti-intellectual workshop of capitalist efficiency, the tyranny of the practical and profitable, and the narrowing of the human sphere: a protest in short, against the fate of philosophy, which had been prematurely condemned to death by a philistine general culture."[5]

Theatre/performance theory and practice as modes of thinking

Following this insight, I wish to contend that theatre or performance theory (the way one thinks critically and dialectically about things) and practice (the way one does things) are modes of thinking. These modes of thinking acquire material shapes in a space where theatre is viewed not in terms of Aristotelian poetics, utopian performative, or scientific desire for certitude, but in terms of an autonomous practice, which betrays the established reality or the ordinary realm of approved knowledge. This autonomous practice is only entrusted to the constancy of its specific representational acts.

Representational practice: three fragments

Traditionally, representation in theatre was defined in terms of: (1) imitation of nature (Aristotle, *Physics*, 199a) or the process of doubling of the "one that becomes two" (Plato, *Phaedo*) delimited by hierarchism of optical geometry, that is, by Leon Battista Alberti's 1435 rules of a single-point perspective ordering a transfer of objects from a real space to an imaginary stage; (2) the process of making the subject transparent to monocular vision of the identified community to which it belongs: the nation, the city, the ethnic group, etc.

This concept of representation was however championed and problematized at the beginning of the twentieth century, because of the fragmentation and split evident within the subject. The "I" and "we" ceased to be valued as universally defined nouns. As a corollary, representation was no longer able to express the subject's desire to impose linear transfer and ideological order upon both human beings and objects that were to appear in theatre and drama. Once the authority of the subject to control the standards for seeing the objects was undone, representation was replaced by the objects or their fragments floating in a dynamic space wherein different, often contradictory, possibilities were enunciated. Within this field of specifiable political, cultural, and social enunciations, a simultaneous interplay of multiple discourses on representation can be discerned. To substantiate this point, consider, for example, three transformations that had a considerable impact on the perception of the objects now altered by the changes in the understanding of time, space, and matter in Western culture and history. New perceptions of time and space at the beginning of the twentieth century, the events of World War II, and the postmodern sociology of the body are examples *par excellence* of the complex interplay between theory and material practice.

Positivist representation was challenged by philosophers, physicists, and artists in the second half of the nineteenth and the first decades of the twentieth century. Among the changes introduced, those in the perception of time and space were the most assertive. The realm of intellectual inquiry was infiltrated by Nicolai Lobachevsky's and János Bolyai's systems of non-Euclidean geometry, Bernhard Riemann's n-dimensional geometry, Alfred Einstein's special theory of relativity, and Werner Heisenberg's indeterminacy principle.[6] All of these theories provided support for Einstein's famous dictum that "time and space are modes by which we think and not conditions in which we live."[7] If space and time are modes of thinking, this can only mean that the definition of what space and time are is no longer absolute, but is in flux and needs to be elucidated. In the fine arts, experiments with spacetime, and specifically with its speed, direction, shape, rhythm, and density were the most revolutionary formal devices in cubism, futurism, dadaism, surrealism, and constructivism, as evidenced by their manifestos.[8] Non-developmental dialogue, simultaneism, transrational language, collage, montage, automatic writing, and phonic exercises were frequently random combinations of a certain number of elements from other works, objects, and pre-existing messages which were put together to constitute a new creation. As Georges Braque's paintings, animating the discrepancies between vision and cognition, Luigi Russolo's dynamic paintings of color zones and the objects positioned within them, Marcel Duchamp's experiments with *l'objet prêt,* or Kurt Schwitters' *Mertz* construction exemplified, the new work of art was now believed to be "real" in itself, an independent reality that existed nowhere else. These processes of grafting emphasized the subjectivity of perception and the interplay of domination and subjugation between artistic expressions and the experience of the everyday world. As Hugo Ball noted about the dada soirees at the Cabaret Voltaire in Zurich in 1916:

> Our cabaret is a gesture. Every word that is spoken and sung here says at least this one thing: that this humiliating age has not succeeded in winning our respect. What could be respectable and impressive about it? Its cannons? Our big drum drowns them. Its idealism? That has long been a laughingstock, in its popular and academic edition. The grandiose slaughters and cannibalistic exploits? Our spontaneous foolishness and our enthusiasm for illusion will destroy them.[9]

The events of World War II cleaved the subject into irreconcilable fragments. Both Theodor Adorno's "Commitment" and Jean-François Lyotard's "Discussions, or Phrasing 'after Auschwitz'" put forth the necessity for re-evaluating all the phrases, both secular and theological, that lost their right to exist after Auschwitz, unless it was acceptable that genocide become a part of Western culture.[10] More importantly, how could suffering find its voice without being appropriated or assimilated by bourgeois subjectivity and its systems of power, without which there could have been no Auschwitz? According to Adorno, autonomous works, that is, works that are governed by their own inherent structure, rather than social psychology, provide an answer.[11] "They are knowledge as nonconceptual objects. This is the source of their greatness. It is not something of which they have to persuade men, because it should be given to them."[12] Jean-François Lyotard, on the other hand, draws attention to phrases such as "we," "die," and "I decree it" which, as he asserts, lost their power as immobilizing normative statements because of the destruction of the legitimate or legitimating authority. How could "we" be the whole if the SS and the prisoner in a concentration camp had no common ontological or psychological grounds? When expressed in art, these experiences had to abandon the tradition which defined art in terms of representation affirming the external order of things and its structures of belonging. Samuel Beckett's *Waiting for Godot* and *Endgame*, for example, manifest forms which were freed from the strict laws of construction of pre-war representational art, and were instead always changing and fluid, negating, decomposing, dissolving, deconstructing, or destroying any promise of representation. Tadeusz Kantor's 1944 production of *The Return of Odysseus* was staged in Kraków, Poland, in a room destroyed by the war, since even if it had been possible, placing it in a theatre building would have legitimated the conventions of the Western civilization which had led to the outbreak of World War II in 1939.

Recent theories and practices presented by traditionally marginalized groups, that is, by feminist and lesbian studies, by gay/queer studies, and by cultural "minorities," are engaged in meticulous and systematic analyses of coercive and disciplining modes of representation by producing a space from which the "other" subject can speak. Employing various Marxist, structuralist, psychoanalytic, and post-colonial strategies, they keep re-examining dominant institutions, both real and symbolic, which control, shape, and reproduce traditional narrative and scopic structures of expectations. The political agendas combined in these revisionary approaches are aimed at the present power structures organizing representation—that is, what is to be seen, where it is to be seen, and how it is to be seen. What is essential in them is that they question the representation's power to contain the discourse on visual pleasure, gaze, class and ethnicity, or the construction of sexual difference and gender. Recall, for example, past (and, by now, signature) performances by Carolee Schneemann (*Interior Scroll*), Suzanne Lacy (*Ablutions*), Leslie Labowitz (*Paragraph 218*), Joan Jonas (*Organic Honey*), Karen Finley (*We Keep Our Victims Ready*), Holly Hughes (*Clit Notes*), Coco Fusco (*A Couple in a Cage*), Vito Acconci (*Seedbed*), Chris Burden (*Shoot*), Tim Miller (*My Queer Body*), or Bill T. Jones (*Still Here*) which determine and displace the boundaries delimiting institutionally-defined cultural fields by reworking the structures of expectations that organize and control them to produce images of the other as a construct of a particular group identity.

The endgame of theory and practice: Antonin Artaud and Tadeusz Kantor

The displacement of the temporal and spatial boundaries that define representation, the re-evaluation of the nature of the speaking/performing subject, and the new mode of functioning of the subject have indeed reconstituted representation. Antonin Artaud's theatre of cruelty and Kantor's theatre experiments are two examples of how this penetrative process is accomplished through the endgame of theory and practice—a praxis which can open up the potential for a radical repositioning of the dominant representational practices by exposing art, history, and politics, which are caught in the act of inventing reified forms for the consumption of the culture industry.

In "The Theatre of Cruelty and the Closure of Representation," Derrida provides an insightful reading of Artaud's statement that theatre has not yet begun to exist.[13] According to Artaud, "Western Theatre has been separated from the force of its [unique, not to say, non-theological] essence, removed from its affirmative essence, its *vis affirmative*" by representation in which life "lets itself be doubled and emptied by negation."[14] One of the consequences of this separation is that theatre accepted the functions that were imposed upon it by the external order of things and successive models of representation. Representation imprints the culture within which it is positioned and all attempts at dissolving or destroying representation by, for example, the avant-garde movements—constructivism, futurism, surrealism, and the happenings—cease to be viable as soon as the dominant structures of the culture industry absorb the products of these movements, or their techniques of representation, only to nullify their revolutionary content.

Artaud places his theatre of cruelty in opposition to these practices, viewing it as a site where the complete destruction of representation is possible through the destruction of the structure of belonging. In its stead, the theatre of cruelty produces a non-theological space, which is independent and autonomous and that "must, in order to revive or simply to live, realize what differentiates it from text, pure speech, literature, and all other fixed and written means."[15] Theological space, for Artaud, is the stage dominated by speech/logos and an author-creator who "lets representation represent him through representatives, director or actors, enslaved interpreters who represent characters, who primarily through what they say, more or less directly represent the thought of the 'creator.'"[16]

Released from these constraints, the theatre of cruelty will no longer re-present a known present, but will produce an experience which produces its own space. Spacing (*espacement*), that is to say, the production of a space that no external authority or systems of conventions can comprehend or appropriate—and, thus, which functions beyond the confines of what a given tradition or ideology wants this space to be or signify—is an answer to Aristotelian imitation of nature or Platonic process of doubling. The constitution of a closed space of representation, that is, "a space produced within itself and no longer organized from the vantage of an other absent site, an illocality, an alibi or invisible utopia,"[17] will allow for the experience of the elements positioned within it. By so doing, Artaud's is a theatre that critiques and rejects forms accepted in a culture, rejects logocentrism articulated in and by language, and rejects social norms that control individuals.

Whereas Artaud's statements are primarily about non-theological representation, Kantor's theatre experiments in the period between 1944 and 1990 provide a visual example of speaking within a representation. It should be noted here that although their philosophical systems are incompatible—since Artaud's project tried to restore an affirmative essence permitting access to a life before and after the death of Western theatre, while Kantor's theatre was about collecting the objects wrenched from reality—both of them advanced considerably a discourse about the closure of traditional representation.

In his experiments, in the period between 1944 and 1990, which were labeled the Autonomous Theatre, the Informel Theatre, the Zero Theatre, the Happening-Theatre, the Impossible Theatre, and the Theatre of Memory, Kantor insisted that traditional theatre was an anomalous institution where "the gaping ritual was staged for the faithful."[18] In its stead, he wanted to create a theatre that would have a primordial power of shock

TAKING PLACE AT THE MOMENT WHEN, OPPOSITE A HUMAN (A SPACTATOR), THERE STOOD FOR THE FIRST TIME A HUMAN (AN ACTOR), DECEPTIVELY SIMILAR TO US, YET AT THE SAME TIME INFINITELY FOREIGN, BEYOND THE IMPASSABLE BARRIER.[19]

Kantor insisted that a performance space be treated as a place producing its own space where the thinking and the vision of the ever-present artist were executed.[20] The experiments with the so-called places of "the lowest rank," a bombed room, galleries, gyms, and altered theatres, which existed as if outside of the appropriating gaze of the external order, were the structures where he discussed the disintegration of theatrical illusion, performing, and representation. Accordingly, the 1944 production of *The Return of Odysseus* was staged in a room of a house destroyed by the war into which Odysseus, a man in a military uniform, returned from a siege of Stalingrad. In "The Zero Theatre Manifesto" (1963), Kantor evoked on stage negative emotions such as apathy, melancholy, and depression in order to question patterns of traditional Aristotelian plot development. "The Theatre of Real Space Manifesto" (1967) postulated that, during a performance, the actors ought to perform activities and characters in a way that agreed with the reality of a selected performance site and its characteristics. "The Theatre of Death Manifesto" (1975) introduced the impassable barrier between the auditorium and the performance space in order to create a place for the exploration of the intimate world of Kantor's memories. The concept of "The Room of Memory" explored in *Wielopole, Wielopole* (1980) presented the audience with the spatial dimensions of immaterial memory enacted by actors on stage. "The Theory of [Film] Negatives" introduced in *Let the Artists Die* (1985) suggested that events/memories "acted out" by the actors could not be presented in a linear fashion. The idea of "The Inn of Memory" presented in *I Shall Never Return* (1988) created a meeting ground for Kantor and his memories/actors. Finally, the notion of "The Found Reality" made visible in *Today is My Birthday* (1990) explored the consequences of Kantor positioning himself in the liminal space between reality and illusion.

Kantor's theoretical writings not only challenged what he had perceived as official art or mass culture in a socialist Poland, but also probed into the traditional notion of representation by giving visibility to the objects that could no longer be or were not yet appropriated by the artistic convention or had a use-value assigned to them. Instead, the objects articulated and re-articulated their functions while establishing relationships with other objects and people in a performance space, which were accidentally formed and could not be foreseen. The object, which was bereft of the security of its structure of belonging, "enters into the closest possible relationship with its equivalents."[21]

In order to accomplish this, Kantor introduced the notion of annexing reality, or the process of incorporating ready-made elements—the objects, the events, and the environment—into an artistic activity. The strategy of annexing reality signified the process of wrenching these objects from that reality where they were "named" and placing them in a space where their objectness or their own inherent structure, to use Adorno's phrase, could be explored in the encounter with other elements positioned within that space. Thus, the objects were non-conceptual in Adorno's sense of the principles that govern autonomous works of art. The focus was on their inherent structure, rather than on the totality of the effects; on a manual process of signification, rather than the visual sovereignty of the eye producing the representational image in a classical, three-dimensional space; on that which "refuses the consolation of correct forms, refuses the consensus of taste permitting a common experience of nostalgia for the impossible, and inquires into new presentations."[22]

Using poor objects, matter, marginalized objects, degraded objects, which are positioned within a dynamic, fluid, and open space, Kantor offered a praxis which troubled the recognized reality by bringing to the fore its unknown, dismissed, or illegitimate aspect. Kantor by no means transformed reality, the real, or the everyday. He took it up in order to rethink its singularity, rather than to explore its relation to the mimetic program of realism. If indeed reality was taken up, rather than transformed, both it and its content were viewed as the ready-mades. Their pre-existing configurations were disfigured by subjecting both actions and objects to repetitive operations, by liberating them from the bondage of moral or aesthetic utility, and constructing new relationships between them in order to exhibit their inherent structure, thus, mediality. Existing-in-a-medium consumed the energy necessary for creating an object in the image of the Object so that it could become a subject of an artistic creation. Bereft of this energy, an object or an action, existing-in-a-medium, was autonomous and non-conceptual.

Kantor, thus, created a praxis which, indeed, went beyond the "ordinary" realm of established interests and differences. His theatre was a radical departure from, or rupture within, the normative representational theatrical categories or structures. It created a possibility of seeing that which cannot really be grasped or understood using a traditional idea of a transfer from a real space to an imaginary stage, because in its most concrete stage form it showed "nothing." Kantor's poor/real objects, reality of the lowest rank, an autonomous work of art, zero zones, the impossible condition, and the complex mnemotechnics, were a critique of instrumental reason. They elaborated the concept of an initial forgetting—that forgetting which happens every time an object is transformed into a form with a pre-assigned commercial or artistic use-value.[23]

Theatrical event as condition of possibility

Artaud's and Kantor's theory and practice restored a theatrical event to its condition of possibility by cracking a smooth surface of the visible and intelligible wide open in order to show a potential for radical rejection of the dominant representational practices in service of the culture industry and its imaginary. Artaud's theory/practice puts forth the idea of experience which produces its own space (*espacement*) wherein words, bodies, and objects betray their structures of belonging. Kantor's theory/practice brings to the fore that which has been marginalized, degraded, forgotten, erased, or damned to be irrelevant—shards, which come back, despite everything, on the edges of discourse. These remainders gather to remind us that, indeed, there is a world elsewhere where a theatre practice will always be an answer to, rather than a representation of, reality.

Notes

1. Emily Eakin, "The Theory of Everything, R.I.P.," Section 4: Week in Review, *The New York Times* (Sunday, October 17, 2004), 12.
2. Francis Fukuyama, "The End of History," *The National Interest*, 16 (Summer 1989), 3–18.
3. Paul Bové, *In the Wake of Theory* (Hanover: University Press of New England, 1992); Terry Eagelton, *After Theory* (New York: Basic Books, 2003); Michael Payne and John Schad, eds, *life. after. theory* (London, New York: Continuum, 2003).
4. Eagleton, *After Theory*, 1. All references are to page numbers in this volume.
5. Timothy Brennan, *Wars of Position: The Cultural Politics of Left and Right* (New York: Columbia University Press, 2006), 8.
6. For a discussion of these theories and experiments see, for example, Max Jammer, *Concepts of Space* (Cambridge, MA: Harvard University Press, 1969); Milič Čapek, *The Philosophical Impact of Contemporary Physics* (New York: Van Nostrand Reinhold Company, 1961); Stephen Kern, *The Culture of Time and Space* (Cambridge: Harvard University Press, 1983).
7. Aylesa Forsee, *Albert Einstein: Theoretical Physicist* (New York: Macmillan, 1963), 81.
8. See, for example, Linda Dalrymple Henderson, *The Fourth Dimension and Non-Euclidean Geometry in Modern Art* (Princeton: Princeton University Press, 1983); J. H. Matthews, *Theatre in Dada and Surrealism* (Syracuse: Syracuse University Press, 1974); Christiana J. Taylor, *Futurism: Politics, Painting and Performance* (Ann Arbor: UMI Press, 1979); Annabelle Melzer, *Latest Rage and Big Drum* (Ann Arbor: UMI Press, 1980).
9. Hugo Ball, *Flight Out of Time: A DADA Diary*, ed. John Elderfield (Berkeley: University of California Press, 1996), 61.
10. Theodor Adorno, "Commitment," in *The Essential Frankfurt Reader*, 300–18; Jean-François Lyotard, "Discussion, or Phrasing 'after Auschwitz,'" in *The Lyotard Reader* (Oxford: Basil Blackwell, 1989), 360–92.
11. While talking about the relationship between the authority and non-autonomous forms, Adorno observes that

   > Newspapers and magazines of the radical Right constantly stir up indignation against what is unnatural, over-intellectual, morbid and decadent: they know their readers. The insights of social psychology into the authoritarian personality confirm them. The basic features of this type include conformism, respect for a petrified facade of opinion and society, and resistance to impulses that disturb its order or evoke inner elements of the unconscious that cannot be admitted. (Adorno, 303)

12. Adorno, "Commitment," 317.
13. Jacques Derrida, "The Theatre of Cruelty and the Closure of Representation," in *Writing and Difference* (London: Routledge & Kegan Paul, 1978), 232–50.
14. Ibid., 233–4.
15. Ibid., 237.
16. Ibid., 235.
17. Ibid., 238.

18. Tadeusz Kantor, "Credo 1942–44," in *A Journey Through Other Spaces: Essays and Manifestos, 1944–1990*, ed. and trans. Michal Kobialka (Berkeley: University of California Press, 1993), 34.
19. Kantor, "Theatre of Death Manifesto," in *A Journey Through Other Spaces*, 114.
20. See Kantor, *A Journey Through Other Spaces* for the texts of these manifestos.
21. Walter Benjamin cited in Douglas Crimp, "This is not a Museum of Art," in *Marcel Broodthaers* (Minneapolis: Walker Art Center, 1989), 72.
22. Jean-François Lyotard, *The Postmodern Explained*, trans. Don Barry, Bernadette Maher, Julian Pefanis, Virginia Spate, and Morgan Thomas (Minneapolis: University of Minnesota Press, 1993), 5.
23. The concept of an initial forgetting comes from Jean-François Lyotard. See Lyotard, *The Postmodern Explained*, 80.

Part II
Interrogating Theory in Theatre Practice: Productive Tensions, Questions, and Implications

Introduction: Part II

Megan Alrutz and Julia Listengarten

The chapters in Part II, "Interrogating Theory in Theatre Practice," introduce productive tensions, questions, and implications raised by the practical application of theory within theatre practice. Stressing the empowering nature of reflection, contradiction, and tension for theatre makers, the entries in this part invite us to contemplate the ways in which theory, when applied to a creative process, can propel us to move forward, to continue to (re)imagine and (re)build new ways for making art and ultimately engaging the audience. Together, the authors in this part foster a dialogue around the application of various theories across theatre disciplines to raise complex issues around theatre making, meaning making, and spectatorship.

While investigating some of the significant impacts of theoretical discourse for theatre makers, the chapters in Part II also point to the role of theory in propelling the emergence of new methodologies for and from the creative process. Despite this part's broad scope in approaching the role of theory in practice, throughlines in emphasis emerge from the collection of chapters. Several authors in this section draw on recent developments in science, noting the growing influence of cognitive theory and neuroscience on both theatre theorists and practitioners. Other authors expound upon cultural theory and its connection to practice, reminding us that cultural and historical perspectives as well as issues of power, identity, and authenticity remain relevant to theatre practice and continue to offer innovative and useful ways to think about, imagine, and create theatre. As theatre artists engage recent scientific developments and weigh the value of cultural theory within theatre practice, the chapters in Part II invite the reader to consider how theoretical landscapes complicate representational practices and our ability to engage audiences. By interrogating theory in theatre practice, through an examination of questions, tensions, and contradictions around this complex and often disputed relationship, the authors in Part II contemplate the role of theory in facilitating what Jill Dolan refers to as "productive misunderstandings" for both theatre makers and audience members.[1]

The first four chapters in this section offer a variety of perspectives drawn from media theory, theories of authenticity and nationalism, as well as recent developments in neuroscience to further investigate the relationship between performance, performer, and audience. These chapters examine theory in relation to performance making on a relatively general level, encouraging us to consider how various theories can lead us to new, productive choices as we make theatre. Pondering the use-value of theory, whether implicitly or explicitly, some of this work also stresses notions of responsibility and power of theatre, thus continuing the debates around fundamental perspectives on the role and place of theory in theatre that are introduced in Part I. The second group of chapters, which are further addressed in the latter half of this introduction, focus more specifically on the creative process within dramaturgy, design, acting, and directing, and highlight the intersection(s) between intellectual thought and creativity, as well as various possibilities for theoretical discourse to invigorate theatre practice.

Sarah Bay-Cheng opens Part II with an exploration of the intersections of body (biology) and media (technology) in both the creation and reception of live and digital performance and culture, specifically considering the effects of "media body theory," with all its embodied tensions and contradictions, in the work of Belgian artist Kris Verdonck. Her chapter suggests a dialectic relationship between media theory and theatre, interrogating the ways in which media discourse can inform, challenge, and shape emerging theatre practice, and offering clear examples of how theatre can become a literal embodiment of theoretical discourse.

Individual chapters by Stephani Etheridge Woodson and S. E. Wilmer follow with investigations of responsible representation from differing perspectives, specifically revolving around concepts of authenticity and nationalism. Woodson focuses her discussion about responsible representation on the ethical ramifications of an untheorized understanding of authenticity, thus fostering the concept of theorized practice suggested earlier in Part I in Michal Kobialka's discussion of the works of Antonin Artaud and Tadeusz Kantor. Reflecting on how our approach to, and understanding of, authenticity is intrinsically connected to meaning making and identity construction, Woodson points to the significance of intellectual and artistic choices in assigning value to an ideology, a social system, and/or cultural narrative. She examines authenticity as a theoretical statement that signifies power and is concerned with inherent "meaning, moral merit, and intrinsic value." Wilmer continues the discussion on social, cultural, and ideological ramifications of representational choices by examining the ways in which theoretical debates on nationalism impact theatre artists' relationship to national identity. Exploring the role of nationalism and nationalist theories in establishing, reinforcing, and/or disrupting nationalist ideals and beliefs through theatrical representation, Wilmer suggests ways that embodied theoretical discourse can construct and/or subvert identity formation, as well as (re)build and/or disrupt communities. Describing a wide range of productions/theatrical events throughout the last two centuries in which theatre artists critique nationalist expression, embrace nationalist ideals toward the purpose of the state, or employ a subversive strategy of over-identifying with extreme nationalists to disrupt their chauvinist dogma, Wilmer foregrounds the influence of theatre practitioners on the development of nationalist discourse in its many different manifestations, thus further underlining a dialectic relationship between theory and art.

Stephen Di Benedetto follows this discussion with a chapter on senses and reception, examining how the application of theories drawn from cognitive science and neurobiology can shape an intentional creative process for theatre makers. Specifically, Di Benedetto encourages us to attend to the implications of sense (perception) theories, offering questions and examples that address performers, directors, designers, and spectators as they make choices to affect an audience. Similar to the earlier chapters, Di Benedetto's essay thus addresses the relationship between theory and intentionality in our production work, pointing to theory as a framework for conscious and purposeful theatre making. Moreover, by considering scientific evidence and theory as a framework for making artistic decisions, this chapter builds a foundation for artists to rethink attention to senses and neurocognitive engagements in theatre, subjects that are also discussed later by contributors to this part.

Lenora Inez Brown's chapter on active dramaturgy marks a shift in Part II, pointing to chapters that engage in more discipline-specific (such as dramaturgy, design, acting, and so on) explorations of the creative process in relation to theory. Brown addresses the potential of academic and theoretical research to complicate our production process from a dramaturgical perspective, offering a frank interrogation of the usefulness of theory during the rehearsal process. Specifically, she provides a skeptical view of theory in the rehearsal hall, suggesting that theoretical discourse can offer important contexts for a production team, but rarely translates directly into active, playable material for the stage. Considering approaches to active and creative dramaturgy, Brown views theory as an inspiration for action, expands definitions of theory to include research and criticism in a broad sense, and ultimately proposes a methodology for evaluating the relevance of theoretical frameworks to dramaturgical practice.

The remaining chapters in this part explore the contradictions and complexities of the creative process through various theoretical lenses primarily drawn from neuroscience, while questioning the value of binary thinking that separates mind and body, emotion and reason, intuition and intellect. In conjunction with one another, these chapters establish a dialogue about the relevance of new developments in neuroscience for contemporary theatre practice, illuminating Di Benedetto's earlier propositions concerning the interplay between sense theories and theatre making. Interrogating the process of creative practice in terms of its intuitive nature, Harry Feiner employs elements of cognitive theory, specifically current theoretical paradigms of consciousness, and its application to the creative process—a discussion that he later extends to his own scenographic practice. While theorizing the role of intuition, he taps, even if inadvertently, into what French philosopher Pierre Bourdieu refers to as "theory of practice":[2] theory itself becomes a process, a mode of practice, and a framework for re-visioning the binary of thought and creativity. John Lutterbie, too, explores the potential of cognitive theory, along with theories of phenomenology and deconstruction, to shift our understanding of the creative process and ultimately challenge existing paradigms of actor training. His chapter exemplifies what Fortier, in Part I, refers to as "hybrid theory," demonstrating how artists borrow and combine pieces of current theory with past paradigms to intentionally challenge and revise theatre practice. Arguing for a more holistic approach to training actors, Lutterbie continues to question the value and implications of a binary approach to acting training, referring to ideas such as "the inside/outside dualism" or the traditional separation of thought and emotion in the actor's process. Marking an important dialogue with both Di Benedetto and Feiner, Lutterbie points to the inseparability of emotion from rational thought, both of which, he believes, prove integral to the creative process.

Bruce McConachie concludes Part II with a discussion on cognitive theory as a tool for re-animating the progressive politics of Bertolt Brecht's plays for contemporary audiences. He offers the application of cognitive science to Brecht's theories of acting and audience response to "close the gap between a cognitive perspective on theatre and the dialectical theatre of the playwright-director" and to open up possibilities "for a reconsideration of all politically ambitions performance." Employing the concepts of cognitive scientists Gilles Fauconnier and Mark Turner about human beings' ability to experience "conceptual blending," McConachie approaches Brecht's plays from a perspective of both a theorist and director to challenge Brecht's *Verfremdungseffekt* and complicate audience response to Brecht's call for action. His chapter encourages us to rethink our relationship to past theories and to incorporate scientific advances and new theories that markedly shift our understanding of notions of empathy, emotion, and natural behavior, particularly in relation to acting and audience response. McConachie's discussion of Brecht's theoretical contradictions revealed by recent scientific developments points to tensions raised by Fortier and Kobialka in Part I, inviting us to consider whether theory should—or will—be reconsidered given inevitable shifts in time, culture, and context.

While not intentionally responding to each other's theoretical claims and queries, the authors in Part II map out a landscape, albeit partial, of current theoretical propositions and hypotheses and their intimate interplay with theatre practice. Moreover, in arguing for the relevance of new scientific theories in contemporary theatre practice, the authors continue the debates introduced in Part I around value, form, and function of theory in relation to practice and whether theory remains context-specific or a mode of autonomous practice.

As a whole, the chapters in Part II provide us with concrete examples, suggestions, and considerations of how theory can productively complicate our creative choices. In doing so, the authors ultimately raise a series of questions for students and early-career professionals beginning to negotiate the roadmap(s) of intentionally dynamic theatre making. In the process of representing culture and/or shaping identity through production, what determines our relationship to different theories and what ultimately informs our decision to select a certain theoretical model? Furthermore, what concrete ideas does theory offer us for challenging spectators' senses and perceptions or addressing issues of authenticity and nationalism in an increasingly global context? Where do intuition and intellect collide and diverge in our own artistic processes, and how does our understanding of this relationship inform our approach to theatre making? Jointly, these chapters encourage us to explore tensions and questions in our theatre-making process and to consider the practical implications of intentional and/or untheorized theatre practices.

Notes

1. See Jill Dolan's *Geographies of Learning* (Middletown, CT: Wesleyan University Press, 2001).
2. Pierre Bourdieu, *Outline of a Theory of Practice* (Cambridge: Cambridge University Press, 1977). See also Estelle Barrett and Barbara Bolt, eds, *Practice as Research: Approaches to Creative Arts Enquiry* (London and New York: I.B. Tauris, 2010) in which they refer to Bourdieu's theoretical discourse on the logic of practice in relation to the production of knowledge as a central focus of practice as research.

4
Intermediate Bodies: Media Theory in Theatre

Sarah Bay-Cheng

> Can we really put futuristic, 'disembodied' images on stage? Can we show characters whose functions are taken over by an object?[1]

The past 20 years of cultural, performance, and media theory have focused on the question of the body with increasing intensity. As Steve Dixon notes in *Digital Performance*, "The body is the most revered, fetishized, contested, detested, and confused concept in contemporary cultural theory."[2] Given the centrality of both bodies (typically as performers) and technology (lights, sets, architecture, etc.) to the theatre, it is not surprising that these new perspectives in media and cultural theory have had a pronounced influence in theatre and performance studies. Indeed, the emphasis on the body and media theory in theatre and performance is perhaps the fastest growing area of performance scholarship.

While much recent scholarship observes the cultural media contexts in which theatre artists create and the deployment of new technologies in their creative work, critics have paid less explicit attention to the effect of media theory itself on theatrical performance. And yet, as I attempt to demonstrate here, there is ample evidence that key media concepts play a significant role in new theatre work that articulates the cultural changes in bodies, machines, and technology. This chapter considers the effects of media body theory in recent theatrical performance, particularly the work of Belgian artist Kris Verdonck. Specifically, I explore the intersection of the body and machine theory in the creation of live performance and the ways in which the media discourse informs, challenges, and shapes emerging theatre practice in the twenty-first century. Of course, as Ralf Remshardt notes in his recent essay on posthuman performance, "theory is not clearly a priori or a posteriori to the practice, but rather emerges from a constant, and constantly accelerating feed-back loop of theory and practice."[3] It would be difficult, if not impossible then, to argue for such a unidirectional influence of media theory in theatre. Nevertheless, one can point to certain salient aspects of media theory, particularly its focus on the body, as animating features of contemporary performance, particularly in the work of artists who draw from theoretical sources for their work.

The most significant of these sources is the mediated body—that is, the body as it has evolved in media theory over the second half of the twentieth century—in contrast to the theatre's theoretically immediate body—that is, a body presented in physical proximity to an audience. Media-based theories of the body include a wide array of emphases, including the cyborg—a cybernetic organism—the post-human, and virtual bodies, among others, while performance theory tended to assert the live, performing body as the ontological root of performance. Peggy Phelan's influential *Unmarked: The Politics of Performance* (1993) set the stage for this essential presence, and numerous theatre theorists have reiterated it since. As I argue here, media theory serves as a trigger for new forms of theatre, one that fundamentally revises the role of the performing body on stage. I call this the intermediate body because it engages media theory within the space of live interaction and, most importantly, physical vulnerability. Within these media-based theories of the body, technology, and presence, Verdonck provides a potent example through performances that highlight the tensions among human performing bodies, their status as indeterminate objects, and the technological environment of both the performer and audience. Engaging both technological and theatre theory, Verdonck uses the body as a bridge between mediated representation and sensual experience.

The mediated body

Within the diverse field of media and cultural theory, it is difficult to identify a more ubiquitously studied subject than the sometimes abstract, sometimes concrete notion of what is often identified as *the body*. This focus on the body has emerged from a range of media theories, particularly Marshall McLuhan's *Understanding Media: The Extensions of Man* (1964). Though often cited for its argument that the medium is the message, McLuhan's book also argued that, "Any invention or technology is an extension or self-amputation of our physical bodies, and such extension also demands new ratios or new equilibriums among the other organs and extension of the body."[4] McLuhan's notion of media as simultaneously an extension and an amputation of the body raised the central question regarding the body's relation to media and its enhancement (and potential obsolescence) through media. Writing within a year of McLuhan, neurophysiologist and cybernetician Warren McCulloch observed that whereas "the industrial revolution concludes in bigger and better bombs, an intellectual revolution opens with bigger and better robots."[5] The threat was thus not only to human bodies, but also to their brains; a threat to "us, the thinkers, with technological unemployment, for it will replace brains with machines limited by the law that entropy never decreases."[6]

In addition to techno-enthusiasts like McCulloch, feminists and political thinkers also saw potential within enhanced technology for new relations among bodies and media. Donna Haraway, for instance, argued that cyberspace and the figure of the cyborg offered a new radical potential: "a cyborg world might be about lived social and bodily realities in which people are not afraid of their joint kinship with animals and machines, not afraid of permanently partial identities and contradictory standpoints."[7] Including connections between not only machines, but also animals (whose bodies are often eclipsed in discussions of the body), Haraway introduced a broad conception of the cyborg, an idea in concert with N. Katherine Hayles' later arguments on the post-human. In her provocatively titled *How We Became Posthuman*, Hayles theorized the post-human as both "the union of the human with the intelligent machine" and a conception of the body understood "simultaneously as an expression of genetic information and as a physical structure."[8] Like Haraway's cyborg, Hayles envisioned her post-human subject as "an amalgam, a collection of heterogeneous components, a material-informational entity whose boundaries undergo continuous construction and reconstruction."[9] This post-human figure would be free from essential and biological determinism, thereby allowing individuals to redefine their identities, bodies, and relationships to power. For Haraway, Hayles, and other feminist critics of science, as well as performance scholars such as Sue-Ellen Case, the post-human contains the potential for a revision of humanistic thought, rather than the decline of humanity itself.[10]

In the wake of Haraway's cyborg and Hayles' post-human subject, media theorists continued to wrestle with the relations among bodies, technologies, and representation. In his *Bodies in Code* (2006), for instance, Mark Hansen argued for a "mixed reality paradigm in our contemporary technoculture," in which "the irreducible body or analog basis of experience . . . has always been conditioned by a technical dimension and has always occurred as a cofunctioning of embodiment with technics."[11] This blending of technology and embodiment—especially the argument that the two are conditionally related—has recurred in media theory since the early 1990s. Media artist Jeffrey Shaw claimed that, "Representation is, and always was, the domain of both our embodied and disembodied yearnings. It is in the friction of this conjunction that we experience the euphoric dislocation of our present condition."[12] This perspective invited a radical rethinking, such that, "life is not simply a force that inhabits the organism but a network coextensive with information gathering, retrieving, storage, manipulation and management techniques,"[13] or, as Bernadette Wegenstein observed, "there is no body as 'raw material.'"[14] Thus, the body in media theory had become virtually indistinguishable from the mediated technologies themselves. If McLuhan had seen media as the extensions of man, humanity was now the logical extension of media.

But if the body's status changed so thoroughly from an autonomous being to one constituted by media, what impact does this have on performance? For artists like Shaw, new technologies repositioned the role of the audience as an embodied participant, an "experiencer" appropriated from Maurice Merleau-Ponty's argument that the body was the medium for perceiving the world.[15] For others, questions of the body were "replaced by issues regarding mediality itself."[16] For much of theatre studies, however, the argument was precisely the opposite. If media theory saw the distinctions between the body and media eroding productively, performance theorists saw media primarily as a threat to the performing body as an original and authentic material, what we might call an immediate body.

The immediate body

Against theories of the mediated body, theatre tended to position itself as the domain of the immediate body. Simon Shepherd summed up the emphasis of much of this work when he wrote, "theatre is, and has always been, a place which exhibits what a human body is, what it does, what it is capable of."[17] This live, theatrical body stretched back to Peter Brook's 1968 argument for an immediate theatre (in contrast to cinema) that "always asserts itself in the present,"[18] and recurred in Phelan's assertion that "Performance's only life is in the present."[19] Phelan's work joined other performance theory throughout the 1980s and 1990s that prioritized the role of live, performing bodies on stage, including those working in mediated forms of theatre. Dancer, theorist, and media artist Johannes Birringer, for example, wrote about "digital bodies," one type of mediated body, even as he strove to preserve the status of the live, human, performing body and its inherent (essential?) subjectivity:

> The cyberspatial dismissal of psychological depth, narrative, and subjectivity strikes me as one of the unacknowledged dangers of the dynamics proposed by the synthesis of virtual realities and artificial languages.[20]

To compensate for this potential loss, Birringer often situated his own performing body as a medium capable of realizing the various subject positions and sensations threatened by the virtual, as in his productions such as *AlienNation* and *From the Border*. He argues, perhaps ironically, that by performing, filming, and then reviewing his own performances, "I become more aware of my production and of the particular subject positions I assume in taking up my body."[21] If in media theory, the medium had become a body, theatre could still articulate the body as unalterable media. Birringer's irony, of course, is that in order to see it, the performer himself would need to rely on media.

The primacy of live performance similarly came under scrutiny in Philip Auslander's *Liveness: Performance in a Mediatized Culture* (1999). In this now oft-cited book, Auslander challenged the ontological significance of "liveness." Explicitly rejecting Phelan's ontology of performance as live, Auslander located performance in a context much like Hansen, arguing that performance and any conditions of liveness were predicated already on mediatized culture, thus omitting "clear-cut ontological distinctions between live forms and mediatized ones."[22] Auslander's book articulated the key tension for theatre in a mediatized context, or what Hans-Thies Lehmann called *The Postdramatic Theatre* (1999). Published in German the same year as Auslander's text and translated into English in 2006, Lehmann's book similarly considered the shifting relations between the body, text, and media, cogently arguing that it was "the spread and then omnipresence of the media in everyday life" that ultimately inspired "a new multiform kind of theatrical discourse."[23] Although contemporary performance may be indebted to developments in the historical avant-gardes and increased emphasis on performance over dramatic literature in the 1960s, Lehmann's postdramatic theatre was the result of what he calls "the caesura of the media society," an epistemological break with the dramatic texts of the past and a reaction to media's emergence.[24]

This tension between media and theatrical theories of the body are rarely more evident than in the work of Verdonck. Explicitly drawing inspiration from machine theory, new technologies, robotics, and theatre, he radically revisions the role of the performing body on stage in ways that explicitly perform the post-human. His *Variation IV* (2002–5),[25] for example, questions the fundamental ontology of the performing body, the role of the actor, and the function of live performance. Verdonck's mediated and technological bodies embark on struggles between their position as autonomous, subjective individuals and manipulated objects of technology and art. As such, Verdonck's bodies suggest a new status between wholly mediated representations and immediate live bodies, and provoke new visions for how theories of the post-human can play out in physical performance contexts.

Intermediate bodies: Kris Verdonck

Verdonck is emphatic that he is not interested in a dramaturgy of pain, but it can be difficult to reconcile this assertion with the images he presents. Some of his performances literally drown his performers in stimuli; others in mediated deprivation. Often, he creates situations that compel his performers to endure both over-stimulation and deprivation. His performance installation *Man* (2005) exhibits a human figure deprived of visual sensation, yet nearly overwhelmed by auditory input. With his head encased in a large, black sphere, a half-dressed dancer in latex gloves tentatively looks for his clothes, using only the input digitally inserted into the helmet to guide his way. As Verdonck describes it, the performer's "'sensory deprivation' turns into a 'nearly drowning' in an excessive quantity of unknown impulses in which he literally has to find his way."[26] In a related piece *Patent Human Energy* (2005), Verdonck encases a female performer in a three-dimensional box built from steel rods. The rods surround and entrap her body such that her movements are limited and the spectator's view of her is fragmented, almost ethereal. The audience cannot see the performer clearly, and like a mirage, the closer one draws, the more obscure the view. At the end of the rods around her body are sensors turning her limited movements into sounds that reverberate throughout the space. Based on the Microsoft Corporation's actual patent for turning human energy into power for handheld electronics, Verdonck's own *Patent Human Energy* literally traps the body in a dense structure of technology, in which the performer's energy is transformed into electronic signals without clear meaning or purpose.

The impact of works like these is a haunting sensation of pain and anomie. Yet, this is explicitly not Verdonck's aim. In a discussion regarding his work with actors, Verdonck asserts that his only direction to the actors, who as he notes perform not as "characters," but as "figüren" (figures), is to "try not to be victimized by the machine." It is their inevitable failure that renders these figüren as "tragic personages."[27] His installation *Box* (2005) creates this effect on the audience by enclosing them in a small space with the glass box containing the strongest possible light source in the relatively small area. Protective glasses are needed and the air around the box quickly warms to uncomfortable temperatures, while Heiner Müller's apocalyptic texts play in the background. Rather than exercising pain in all these works, Verdonck ironically positions the vulnerable bodies of his performers (and audiences) as sites of resistance against technology. Although experiencing his performances and installations, one might wonder who Verdonck is rooting for in the end.

The tension that Verdonck displays is thus not only between the body and the machine, but also between the performer's autonomy and Verdonck's deployment of the machine. The performance *In* (2003) takes Verdonck's drowning reference in *Man* even further by submerging a fully dressed performer within a large water-filled transparent tank and connected to an external oxygen supply by a single tube. Almost totally unmoving, eyes open (sometimes blinking), the person in the tank quickly takes on the properties of an object as the audience gathers around, moving closer to both the walls of the tank and the oxygen source vulnerably placed outside it. Within the space, unseen microphones amplify the sounds of the body, highlighting the mechanically dependent body systems of breath and heartbeat—a soundscape of a body under stress. In yet another, *Heart* (2004), a woman is thrown repeatedly against an upstage wall every 500 beats of her own heart. As the audience listens to her heartbeat (amplified from a monitor on her right hand), the actor is pulled both upward and backward by a cable affixed to a harness beneath her dress. The unsettling sound of her striking the wall and the sound of her falling again and again to the stage floor are punctuations in the continuous sound of her heart, beating faster as the audience arrives in the space, and faster still with the rush of adrenaline as she is pulled back against the wall.[28] Whereas *Man* and *Patent Human Energy* enclose the performer's body in an impenetrable infrastructure of mechanics (simultaneously playing with commercial software as Verdonck's technologies of choice), *In* and *Heart* go into the bodies of the performers themselves, turning their involuntary responses and uncontrollable organic functions into consumable art objects.

What is most striking about the individual pieces in Verdonck's *Variation IV* (including installations from 2002–5; performed 2008) is the way in which the technology both penetrates the performer's body and manipulates it. *Heart* connects the physical trauma of the machine to the performer's own involuntary movements. In this sense Verdonck reverses an earlier tendency in dance and technology, in which performers used their own bodies (including heart rhythms) to register visual or auditory impressions. For example, Mikhail Baryshnikov's *HeartBeat: mb* (1998) used Christopher Janney's HeartBeat sound system to translate the electrical impulses of Baryshnikov's heart into a soundscape in which he performed. As technology became available, dancers were frequently tapped for virtual reality projects, such as *Ghostcatching* with Bill T. Jones (1999), or even Merce Cunningham's early collaborations with Nam June Paik.

The difference with Verdonck's work is that the performer, although the one generating the sound, is not free to respond to it. Her role, in stark contrast to the controlled physique of Baryshnikov, for example, is one of submission. As Verdonck's dramaturge Marianne Van Kerkhoven writes, *Heart's* performer "cannot help but surrender to the machine of her own heart."[29] This emphasis on the interiority of the performer, with the tongue-in-cheek romanticism of a woman literally carried away by her heart, makes the body itself a visible system to the viewer, or, as Verdonck puts it, a body that the audience "can read." He thus positions the body at the intersections of media and performance theory, in which the body of the performer is simultaneously a mediated subject—the audience sees the images from the camera projected behind *Man* and hears the bodily systems of the performer in *In* and *Heart*—and an immediate human presence, or as Müller called it, "the potentially dying person" of the theatre.[30] Even if not putting his actors in danger (as he adamantly insists he is not), Verdonck clearly embraces a context of technological risk in which the mediated body is made, ironically, more vulnerable, more visible, and perhaps even more organically human, by the layers of mediation.

Playing (dangerously) with theory

Verdonck draws inspiration for his work from a range of technological and media theories, including work by Paul Virilio, Marina Grzinic, as well as reflections by playwrights such as Samuel Beckett and Heiner Müller. In *Man*, for example, Verdonck quotes from Virilio: "We have to change our view to survive, just like we have to change our existence to stay alive. It is no longer sufficient talking in negative terms about 'zero expansion', we have to exert ourselves positively to reinvent our perception of the world."[31] One can immediately see the humor in Verdonck's literal embodiment of Virilio's attempt to "reinvent our perception" by using the black sphere helmet and the performer's fumbling attempts to find his way as a potentially positive assertion in the world. And yet, a darker meaning hovers over the association with Virilio. The text from which Verdonck pulls the quote is Virilio's *Negative Horizon: An Essay in Dromoscopy* (1986), in which he observed that increased technological speed (drawn from the Greek dromos or "race") and improvements in vision (the scopic) have evolved to benefit the domination of the fast over the slow, particularly in the technologies of war. Tracing the evolution from feudalism to capitalism, Virilio observed the increased integration of technology and death, resulting in what he calls the "death machine" and has elsewhere asserted that "history progresses at the speed of its weapons systems."[32] Verdonck optimistically quotes Virilio's change in perception as a key to survival, "We have to change our view to survive," even as he appropriates technological enhancements intended to support sensory-deprived bodies. The video-audio technology that Verdonck employs is The vOICe, a Dutch program designed to translate visual images digitally into audio output, thus allowing the blind to see. And yet, Verdonck seemingly mocks this enhancement by turning it into an act of drowning.

It is no coincidence that Verdonck introduces *Variation IV* with an excerpt from media theorist and artist Grzinic, who relates the contemporary human condition to "mechanized serial production," and compares current relations between bodies and technology to the development of the lobotomy procedure. Rather than posing a division between the biological and the technological, Grzinic draws attention to the ways in which the body has become like a machine and indeed may find its technological (even spiritual) destiny in biological destruction. The brief excerpt concludes with Grzinic's inarguable assertion that "Partly angels, we are already inevitably future cadavers!" (Partiellement anges, nous sommes inéluctablement prêts à devenir cadavers!).[33] Given these parameters, it might be tempting to equate Verdonck's work with that of Stelarc (Stelios Arkadiou) the Greek-Australian performance artist and media theorist who began his career by staging his own body in danger (e.g., suspending himself in the air by hooks piercing his skin) and later developed a series of mediated and technological appendages, such as his robotic *Third Hand Project* (1976–81). According to Stelarc, "the body is obsolete," a system or "architecture," as he sometimes calls it, to be upgraded and amended with increasingly sophisticated technology.[34]

But there is something fundamentally different about Verdonck's work. Whereas artists like Stelarc revel in the technological possibilities, and theatrical defenders of the performing body warn against its dangers, Verdonck derives his work precisely from the dangers of technology and the vulnerability of his human figures. In this sense, Verdonck directly incorporates questions of media theory as the basis for his bodily experiments. If the question for so much media theory is the relation between the body and technology, Verdonck directly embodies these emerging ideas as the basis for his work. Indeed, so entangled are his performances with contemporary media theory, that it is impossible to imagine his work emerging from another context. As Kerkhoven explains, "One of the fundamental paradoxes Verdonck stages for us in his work, is the one between the technological representation and the re-production capacity on one hand, and on the other hand the singularity of a theatrical presentation, the here and now of a live performance."[35] It is this tension that relates his work so closely to that of the post-human. By positioning bodies between technological immortality and biological vulnerability, Verdonck draws on, and perhaps even intentionally stages, Hayles' notion of the post-human as the key to human survival.[36] In her notes to *Variation IV* Kerkhoven asks, "Can the 'human' be defined then, as 'making mistakes', as failing, stumbling and stuttering? Can one reduce the essential difference between man and robot to the fact that a human being can fail and a robot cannot?" In Verdonck's work, the body is powerful only so far as it makes mistakes: greatest of all is its potential to die. Looking at Verdonck's performing bodies, then, is to observe bodies caught in a moment of transition, stretched almost to the breaking point between technological determinism and biological breakdown. After facing criticism that he treats his performers as robots, it may come as no surprise that Verdonck's next works address the end (obsolescence?) of humanity (e.g., *End*, 2008) and replace human actors with robots (*Actor #1*, 2009). Although it might be a relief not to watch bodies imperiled, one wonders if Verdonck's work will have power without humans. Can the death of a robot be mourned; can its injury be feared? To return to Verdonck's central question raised at the opening of this essay, it seems clear that performing objects can take over the function of the human, just as humans can be turned into objects; the question remains whether objects can take on the vulnerability of the human. What is clear, however, is that media theory has become a powerful, animating force in contemporary, theatrical performance.

Notes

1. Kris Verdonck, notes to *Variation IV*.
2. Steve Dixon, *Digital Performance: A History of New Media in Theater, Dance, Performance Art, and Installation* (London: MIT Press, 2007), 212.
3. Ralf Remshardt, "Beyond Performance Studies: Mediated Performance and the Posthuman," *Cultura, Lenguaje y Representación/Culture, Language and Representation*, 6 (2008), 41.
4. Marshall McLuhan, *Understanding Media: The Extensions of Man* (New York: Signet, 1964), 54.
5. Warren S. McCulloch, *Embodiments of Mind* (London: MIT Press, 1988), 72.
6. Ibid.
7. Donna Haraway, "A Cyborg Manifesto: Science, Technology, and Socialist-Feminism in the Late Twentieth Century," in *Simians, Cyborgs and Women: The Reinvention of Nature* (New York; Routledge, 1991), 154.
8. N. Katherine Hayles, *How We Became Posthuman: Virtual Bodies in Cybernetics, Literature, and Informatics* (Chicago, IL: University of Chicago, 1999), 2, 29.
9. Ibid., 3.
10. See, for example, Sue-Ellen Case's *The Domain-Matrix: Performing Lesbian at the End of Print Culture* (Bloomington: Indiana University Press, 1996).
11. Mark B. N. Hansen, *Bodies in Code: Interfaces with Digital Media* (New York: Routledge, 2006), 7, 8–9.
12. Jeffrey Shaw, "The Dis-Embodied Re-Embodied Body," in Jeffrey Shaw, *A User's Manual—Jeffrey Shaw: Eine Gebrauchsanweisung: From Expanded Cinema to Virtual Reality. Vom Expanded Cinema zur Virtuellen Realität*, eds Anne-Marie Duguet, Heinrich Klotz, and Peter Weibel (Osfildern: Hatje Cantz, 1997), 157.
13. Anna Munster, *Materializing New Media: Embodiment in Information Aesthetics* (Dartmouth: Dartmouth College Press, 2006), 183.
14. Bernadette Wegenstein, *Getting Under the Skin: Body and Media Theory* (London: MIT Press, 2006), 161.
15. Merleau-Ponty's philosophical writing and theories of phenomenology have had a significant and wide-ranging impact on contemporary media and performance theory. Limited space precludes a more detailed discussion of this field of study here. For some representative examples that engage Merleau-Ponty, see Robin Nelson, "Double-Jointed: Implications of Virtual and Bodily Encounters in Contemporary Performance," Theater & Medien: VIII Kongress der Gesellschaft für Theaterwissenschaft, October 2006; and Stanton Garner, Jr., *Bodied Spaces: Phenomenology and Performance in Contemporary Drama* (Ithaca, NY: Cornell University Press, 1994). For a useful overview of phenomenology, see Maurice Merleau-Ponty, *The Primacy of Perception: And Other Essays on Phenomenological Psychology, the Philosophy of Art, History and Politics* (1945), ed. James M. Edie, trans. William Cobb (Evanston, IL: Northwestern University Press, 1964).
16. Ibid., 162.
17. Simon Shepherd, *Theatre, Body and Pleasure* (New York: Routledge, 2005), 1.
18. Peter Brook, *The Empty Space* (London: Penguin Books, 1990), 99.
19. Peggy Phelan, *Unmarked: The Politics of Performance* (New York: Routledge, 1993), 146.

20. Johannes Birringer, *Media & Performance: Along the Border* (Baltimore: Johns Hopkins University Press, 1998), 101.
21. Ibid., 115.
22. Philip Auslander, *Liveness: Performance in a Mediatized Culture* (London: Routledge, 1999), 7.
23. Hans-Thies Lehmann, *The Postdramatic Theatre* (New York: Routledge, 2006), 22.
24. Ibid.
25. Performed at the Festival d'Avignon, July 2008.
26. Kris Verdonck, *Kris Verdonck_Installations/Performances* (Brussels: Margarita Production_stilllab, 2005), n.p.
27. Verdonck, presentation and discussion at Centre National des Écritures du Spectacle, La Chartreuse in Villeneuve-les-Avignon, July 23, 2008.
28. Verdonck acknowledges that in more recent performances of this work, the heartbeat is recorded from earlier performances and replayed due to technical difficulties with the heart monitor connection.
29. Marianne Van Kerkhoven, *Kris Verdonck_Installations/Performances* (Brussels: Margarita Production_stilllab, 2005), n.p.
30. Quoted in Lehmann, *The Postdramatic Theatre*, 167.
31. Margarita Production, "Man [2005] by Kris Verdonck," http://www.margarita production.be/_ENG/KRIS_VERDONCK/MAN/INTRO.html (accessed July 25, 2008).
32. Paul Virilio, *Negative Horizon: An Essay in Dromoscopy* (Continuum, 2006), 68.
33. Marina Grzinic, "The Limit Between Life and Death," in Kris Verdonck, *Variation IV*, Festival d'Avignon, 2008 (Brussels: Margarita Production, 2008), 3.
34. This phrase is a central idea of Stelarc's and may be found in many of his writings, interviews, and in the description of several performance pieces. This phrase also became the title of a short 2007 documentary, distributed by Contemporary Arts Media.
35. Marianne Van Kerkhoven, *Kris Verdonck_Installations/Performances*, n.p.
36. Hayles, *How We Became Posthuman*, 291.

5

Authenticity in Children's Theatre and Art

Stephani Etheridge Woodson

"Not really for children"

I teach a lesson to teachers-in-training on the First Amendment and children's literature in which I put participants in role as an ad hoc committee examining books in a school library. In this scenario, the committee must respond to a citizen's group demanding the removal of several books they deem "offensive" or "unsuitable" for children. Generally, I am not surprised when in-role participants vote to remove books like Mem Fox's *Feathers and Fools,* or Justin Richardson and Peter Parnell's *And Tango Makes Three,* recently, however, a group also voted to remove Robert Munsch's *The Paper Bag Princess,* Dav Pilkey's *Dogzilla,* Jon Scieszka and Lane Smith's *The Stinky Cheese Man and Other Fairly Stupid Tales,* and Neal Gaiman's *The Wolves in the Walls.* While I undoubtedly slant their assessment of these titles through the scenario I use, participants rarely justify the *inclusion* of titles with arguments based on young people's First Amendment rights or access to aesthetic diversity. Rather, they justify the removal of these books with statements like, "it's not really for children." Every single one of these books can be found in the children's section of the bookstore, and are published by imprints or companies specializing in children's literature. So, on a literal level these books are *made for* children.

Recently, I was looking on iTunes for music to use in a first grade drama lesson on addition and subtraction and was surprised by the number of mathematical musical choices. Although many fell into what I would consider to be the category of commercial drivel—the times tables in pseudo rap style, for example—I found several choices reviewed as "kid stuff that grown-ups can enjoy" or "not really for children but

mine love it." What is actually being said or assumed when we judge a book or a song as "not really for children?"

To assuage my own curiosity, I conducted an entirely unscientific poll in my own family, exploring this question with young people and their musical choices. The US National Labor Committee website (www. nlcnet.org) estimates that teens (ages 12 to 17) spend an average of two to three hours a day listening to and/or downloading music. While I was unable to find statistics on children younger than 12, I asked ten kids between the ages of five and 12 about the last three songs or CDs they purchased. I then looked the songs up for genre and discovered that few (less than 20 per cent) were labeled "children's music." Most, in fact, were pop or country. So, does that mean Soulja Boy's "Crank That (Soulja Boy)" is "not really for children?" Six of the ten children in my family bought this song for themselves and the other four owned it already. As of October 2008, there were almost 47,000 videos on YouTube featuring "Crank That (Soulja Boy)." Over 1,500 of the videos have real children dancing to the song and another several hundred videos feature children's cartoons. Does it matter that Soulja Boy himself was 17 when the song hit number one on the Billboard Hot 100 in September 2007? Soulja Boy Tell 'Em, known to his parents and teachers as DeAndre Way, was born in 1990. And according to an article in *The Washington Post*, Way wrote, recorded, and first posted "Crank That" in 2006 when he was 16.[1] Is that enough to make this song "authentic youth music" even though it lacks that marketing label? I want to come back to this question in a moment, but one last story.

For our 2007/8 season, Arizona State University commissioned a new play from Laurie Brooks on immigration for the Theatre for Young Audiences slot. An award-winning playwright, Brooks chose to explore immigration as a historically-situated experience using the 1911 Triangle Shirtwaist fire as a way of drawing parallels with twenty-first century events. Her play, *Triangle*, centers on two sets of sisters, one set from today's world and one from the world of 1911. In many ways, *Triangle* is a disaster play. The Triangle Shirtwaist fire is considered by labor historians to be the worst US workplace tragedy until the events of 9/11. One hundred and forty-eight garment workers died in the fire, most of them recent immigrants, almost all of them young women between the ages of 14 and 25. As a new play, *Triangle* went through several revisions and incorporated audience talkbacks in both the staged reading and the full production. In both talkbacks and written responses, audiences (composed primarily of young adults) consistently complained that while they "liked the play," they did not believe the production was "really for

children." Their written and verbal feedback cited the play's incorporation of complex labor and unionization issues, the staging of the fire, and
the death of two of the protagonists as reasons for their judgment. I asked
my ten-year-old daughter her opinion, and she too suggested that while
she enjoyed and understood the play, perhaps younger children would
not. Again, what makes something *for* or *not-for* children? Who decides
what counts as "legitimate" children's theatre or children's music or
children's literature? While these questions may seem particular to work
with, for, and by children and youth, I would argue that such questions
are vitally important to representational practices in general. Who says
what counts as "legitimate" or "authentic" art? Do the answers to these
questions reside with makers? Audiences? Marketing departments?

A search on the Theatre Communications Group website[2] for 2007–8
not-for-profit theatre companies identifying themselves as producing
plays or programming for young audiences turns up 95 separate companies. And that number represents only the tip of the iceberg, as it does
not include recreation programs, municipal programming, for-profit
companies, or primarily educational groups. While I am most interested
in the specialized field of children's theatre, the question of "authenticity"
in representational art speaks to larger questions of value, ethical artistic
practices, and who has the right to represent whom—theoretical implications. Would a Hispanic director's interpretation of *Ma Rainey's Black
Bottom* be less "authentic" than an African American director's? Does
one need to be Jewish to produce a Holocaust play? Should someone be
Irish if s/he is to direct *Dancing at Lughnasa*? Taken to an extreme, these
questions become preposterous, but questions of authenticity touch on
both ethical and aesthetic practices. In particular, read through the lens
of "for-children" and "not-for-children," these questions can illuminate
some of the most difficult philosophical issues of representational art
forms in a diverse world.

Authenticity, hermeneutics, and exploring "legitimacy"

Each of the examples above revolves around questions of authenticity—
authenticity in children's literature, authenticity of children's music,
and authenticity in children's plays. In the field of theatre for youth,
we say: "theatre *by*, *with*, and *for* young people." How does authenticity
function within each of those prepositions? "Not really for children" is
code for questioning the complexity and/or subject matter of certain
forms of children's entertainment and art, as well as for questioning
young people's capacity to engage genuinely in such forms. And perhaps

not just young people's capacities; I was once introduced by a well-meaning neighbor as "and this is Dr Woodson, but don't worry its only in children's theatre."

Moving from a consideration of childhood as a sociological and cultural space rather than a biological imperative, I am interested in thinking through the intersections of authenticity and art for young people. What does it mean to make *authentic* children's art? What qualifies a book or play as *for* children? Do some pieces qualify as more genuinely children's art than others? Are child makers more authentic than adult makers? Are some companies or artists more legitimate than others? In order to explore these questions more fully, I use a hermeneutic approach, a method of interpretation associated traditionally with St Augustine and biblical exegesis. In the classical form of hermeneutic exploration, scholars focus on the written texts, or terms, moving from the literal through to more subjective and connotive meanings layered beneath literal meanings. Philosophical hermeneutics, developed from the work of Martin Heidegger, Hans-Georg Gadamer, and Max Weber, deepens the inquiry/interpretive process into more ontological and existential realms, exploring context and text as a reciprocal relationship (what Heidegger called the "hermeneutic circle").[3] Moving through both classical and philosophical hermeneutics allows me to concentrate on both the literal meanings of "authenticity" and the relationships, unspoken understandings, and performative iterations of the term.

From the literal to the philosophical in *The Wolves in the Walls*

Scholars understand the *Oxford English Dictionary* (OED) as the definitive source on English language usage from first written records into the present era. In the entry on "authenticity," the OED provides four inter-related classifications for the "quality of being authentic, or entitled to acceptance:"

1. as being authoritative or duly authorized;
2. as being in accordance with fact, as being true in substance;
3. as being what it professes in origin or authorship, as being genuine; genuineness;
4. as being real, actual; reality.[4]

While this maps the factual definition of "authenticity," I'm not sure this classification approaches the complexity of the questions considered here.

In order to discover whether or not the above definition is enough for our needs, we have to apply this classical hermeneutic conceptualization of "authenticity" to one of our examples. Returning then to the children's books, I would like to consider Gaiman's *The Wolves in the Walls*.[5] A book handily dismissed by the pre-service[6] teachers as "way too scary for kids," or as one Amazon reviewer proclaimed in 2004, "This is a very bad book, it's scary and not for children!!!!!!"[7]

Published by HarperCollins in 2003, artist Dave McKean illustrates the book with his dark, signature mix of photographs, pen and ink scribbles, and highly saturated sepia tones. A young girl, Lucy, is sure that wolves are living in the walls of her house. The front flap says, "There are sneaking, creeping, crumbling noises coming from inside the walls" and "as everybody says, if the wolves come out of the walls, it's all over." As you can imagine of this whimsically strange book, the wolves do come out of the walls, wreaking havoc in the house. Finally, the family has enough and they run the wolves off with broken chair legs. Gaiman and McKean have collaborated on multiple projects across several media forms. They are perhaps best known for their work in adult graphic novels and comic books. Together, however, they have also produced two other children's books, including a New York Times best-seller and the movie *Mirrormask*. In 2006, the National Theatre of Scotland and Improbable Theatre Company of London adapted *Wolves in the Walls* to the stage, calling it a "Musical Pandemonium."[8] The production received a 2006 Theatre Management Association award for Best Show for Children and Young People, and featured the co-direction of Julian Crouch and Vicky Featherstone, and the music of Nick Powell.

But to return to the question of "authenticity," what qualifies a book or a musical pandemonium as "entitled to acceptance" as for-children or not-for-children? *The Wolves in the Walls* is frightening. In fact, my younger daughter finds the book to be too much for her; we only read it during the day, if at all. In interviews posted on his website and on the HarperCollins site, Gaiman says that the book is about bravery, "about fighting back and dealing with the things that scare you."[9] The tag line for the musical's advertising was "for everyone over seven who is not a scaredy cat." The genesis of the story grew from a nightmare Gaiman's young daughter had, in which she insisted there were wolves in the walls of their home. The book also features a stuffed pig puppet who serves as both Lucy's security object and her best friend. In real life, the pig puppet belongs to McKean's young son and is *his* security object. Does that therefore make the story "duly authorized," "genuine," or "true in substance?" As to authorship, neither McKean nor Gaiman are children themselves, although both are parents. Of course, they don't claim to be children, so the book is exactly what it "professes in origin or authorship." Does that make the book then a more or less "authentic" children's text?

Unfortunately, while the OED's definition of "authenticity" helps map our understandings, it does not help to illuminate the ambiguous values called into play by statements like, "not really for children." When we assert something as inauthentic, we pre-suppose some sort of quality or lack of quality. In this way, the claim of "authenticity" classifies relationships, not just material goods or cultural transactions, and makes theoretical claims of meaning, merit, and value. We evaluate the authenticity of a work on a metaphysical level for inherent meaning and that good's relationship to our platonic ideal; on a moral level, for inherent truthfulness; and on an existential level for significance. In addition, as educational theorist, Mark Evans points out, "The confusion over 'authenticity' really gathers pace when we realize that cultures are not its only subjects. It has been famously employed to characterize an individual's mode of being, especially by existentialist philosophers, but there is less agreement as to what this mode should be thought of as entailing."[10] To announce *The Wolves in the Walls* as not-for-children then, is to make claims about not just processes of meaning-making, but also modes of being. To be clear, to claim this book as not-for-children speaks just as much to the nature of childhood as it does to the book itself. Such an act crosses into a landscape of moral privilege and power relations. Who is entitled to assign meaning and/or form in, or for, an intangible cultural product or good? Who gets to speak for whom? Authenticity is a theoretical statement that points to, or signifies, identity structures.

Considering the question of authenticity as located in linked rings of signification allows us to see the subtle, and not-so subtle, forces at play in determining value. In particular, art *for* children posits internal modes of being. To live an authentic life on an individual and adult plane elides with Westernized conceptualizations of individuality focused on being present, being original, and living up to an unlimited potential. Heidegger points to authenticity as the innate existential condition of acknowledging our unrealized possibilities. Instead of closed identity structures provided to individuals by a unilateral culture, modernity allows us infinite possible identities. In Western culture, the structural project of childhood is the creation of identity structures useful to the culture and to the market—to set apart in order to recuperate later. Here, I find Homi Bhabha's conceptualization of "mimicry" a useful way of discerning how the social structure of childhood operates in a larger cultural environment:

> . . . the discourse of mimicry is constructed around an ambivalence; in order to be effective, mimicry must continually produce its slippage, its excess, its difference. . . . Mimicry is also the sign of the inappropriate, however, a difference or recalcitrance which coheres the dominant strategic function of colonial power, intensifies surveillance, and poses an immanent threat to both "normalized" knowledges and disciplinary powers.[11]

Children are always Other than adult and therefore need regulation, protection, and intense surveillance. To question the authenticity of an artwork created for children—to claim "not for children"—is to posit an identity structure for children that speaks to their inherent internal life. In other words, to make such a claim is to practice a form of discipline upon the Other related to appropriate and inappropriate identity structures. As artists, the importance of this understanding cannot be overstated. If makers produce untheorized or under-questioned art for young people, assuming incompetence, we in effect practice censorship and limit the aesthetic possibilities of our work.

The manner in which power precipitates in childhood lends itself to an understanding of children as lesser than they really are. One of the axis along which power plays out in childhood is age. Older children have more power, rights, and responsibilities than younger children. "Don't be a baby" is an unparalleled insult in elementary school. A construction of age as power fosters a habit of mind, interpreting children as unfinished, in process, and becoming. Within such a construct, those younger than yourself will always be lower on the developmental scale than you. They will be less finished, less mature, and less capable. The corollary too is that those younger need extra guidance, help, and supervision. We like to believe that more education, plus more experience, equals more capability. The equation is not that simple, however. For one, capability and competency have no upper limit. So, we cannot point to a particular birthday or life event and say, "there—that's when I became competent;" instead competency is a process. And to become competent at one skill does not guarantee an equal competency at others. While I am an able artist and a capable teacher, I am horrible at plumbing. We all know someone, too, with great skill in the professional realm but great incompetence in his or her personal life. An unquestioning acceptance of age as power, in effect, posits that adults constructing art and media for children's consumption are more authentic, more appropriate creators *and receivers* than children themselves.

Epistemological and existential authenticity in the cultural marketplace

In his 2008 book, *Culture and Authenticity*, Charles Lindholm points out that, "At minimum, [authenticity] is the leading member of a set of values that includes sincere, essential, natural, original, and real."[12] This "authenticity" collection naturally excludes artifice, pretense, and deception. In the US, authenticity generally is understood in one of two related ways: (1) as associated with a material or cultural good; (2) or an individual's mode of being-ness. In other words, we can talk about a work of art being an authentic example of a culture or artist, and we can talk about authentic people or how to live an authentic life. In both cases, authenticity as a notion "connects the metaphysical concern of being and reality, the moral concern of truth, meaning, and value, and the existential concern of significance and credibility."[13] Authenticity exists as a multi-layered and dense concept, but at all layers that the word speaks to are concerned with inherent meaning, moral merit, and intrinsic worth. So, when we talk about an "authentic" artistic good, like a Hopi pot, or an "authentic" cultural experience, like attending the bullfights in Madrid, we judge that event or good within a range of criteria—only some of which reside in the event or good itself. For example, the identity of the artist becomes quite important, as does the good's relationship to the source community. A Hopi pot needs to be created by a Hopi artist. A Hopi pot also should have a clear relationship with its source community, in this case of course, Hopi. Perhaps the artist mines the clay in a traditional location or fires the pot in the time-honored manner. Perhaps the pot appears in a cultural ceremony or uses an established motif or shape. Importantly, authenticity rests not just in the characteristics of the pot itself, but in that pot's complex representation of, and relationship to, a particular culture at a particular time. But as copyright lawyer, Susan Scafidi reflects, "authenticity is a label applied only when a cultural product comes into contact with the outside world."[14] This notion points us back to the concern with being-ness, and how we define identity and belonging. I suggest that within the parameters of theatre *with* and *by* children, authenticity exists in the processes of construction, devising, and creation in which actual children and/or youth are involved. Only when adults come into the picture as producers, intermediaries, or consumers does the puzzle of authenticity play out—art *for* children and youth or the consumption of art *by* children and youth. On a pragmatic and programmatic level however, art *for* and even art *with* and *by*, kids *always* and *already* engages market culture—adult culture.

Again for a material good or cultural event to be considered "authentic," we evaluate that work on a metaphysical level for inherent meaning and that good's relationship to our platonic ideal; on a moral level, for inherent truthfulness; and on an existential level for significance. This philosophical dance becomes even more complex when we discuss a dispersed culture like childhood. Unlike the Hopi, children do not share explicit boundaries. Literally, Hopi has physical boundaries, membership identification, shared language and narrative, world view, and religious affiliation. While childhood can be considered a subaltern culture—it is certainly a social system—membership is a function of time, not language or blood quantum. Perhaps, then, we would be most accurate discussing the authenticities of child art rather than the authenticity. Regardless, arguing for or against a cultural product or material good's authenticity reflexively engages theory in the form of relationships, identity formation, and interplay of value and merit. Returning to our case studies, in order to map authenticity as a relational category, I argue that we need to consider (1) the identity of the artist(s); (2) the connection(s) to the source culture; (3) the characteristics of the thing itself; and (4) the "outside world" in which the good is exchanged.

Conclusions

To claim or question authenticity engages meaning, moral merit, and intrinsic worth in complex relational structures and modalities. For each of our case studies then, I would argue that the work *is* authentic art by, with, and for children and youth. "Crank That (Soulja Boy)" was created by a youth. The evidence that the song's aesthetic form speaks to and engages other youth is overwhelming—so the piece is created by youth and claimed by children and youth in a form enjoyed by children and youth. That is not to say I approve of this song. In fact, after researching the metaphors[15] used by Way for this essay, I promptly deleted the song from our music library. While I find Way's lyrics vile, I do not question their authenticity as expressive youth art. And even though *Triangle* is a disaster play in which fully half of the protagonists die, I claim the piece as authentic children's theatre. The playwright is a professional Theatre for Young Audiences author, the play was commissioned and produced as a piece of theatre *for* youth, features youthful protagonists, functioned in the economy of theatre for youth, and the community of theatre for youth artists. To say this play is not-for-children posits a closed and deterministic identity structure for a whole class of people to whom I no longer belong. In a similar manner, *Wolves in the Walls* is an authentic children's book; to say otherwise is to limit the unrealized possibilities of another's true self. True, my six-year-old doesn't care for the book, but that does not eliminate the book categorically from the realm of children's literature.

Theatre with, by, and for children and youth offers a unique perspective to questions of authenticity and identity. Unlike most fields, children's media is not produced, controlled, or even purchased primarily by the individuals that comprise the target audience. All representational artists, however, create art with, by, and for others/Others, which at heart is as much an ethical proposition as an aesthetic one. Can a white, Jewish man direct *The Color Purple*? Of course. Will his version be a less authentic version than a black woman director's? Not necessarily—authenticity is a relational category, not an ontological one. The difficulty, however, lies in an untheorized practice in which we never ask the difficult questions or address the inherent structural differences of being Other and being authentic.

Notes

1. Richard Harrington, "Soulja Boy Cranks it Up Big-Time; DIY Rapper is Making All the Right Moves," *Washington Post*, 21 December 2007, Weekend section; Pg. WE12.
2. http://www.tcg.org/tools/profiles/member_profiles/main.cfm?CFID=12423872&CFTOKEN=56351801 (accessed 16 September 2008).
3. Martin Heidegger, *Being and Time: A Translation of Sien und Zeit.* [first published 1927], Trans. Joan Stambaugh (Albany: State University of New York Press, 1996).
4. "authenticity" *The Oxford English Dictionary*, 2nd edn, 1989. OED Online. Oxford University Press, <http://dictionary.oed.com/> (accessed 16 September 2008).
5. Neil Gaiman, *The Wolves in the Walls*, illustrated by Dave McKean (New York: HarperCollins, 2003). All quotes are taken from this edition.
6. "Pre-service" refers to individuals who are in training programs designed to prepare them for teaching careers.
7. http://www.amazon.com/review/product/038097827X/ref=cm_rdphist_1?%5Fencoding=UTF8&filterBy=addOneStar (accessed 16 September 2008).
8. For a collection of production photos, reviews, musical selections, and a video introduction to the play see http://www.improbable.co.uk/show_example.asp?item_id=14 (accessed 16 September 2008).
9. http://www.harpercollins.com/author/authorExtra.aspx?authorID=3417&isbn13=9780380978274&displayType=bookinterview (accessed 16 September 2008).

10. Mark Evans, "'Authenticity' in the Jargon of Multiculturalism," in *Multiculutralism, Identity and Rights*, eds Bruce Haddock and Peter Sutch (New York: Routledge, 2003), 63.
11. Homi Bhabha, *The Location of Culture* (New York: Routledge, 2004), 85–92.
12. Charles Lindholm, *Culture and Authenticity* (Malden, MA: Blackwell, 2008), 1.
13. Xunwu Chen, *Being and Authenticity* (New York: Rodopi, 2004), 1.
14. Susan Scafidi, *Who Owns Culture? Appropriation and Authenticity in American Law* (New Brunswick, New Jersey: Rutgers University Press, 2005), 63.
15. I suggest using www.urbandictionary.com.

6
Theatrical Nationalism and Subversive Affirmation

S. E. Wilmer

Nationalism has been an important facet of theatrical expression since the Greeks. The earliest extant Greek play, *The Persians* by Aeschylus, reveals the ingenious tactics of the Greeks in defeating the Persians in the battle of Salamis, and much of Greek tragedy emphasizes the superiority of the Athenian city state to other polities. Cultural nationalism flourished particularly in the nineteenth century, following the American and French revolutions, the partition of Poland, and the Napoleonic invasion of much of Europe. Nationalist movements developed in many parts of Europe, claiming the distinctiveness of their nations and, in some cases, calling for independence from a foreign oppressor. They used theatre as a powerful means of formulating and solidifying notions of national identity. They helped to establish national theatres, especially in countries that were not yet nation states, to further their aims. In the twenty-first century, national theatres continue to play an important role in conserving national cultures, serving, as Louis Althusser suggested, as a state ideological apparatus, and cultural nationalism remains a recurrent motif. In this chapter, I will discuss some of the earlier features of nationalism that were developed in the theatre and show how they have been retained by theatre artists today, especially in the National Theatre of Scotland. I will also demonstrate how other theatre artists have turned the tables on cultural nationalism, ironizing it and rendering it obscene through techniques, such as subversive over-identification, as in the work of Christoph Schlingensief in Austria and Janez Janša in Slovenia.

Nineteenth-century cultural nationalism applied to theatre

Nations and nation states are somewhat arbitrary constructions that result from wars, invasions, and other historical events. The geographical and cultural contours of these entities have changed over time, but have been legitimated through nationalist discourse in the theatre, emphasizing the homogeneity and distinctiveness of their population and disguising their disharmonies. Nationalism, according to John Hutchinson and Anthony Smith, is "a doctrine of popular freedom and sovereignty" that promotes "autonomy, unity and identity" and has been "pursued by nationalists everywhere since Rousseau, Herder, Fichte, Korais, and Mazzini popularized them in Western and Central Europe."[1] Hutchinson and Smith elaborate on this doctrine as follows:

> The people . . . must determine their own destiny and be masters in their own house; they must control their own resources; they must obey only their own 'inner' voice. . . . The people must be united; they must dissolve all internal divisions; they must be gathered together in a single historic territory, a homeland; and they must have legal equality and share a single public culture. . . . Only a homeland that was "theirs" by historic right, the land of their forebears; only a culture that was "theirs" as a heritage, passed down the generations, and therefore an expression of their authentic identity.[2]

Thus nationalism exhibits both political and cultural features. On the one hand, it expresses the need for political self-determination and, on the other hand, it glorifies the unique features of a national culture, notably its dominant language. In seeking to formulate their own notion of what tied their people together and made them unique, cultural nationalists to some extent reinvented the past, often writing ancient national histories that came to justify the creation of separate nation states. Benedict Anderson has observed, "If nation-states are widely conceded to be 'new' and 'historical,' the nations to which they give political expression always loom out of an immemorial past."[3] Likewise, Ernest Gellner argues, "The cultural shreds and patches used by nationalism are often arbitrary historical inventions. Any old shred would have served as well. . . . Nationalism is not what it seems. . . . The cultures it claims to defend and revive are often its own inventions, or are modified out of all recognition."[4] While Anderson speaks of nations as "imagined communities" and Gellner refers to them as "inventions," as if they were quite arbitrary fabrications, Smith cautions that nations do not appear out of nowhere. They manifest a shared history, a specific topography, and common customs and practices. According to Smith, there are a variety of factors that tie a nation together, such as "song, dance, costume, ritual object, artwork," as well as "landscapes, monuments, buildings, tomb-styles," etc.[5]

One of the early proponents of cultural nationalism was Johann von Herder who rejected the dominance of French culture in German-speaking lands and urged his compatriots to acknowledge the German poets of the past. He developed a theory of the organic growth of the nation, its language and Volksgeist (national spirit), as distinct and unique, placing his faith in cultural, rather than political, unity. He encouraged research into German folklore, myths, legends, and local history and argued that German culture would never come into its own unless it was based on traditional popular German culture. To this end, he encouraged Germans to make a "complete critical study of the chronicles and legends of the Middle Ages."[6] As a result of his endeavors, Herder fostered a new respect for the German folk traditions, gaining Johann Wolfgang von Goethe and Friedrich Schiller as allies, and promoted a notion of national cultural unity. At the same time, he encouraged other nations to do the same, arguing that each nation was organic and distinct, and needed to develop its own national spirit. Cultural nationalists in many countries in Europe read his works avidly and adopted his methods and attitudes.

In attributing specific distinct traits to the nation, nationalists essentialized national characteristics and legitimized the boundaries surrounding the nation; in addition, they emphasized the borders between those to be included or privileged, and those to be excluded or underprivileged in the nation. For those who were privileged according to these distinctions, it provided a sense of belonging and identity. But for those who were underprivileged, it necessitated their marginalization or disenfranchisement on the basis of such differences as gender, class, ethnicity, language, and religion.

Influenced by nationalist theories and nationalist discourse, theatre artists used common techniques to convey nationalist ideologies. Historic plays portraying heroic national characters from the past or images from national folklore or rural life, in the vernacular language, asserted the uniqueness of their culture, and in some cases challenged the dominant discourse of imperial rule. For example, Schiller's *The Maid of Orleans* and *William Tell* focus on historical periods with nationalist heroes striving to free the French and Swiss nations from oppression at a time when there was not yet a German nation state, German-speaking lands being fragmented among many principalities, dukedoms, free cities, etc. and, for a while, under Napoleonic rule. Schiller, who characterized the theatre as a forum of human knowledge and "a school of practical wisdom," argued in his essay "The Stage as a Moral Institution" that theatre could form, as well as represent, the nation, concluding that "if we had a national stage, we would also become a nation."[7]

In most cases, such nationalist plays would focus on male heroes fighting for the author's native land and perhaps dying for it. In the case of *The Maid of Orleans*, there are a couple of unusual features: Joan of Arc is a female warrior, and the play is about a country other than that of the author's. Nevertheless, one can see the typical nationalist rhetoric emerging in the play as the English soldiers are vilified as oppressors and the French are rallied to regain what rightfully belongs to them. The traditional symbols of national flags and Christian icons have a potent effect, as does the image of the heroine dying for her country. Because of her international fame, Joan of Arc has been used as a cross-cultural archetype to serve nationalist purposes, not only in her home country, but also as a metaphor for nationalist struggles in other countries, especially the righteous battle against a foreign oppressor. Although anomalous in being a woman soldier, Joan of Arc also feeds into the normative nationalist iconography that depicts women as representing the nation. Such mythical characters as Britannia, Germania, and Marianne in France have often been represented in monuments and paintings as militant figures (echoing classical images of Artemis, Athena, and Penthesilea), though more passive virginal or motherly depictions of the nation are more common.

Opera was also employed for nationalist purposes, perhaps best seen in the works of Giuseppe Verdi and Richard Wagner. In such operas as *Lohengrin, Tannhäuser, Parsifal,* and the cycle of *Der Ring des Nibelungen,* Wagner employed Nordic legends and folk heroes to convey Germanic identity through music and drama. He celebrated the traditional poets and singing contests of Germany in *Tannhäuser* and *Die Meistersinger,* as well as employing the legend of the Nibelungenlied (though, perhaps surprisingly, the Nordic rather than the German version[8]) for his four-opera masterpiece *Der Ring des Nibelungen,* in which a strong sense of German topography is evoked by the images of the Rhein and the Alps. Wagner wrote in words echoing Herder, "To the operatic poet and composer falls the task of conjuring up the holy spirit of poetry as it comes to us in the sagas and legends of past ages."[9] He also advised that artists focus on pre-Christian myths because, like Herder, he argued that Christianity had diluted the original popular spirituality. "Through the adoption of Christianity the folk has lost all true understanding of the original, vital relations of this mythos."[10] Notorious for his notions of the superiority of the Aryan race, Wagner took nationalistic feelings (and egotism) to an extreme. "I am the most German of beings. I am the German spirit. Consider the incomparable magic of my works."[11]

W. B. Yeats, one of the founders of the Irish National Theatre, was heavily influenced by Wagner and cultural nationalism. He and Lady Gregory published several volumes of folk tales in the late nineteenth century before co-founding the Irish Literary Theatre with Edward Martyn, asserting in their manifesto that the new theatre would no longer demean the Irish people in the way that the British theatre had done in the past. Thus, Irish nationalist theatre at the beginning of the twentieth century employed historic struggles, folklore myths, and stories of idyllic rural life as a means of showing the distinctiveness of Irish (as opposed to English) culture. Yeats' *Cathleen Ni Houlihan* managed to combine all three of these features, showing the mythical figure of Cathleen Ni Houlihan calling out young Irish peasants to fight in the 1798 uprising against British rule.

In nationalist discourse, rural characters are often depicted as pure and wholesome, unsullied by the grime and squalor and malevolent influences of the city. J. M. Synge, however, was not a writer to conform to nationalist rhetoric and frequently depicted the ugly sides of rural life. When *The Playboy of the Western World* was staged by the Irish National Theatre Society at the Abbey Theatre, the portrayal of Christy, who is celebrated by the young women of Mayo as a hero for allegedly killing his father, was regarded as unacceptable and caused riots in the theatre. The nationalists in the audience interpreted the play as being both an inaccurate and an unwelcome depiction of Ireland at a time when they were attempting to assert the superiority of their culture to England's. Having been depicted by English dramatists as wild men and figures of fun for years, Irish nationalists regarded *The Playboy* to be even more demeaning, especially because it was the National Theatre that was now presenting this travesty. The director of the theatre, Yeats, defended the right of the Irish National Theatre Society to present such a play and insisted that it should continue to be performed for the rest of the week (with the aid of a police presence) while the audience continued to riot. However, in subsequent years the play became canonized as one of the most often performed plays in the national repertory, thereby querying the relationship between nationalist rhetoric and national culture. As is manifest in *The Playboy* riots, theatre has equally been a site for disrupting nationalist discourse and challenging national stereotypes. Henrik Ibsen's *Peer Gynt* also depicted a rogue figure and satirized the nationalist movement's language reform in the middle of the nineteenth century. Nevertheless, despite Ibsen's critique of nationalism and an initially hostile reaction from nationalist readers when it was first published, the play rapidly became canonized as one of the most frequently produced plays in Norway, particularly as a result of Grieg's beautiful music, which was written subsequently to accompany it in performance. Both Synge and Ibsen were challenging the nationalist rhetoric of the day in their portrayals of Christy and Peer, and contemporary audiences reacted negatively to the insults that they perceived to their national values. However, it is interesting that these anti-heroes could later become appropriated into nationalist discourse as folk heroes by being presented as lovable rogue types in more saccharine productions.

Extreme nationalist theatre in the twentieth century

In Nazi Germany, nationalist theatre was taken to an extreme. Specific kinds of new drama were encouraged. Plays on historical topics which could serve as analogies for the nationalistic struggle tended to be favoured, such as those supporting "the 'Führer Idea,' heroic sacrifice for the 'people's community' and the inevitability of the 'racial struggle.'"[12] According to Barbara Panse, "Historical conflicts and situations were to be portrayed in such a manner that they could be seen as mile stones on the way to the creation of the German National State."[13] One of the major themes was the historic conflict between the German Reich and the Catholic Church, often depicting a German character heroically fighting against the influence of the Vatican, such as in *Thor's Guest* by Otto Erler, *Uta von Naumburg* by Felix Dhünen, and *Gregor and Heinrich* and *Heroic Passions* by Erwin Guido Kolbenheyer.[14] The audiences of such drama were to witness "no new material or characters, but the old and accustomed through an everlasting regeneration of the human soul."[15] The Nazis also promoted plays that preached national unification and racial purity, such as *The Homecoming* by Sigmund Graff and *Der Gigant* (*The Giant*) by Richard Billinger, as well as plays with cross-cultural historical heroes such as *Isabella von Spanien* (*Isabella of Spain*) by Hermann Heinz Ortner and *Thomas Paine* by Hanns Johst.[16] Performances were obliged to display reverence for German history.

One of the most original dramatic forms developed under the Nazi government was the short-lived *Thingspiel*. Evolving from the earlier ideas of Gottfried Keller's "Stone of Myth," and a "sacred space" around national monuments for open-air performances, the *Thingspiel* centred on the concept of a national community theatre (Volksgemeinschaftstheater). The *Thingspiel* plays incorporated a number of German nationalist ideas about theatre: mass open-air Gesamtkunstwerk performances with choral speaking and music, using stories of German heroes who sacrificed themselves for the fatherland, played in front of huge audiences, who participated in a cultic ritual in which they identified with the actions on stage. The *Thingspiel* plays required a new dramaturgy as well as specially constructed venues on historical sites. The Ministry for Propaganda created Thing festivals, and play and chorus competitions, and invited dramatists to observe model performances and learn about the new style. The government also constructed 20 Thingplätze all over Germany, bearing a striking resemblance to ancient Greek theatres such as at Epidauros, and holding up to 50,000 spectators. Altogether, 400 Thingplätze were envisaged, but the government terminated these plans after acknowledging that the art form was not achieving the success for which it had hoped.[17]

> George Mosse argues that plays in this style of new Nazi drama failed because the National Socialists "made them into large popular spectacles wherein the dramatic content of the performances was transformed into intense expressions of mass veneration for the actors on the stage. Typically enough, the National Socialists formalized the rites so as to eliminate virtually all aspects of true theatre. Theatrical versions of the Nazi ideology's doxology were staged instead, replete with confessions of faith and pledges of allegiance."[18]

Cultural nationalist plays in the twenty-first century

In the twenty-first century, there are obvious echoes of the cultural nationalist movement of the nineteenth and early twentieth century. For example, the creation of the National Theatre of Scotland (NTS) heralds a Romantic nationalist spirit at a time when the possibility of political independence has appeared on the horizon. In the Scottish Parliament in 2003, Frank McAveety, the Minister for Tourism, Culture, and Sport, revealed the important implications of establishing the new theatre by asserting that it was "emblematic of much of the debate about Scotland's identity and cultural future."[19] The nationalist impulse behind the enterprise became clear when the National Theatre explained its intended goals in its newsletter later in the same year: "The National Theatre of Scotland will develop a quality repertoire originating in Scotland. This will include new work, existing work, and the drama of other countries and cultures to which a range of Scottish insights, language, and sensibility can be applied."[20]

Without a theatre building, but with a six million euro subsidy from the Scottish Parliament, in 2006 the National Theatre of Scotland launched a series of events in ten venues around the country under the title "Home." This turned into an opportunity in specific instances for nostalgic reminiscence and for identifying what was culturally distinct about particular areas of Scotland. One of the pieces, *Home Shetland*, was a multimedia event aboard a ship that travelled between Shetland and the mainland of Scotland, and featured Scottish music and local stories about Shetland Islanders. According to one of the reviews, "It was therefore a perfect choice for the 'launch' of the National Theatre of Scotland in Shetland, and the performance transported the small audience groups on a stunning and very personal emotional journey."[21] According to Robert Leach, the National Theatre reflected "a new Scottish consciousness [that] had emerged. Scots began to re-examine their past, and to seek alternative historical narratives, different from those that had been accepted for so long."[22]

Following the series of events on the theme of "home," the NTS produced over 20 productions in their first year, often with national historical themes about Scotland, such as Schiller's *Mary Stuart* in a version by the Scottish playwright David Harrower and *Project Macbeth*, a devised piece with "[t]he real Macbeth at war with Shakespeare's myth in a battle to redefine his twenty-first-century identity."[23] Perhaps the most notable production was *Black Watch*, a new play commissioned by the NTS from Scottish playwright Gregory Burke, about a Scottish regiment that was being amalgamated with other regiments after 300 years of distinguished service. At the same time as being a well-choreographed and dynamic piece of theatre, it was also an exercise in nostalgia and national pride, recounting the history of the Black Watch regiment, as well as its final deployment in Iraq. Owen Humphrys commented in a review for the Royal United Services Institute journal:

> Running as a 'red thread of courage' through the play is the Black Watch's ever-famous and exclusive red hackle. The Watch's pipe-tunes and their songs are used, and adapted, from the 'Black Bear' to '[en]list bonnie laddie and come away' wi' me.' And in one five-minute scene, three centuries of Black Watch history are played out on a red carpet that is rolled out down the drill hall. One soldier is kitted out successively in the garb of 1739, the uniform of Waterloo and the kilt apron of the trenches in 1915. It is a magical moment.[24]

Scottish iconography abounds on stage, with Scottish flags, kilts, bagpipes, and songs, not to mention the accents and speech patterns of the soldiers, providing a strong visual and aural Scottish presence that contrasts strikingly with the documentary video footage of the soldiers' military deployment in the Middle East projected on large screens.

Behind the individual experiences of the soldiers lies a tension between Scottish and British identities. This comes to the fore when two of the actors, impersonating Alex Salmond, head of the Scottish National Party, and Geoffrey Hoon, the British Defense Secretary, trade insults over the redeployment of the Black Watch regiment from Basra to relieve the American troops in Falluja. Salmond opposes this redeployment, which results in the deaths of three soldiers, arguing that the Black Watch has been given "an impossible job"[25] (having to replace a much larger force of American soldiers who are better equipped and have greater backup). He accuses the British government of putting the Scottish soldiers at risk in order to cater to the needs of the Americans, and specifically to aid President Bush's campaign for re-election in 2004. "I think it will give way to a wave of anger as Scotland and the Black Watch families compare and contrast the bravery of our Scottish soldiers with the duplicity and chicanery of the politicians who sent them into this deployment."[26] The redeployment leads to the most horrific sequence in the play, during which three Scottish soldiers are blown sky-high by a suicide bomber.

The play conveys considerable resentment toward the British government for this redeployment, as well as for the controversial decision to amalgamate the Black Watch with five other Scottish regiments, thereby undermining its local and distinctive identity. Ian Jack commented on this amalgamation in *The Guardian*: "Given what the British government was asking the Black Watch to do in the desert of Iraq, the decision was seen as a betrayal, a poor piece of bureaucratic judgment that would damage the Black Watch's already sinking morale."[27] A soldier exclaims in the play: "It takes three hundred years to build an army that's admired and respected around the world. But it only takes three years pissing about in the desert in the biggest western foreign policy disaster ever to fuck it up completely."[28] This expression of resentment is significant and comes close to subversion in challenging British policy during an ongoing war. It sets out a distinctive Scottish agenda in opposition to British military policy, although this is complicated by the Scots being part of the British army. According to Joyce McMillan, the production of *Black Watch* reveals the "National Theatre as a force that can reassert a strong grass-roots Scottish perspective on parts of our story which, until now, have been filtered mainly through institutions of the British state."[29]

On the one hand, the play can be regarded as a piece celebrating local history and culture as well as a military way of life (although the play contains numerous anti-militarist touches). On the other hand, *Black Watch* mourns the passing of an important aspect of Scottish society, like the clothing, mining, shipbuilding, and fishing industries, which have virtually disappeared. Once again, the Scots have become the victims of British political decisions. Thus, the play can be read as a nationalistic performance, expressing pride in a distinctive aspect of Scottish history and culture, and attacking the British government for neglecting Scottish cultural traditions and ignoring the welfare of brave young Scottish men. It is not surprising that Salmond, who has been gearing the Scottish people toward a referendum on political independence, takes great pride in the production and told me in an interview that he would like to send *Black Watch* "around the world."[30] He has used the play "not once but three times to celebrate the opening of the Scottish Parliament and the Scottish National Party's first crack at government."[31] Thus, the NTS, through such plays as *Home Shetland* and *Black Watch*, which are situated in local geographical environments and feature local characters, stories, imagery, and language, is effectively aiding the cause of Scottish political and cultural autonomy. We can see echoes of the past in this, with the NTS replaying the role of theatres in emerging nations in the nineteenth and early twentieth centuries. Plays such as *William Tell*, *Cathleen Ni Houlihan*, and *Black Watch* provide a common approach in stressing the distinctiveness of national identity and supporting the case for independence.

Challenging nationalist ideologies

By contrast with the role of the NTS many theatre artists have ironized and critiqued nationalistic expression. For example, in Germany, Bertolt Brecht and Rolf Hochhuth overtly criticized the virulent nationalism of the Third Reich by showing its evil effects in such plays as Brecht's *Fear and Misery in the Third Reich* and Hochhuth's *The Representative*. Another tactic, which I want to consider in some depth, is that of subversion through over-identification with nationalism, which features in the work of Schlingensief and Janša. Both artists, working on the former border between Western and Eastern Europe in Austria and Slovenia, have devised performances to call nationalistic expression into question by imitating and exaggerating it.

In 2000, Schlingensief created an event in a main square outside the opera house called *Bitte liebt Österreich* (*Please Love Austria*) for the Vienna Festival to focus attention on Austrian attitudes about immigration. Staged shortly after the election of a coalition government that included the right-wing party of Jörg Haider (and caused the EU to impose diplomatic sanctions against a member country for the first time),

Schlingensief placed 12 immigrants in an industrial container and asked the public to decide which of them should be deported and who should be allowed to win prize money, marry an Austrian, and gain the right to remain in the country. Slogans associated with Haider's party were affixed to the outside of the container such as "Ausländer raus" ("foreigners out") and the Nazi motto "Unsere Ehre heißt Treue" (Our pride is loyalty), while the activities inside the container were transmitted via the Internet, which participants could watch live via video streaming. The event was modeled on the popular Big Brother reality TV show, during which contestants live with each other in a confined environment called "the container," and the TV show emphasized that the public could interact with the program by voting whether the contestants should leave or remain in the container (the news programs announced every night who was allowed to remain in the show). In the case of the Vienna performance event, Schlingensief raised the stakes by using contestants who, he claimed, were highly qualified political exiles from various parts of the world (such as China, Iraq, Iran, Kosovo, Sri Lanka, Kurdistan, and Nigeria) and who (supposedly) faced danger if they returned to their home country. Of course, the audience could not be sure if the contestants were real or fictional, that is to say if they were real exiles or simply actors playing such characters, especially because contact between the people within the container and the public outside appears to have been controlled by the mediatization of the event. Schlingensief was adamant about maintaining the illusion that the refugees were real so that the event would have greater impact. He claimed that over 70,000 people contacted the program's website, which kept crashing because of the level of popular interest both in Vienna and elsewhere. The event caused a heated discussion in the press, as it raised uncomfortable associations with the Austrian support for Hitler during the Third Reich, as well as with the recent success of Haider's far-right party. Schlingensief himself stood on top of the container with a loudhailer claiming to represent Haider's party and spouting his party slogans. After several days, the container was assailed by a crowd of left-wing protestors, who objected to the performance and tried to liberate the refugees and dismantle the offensive signs. But Schlingensief felt that this was catering to the right wing by cleaning up the event and implying that Austria welcomed immigrants, and so he brought the refugees back to the container and the performance continued.

Schlingensief was using a subversive strategy of over-identification with the opposition in order to render them powerless and exposed.[32] According to the cultural theorist Slavoj Žižek, "By bringing to light the obscene superego underside of the system, over-identification suspends its efficiency."[33] Haider's party called on the festival organizers to stop the show, but the Austrian government seemed uncertain whether to shut it down and risk accusations of censorship, or to allow it to continue despite all the attendant bad publicity for the coalition partners. In the end, it ran for the week of the festival, attracting considerable newspaper and television coverage.

Using a similar strategy of over-identification with nationalist expression, three Slovenian artists decided that they would all change their own names and adopt the name of the right-wing prime minister of Slovenia, Janez Janša. Slovenia forms the eastern border of the European Union, with its neighbor Croatia outside the EU. The prime minister, Janša, has received criticism from the left for promoting national cultural traditions rather than contemporary art and for stigmatizing immigrants and minority groups. Although Blaž Lucan points out that the three artists "have remained silent regarding their decisions and . . . have stated that this was an intimate, personal decision," he goes on to explain, "The three artists did not pick just any name; they chose Janez Janša . . . the front man of the right wing in the Slovenian political arena. No doubt, the choice of name indicates a certain agenda."[34]

By adopting his name and becoming members of his political party, the three artists have over-identified with Janša and at times caused some confusion regarding his authority. For example, Janez Janša (formerly Emil Hrvatin), a theatre director, performed in a dance festival in Germany resulting in the ironic newspaper headline "Janša dances in Berlin."[35] For a photograph taken on top of the Triglav (the three-peaked mountain in Slovenia that serves as a national symbol on the Slovenian flag), the three Janez Janšas clothed themselves in a black cloth with their three heads peering out the top to represent the Triglav on top of the Triglav mountain in a comic doubling of the iconic image, presenting it as a "multiple ('state-forming') jubilee."[36] The categorization of artistic work as "state-forming" is a quality that Rok Vevar says "has lately become a kind of unwritten prerequisite for artistic events in our country to gain any public relevancy."[37] Critiquing cultural nationalistic policies in Slovenia, Vevar writes that "the anachronistic cultural horizon . . . more than 15 years after the creation of the Slovenian state still conceives art as state-forming, because the official (cultural) policy conceives the state as a kind of reserve for the endangered Slovenian ethnic group."[38] Thus, the Janez Janša artists were calling attention to the obligation on theatre artists to engage in work that appeals to national cultural values, and making it seem ridiculous.

These artists take their inspiration from an earlier Slovenian group called Neue Slovenische Kunst (NSK), which used subversive tactics and irony to ridicule nationalist expression in Slovenia, a generation earlier when it was part of Yugoslavia. Rejecting the notion of Slovenian culture as distinct and authentic, NSK claimed that all cultures borrow from each other, and so they would appropriate other cultural elements as a way of asserting (and subverting) Slovenian culture. One of their most sensational acts was to enter an adapted Nazi poster (Richard Klein's *Third Reich*), depicting youths carrying batons and Yugoslav flags in an overt display of nationalist sentiment, into a poster competition for a Yugoslav Youth Day celebration. When the poster won the contest and its source was revealed, the Yugoslav government tried to prosecute the artists for promoting Fascist propaganda![39]

The theatre director Janez Janša (Hrvatin) also directed a play titled *The National Theatre of Slovenia* (ironically copying the name of the main theatre in Ljubljana) which recalled Slovenians shouting abuse at a Romany family and erecting barricades to prevent them from living in their midst, and encouraged in this by Prime Minister Janša's government. Four artists on stage, using headphones and listening to the "extremely vulgar and aggressive language, used by the angry mob"[40] that had been recorded by television news reporters, repeated their statements to the theatre audience without commentary, with Janša (Hrvatin) himself pacing back and forth across the stage for an hour and a half muttering "Gypsies, gypsies." According to Blaž Lukan, the piece recalled the "deportation of a Gipsy family from this village with all of its side effects. This sad story without a doubt stands for one of the most shameful and tainted moments in Slovenian history since Slovenia became independent."[41] By reconstructing the event with all its xenophobic rhetoric, the theatrical performance called into question the role of the government and the local citizens in exiling the Romany family.

Overt political theatre that tries to undermine the excesses of cultural nationalism by showing their "obscene" nature can be criticized for attracting an audience of like-minded individuals ("preaching to the converted"). The advantage of the tactics of over-identification in performances is that they can attract the opposition as an audience. According to Inke Arns and Sylvia Sasse,

> Subversive affirmation is an artistic/political tactic that allows artists/ activists to take part in certain social, political, or economic discourses and to affirm, appropriate, or consume them while simultaneously undermining them. It is characterised precisely by the fact

that with affirmation there simultaneously occurs a distancing from, or revelation of, what is being affirmed. In subversive affirmation there is always a surplus which destabilises affirmation and turns it into its opposite.[42]

The disadvantage of this type of work is, of course, that it gives a voice to ideologies that one is trying to subvert, and may help to sustain them, rather than undermine them. For example, Schlingensief has been accused, not only in *Bitte Liebt Österreich*, but in other performances as well, of providing neo-Nazis with a platform to express their racist views in public.

In conclusion, theatre artists today, especially those sustained by state or corporate finance, often find themselves drawn into nationalist discourses as part of their work, just as they were in the nineteenth century. Sometimes this is for progressive purposes, such as in promoting ideas of national self-determination, and, at other times, for more reactionary purposes, such as expressing exclusionary attitudes and policies. Cultural nationalism is endemic throughout the world, and the theories of such eighteenth-century philosophers as Herder continue to dominate our way of thinking. At the same time, theatre artists can use theatre to subvert the "obscene" excesses of nationalist discourse, either by directly critiquing it, or through such novel tactics as over-identification.

Notes

Some parts of this essay appeared in "Theatrical Nationalism: Exposing the 'Obscene Superego' of the System," *Journal of Dramatic Theory and Criticism*, XXIII.2 (Spring 2009), 77–87.

1. John Hutchinson and Anthony D. Smith, *Nationalism* (Oxford: Oxford University Press, 1994), 4–5.
2. Ibid., 4.
3. Benedict Anderson, *Imagined Communities*, rev. edn (London: Verso, 1995), 11.
4. Ernest Gellner, *Nations and Nationalism* (Oxford: Basil Blackwell, 1983), 56.
5. Anthony Smith, *Nationalism and Modernism: A Critical Survey of Recent Theories of Nations and Nationalism* (London: Routledge, 1998), 139.
6. Johann von Herder, "Ueber die Legende," in *Sämmtliche Werke*, ed. Suphan Bernhard, vol. 16 (Berlin: Weidmansche Buchlung, 1877), 389.
7. Friedrich Schiller, *Werke in drei Bänden* (Munich: Hanser, 1976), vol. 1, 728.
8. See *The Nibelungenlied*, trans. Helen M. Mustard, in *Medieval Epics* (New York: Modern Library, 1963), 215–16.
9. Quoted from Richard Wagner's diary in Harold C. Schonberg, *The Lives of the Great Composers* (New York: W. W. Norton, 1970), 256–7.
10. Albert Goldman and Evert Sprinchorn, eds *Wagner on Music and Drama* (London: Gollancz, 1970), 139. For Herder's discussion of the negative

influence of Christianity on German culture, see Herder, "Von der neuern Römischen Litteratur," *Sämmtliche Werke*, ed. Bernhard Suphan, vol. 1, 365–7.

11. Schonberg, *The Lives of the Great Composers*, 264.

12. Barbara Panse, "Censorship in Nazi Germany: The Influence of the Reich's Ministry of Propaganda on German Theatre and Drama, 1933–45," in *Fascism and Theatre: Comparative Studies on the Aesthetics and Politics of Performance in Europe, 1925–1945*, ed. Günther Berghaus (Providence, Oxford: Berghahn Books, 1996), 147.

13. Ibid., 146.

14. See John London, ed., *Theatre under the Nazis* (Manchester and New York: Manchester University Press, 2000), 23; and Leigh Clemens, "Gewalt, Gott, Natur, Volk: The Performance of Nazi Ideology in Kolbenheyer's *Gregor und Heinrich*" in *Text and Presentation* XVII (1996), 13–9.

15. Quoted in George L. Mosse, *Nationalization of the Masses* (New York: Fertig, 1975), 103.

16. See London, *Theatre under the Nazis*, 23, and Panse, 153–4.

17. For a speculative discussion on why the form was banned, see William Niven, "The Birth of Nazi Drama?" in *Theatre under the Nazis*, 73–90.

18. George L. Mosse, *The Crisis of German Ideology: Intellectual Origins of the Third Reich* (New York: Grosset and Dunlap, 1964), 81.

19. Robert Leach, "The Short Astonishing History of the National Theatre of Scotland," *New Theatre Quarterly*, 23, part 2 (May 2007), 172.

20. Ibid., 174.

21. John Haswell, "Home Scotland," 2006 The British Theatre Guide, http://www.britishtheatreguide.info/reviews/homeshetland-rev.htm/ (accessed December 27, 2007).

22. Leach, "The Short Astonishing History," 172.

23. "Project Macbeth," 2006. National Theatre of Scotland. http://www.nationaltheatrescotland.com/content/default.asp?page=home_Project%20Macbeth (accessed December 27, 2007).

24. Owen Humphrys, "Theatre Review: *Black Watch*", *RUSI*, 25 October 2006, http://www.rusi.org/publication/defencesystems/ (accessed February 13, 2008).

25. Gregory Burke, *Black Watch* (London: Faber and Faber, 2007), 9.

26. Ibid., 8.

27. Ian Jack, "It's in the Blood," *Guardian*, 14 June 2008.

28. Gregory Burke, *Black Watch*, 71.

29. Joyce McMillan, "*Black Watch*," *The Scotsman*, 7 August 2006, quoted in Zoltán Imre, "Staging the Nation: Changing Concepts of a National Theatre in Europe," *New Theatre Quarterly*, 24 (2008), 93, n. 105.

30. Interview with Alex Salmond, Trinity College Dublin, February 13, 2008.

31. Jack, "It's in the Blood."

32. See Inke Arns and Sylvia Sasse, "Subversive Affirmation: On Mimesis as a Strategy of Resistance," *Maska*, XXI.3–4 (Spring 2006), 5–21.

33. Slavoj Žižek, *The Universal Exception* (London: Continuum, 2006), 65.

34. Blaž Lukan, "The Janez Janša Project," http://www.aksioma.org/sec/reference.html (accessed October 15, 2008).

35. Ibid.

36. Rok Vevar, "The More of Us We Are, the Faster We'll Reach Our Goal", http://www.aksioma.org/sec/reference.html (accessed October 15, 2008).
37. Ibid.
38. Ibid.
39. Barbara Orel, "Ideological Observatory, Neue Slowenische Kunst, Rituals and Playing Culture," paper delivered at the IFTR conference in Seoul 2008, privately held.
40. Blaž Lucan, "Janša in Ambrus (Slovene National Theatre by Janez Janša, 2007)," http://www.maska.si/en/productions/performing_arts/slovene_national_theatre/381/reviews.html, accessed 15 October 2008.
41. Ibid.
42. Arns and Sasse, "Subversive Affirmation," 5.

7

Sensual Engagements: Understanding Theories of the Senses and their Potential Applications within Theatre Practice

Stephen Di Benedetto

An awareness of, and marshaling of, one's senses can enrich theatre practice by honing the practitioner's skill in stimulating the attendants' bodies and harnessing their unconscious physiological responses to theatrical performance. As biological organisms we use our bodies and brains to experience performance, and performers make compositional choices to shape that experience. The brain is what it is because of the structural and functional properties of neurons that communicate by transmitting electrical impulses along their axons. It is through these impulses that the brain perceives, monitors, and interprets the data that our senses collect. The fragments of sensations that sight, touch, hearing, taste, and smell deliver to the brain are the means by which we conceive the world around us. I am interested in tracing the potential power of the senses in performance, the ways in which performance affects and influences attendant understandings of artistic expression and the means by which contemporary live performance is made. What are the implications of sense (perception) theories for actors, directors, designers, and attendants? This essay will explore how the application of theories drawn from cognitive science and physiology influence the creative process for theatre makers.

Perception, consciousness, and attention

There are three basic concepts that can help us understand how we process and interpret stimuli generated by an artistic event: perception, consciousness, and attention. Our close proximity to live actors interacting in a constructed theatre space enables us to use our senses to perceive the action of a play as we perceive any other experience. Perception is a process by which our bodies become aware of our environment on the basis of information taken in by our senses, and its function is to interpret sensory data and to process information.[1] Our perception is influenced from both conscious and unconscious mechanisms, and depends on whether the processing bears primarily on the sensory information drawn directly from stimuli, or on the subject's knowledge, expectations, and motivations. As we watch an acrobat fly across the circus tent we expect the performer to complete his leap from one swing to the next but also monitor for anything that may interfere with it. We both assess sensory data that streams into our brain and assess sensory data according to our experience. There is little difference between our perception of fiction or reality, since they share in common the stimulation of neurons that enable our continuous active engagement with the world around us: "The perceiving brain is active and always adjusting itself. Seeing is as active as touching, when we run our fingers over an object to discover its texture and shape. . . . Both our sensory *and* our motor cortices are always involved in perceiving."[2] While most models of theatrical interpretation assume that we can consciously control our understanding though rational means, there is more active interpretation going on unconsciously than we credit. Arlette Steri describes what happens before we make conscious sense of stimuli:

> Information taken in by the sensory systems provokes a sensation. Each system detects only information that is specific to it, and for this reason, it remains incomplete and fragmented. At this level, processing is automatic, pre-wired, essentially inaccessible to consciousness . . . before the stimulus is identified, various grouping together and breaking down processes are performed on the sensory flow according to the perceiver's knowledge. This knowledge is what drives the perceptual structuring process and enables object identification.[3]

Once this process has occurred we become conscious of some of the information generated, and we can begin to make sense of our emotions and our feelings. If we are irritated by an actor's behavior we may think it is his physical actions that are coloring our interpretation because we are conscious of them, however, our feelings and emotions may have been triggered by the amount of time we had been sitting on a cold, hard bench watching. Controlling the context of performance is a biological process of conveying meaning. Attentional processes also are important in determining what information gets focused on. Once an object is identified the brain "generates a series of multimodal representations (visual, auditory, somesthetic and possibly gustatory and olfactory), as well as motor, lexical, and semantic representations."[4] While we watch any Robert Wilson production, as new objects or colors are introduced into the composition they take on enormous significance. Their strange presence demands attention. We become attentive to meaningful somatic stimuli in addition to cues from psychological and literary meaning-making apparatus. As we begin to attend to the elements of theatrical composition that trigger sensations, we pick out significant data that helps us more richly interpret what we are experiencing; a light will catch our eye or a sound will cause us to look at another part of the stage and become conscious of a new element enabling us to pay attention to meaningful details.

Once we have experienced an object, consciousness, as we commonly think of it, is the unified mental pattern that brings together the object and the self. Nevertheless, the precise composition and dynamics of the emotional responses are shaped in each individual by a unique development and environment.[5] As we share a basic biology, artists can be certain that the use of some strategies can ensure a biological reaction to their artwork. If a lighting designer chooses to illuminate a section of the stage after a period of darkness, then he can be sure that the spectators' eyes will be drawn toward that lighting cue because our visual system seeks out light, and they will have an emotional response as a result of that trigger. The ways that humans' responses can transcend culture, as Antonio Damasio explains, "is why in spite of the infinite variations to be found across cultures among individuals and over the course of a life span we can predict with some success that certain stimuli will produce certain emotions."[6] Artistic stimulation directly affects human biology and produces an emotional response that can be instigated.

As our bodies respond to the world, our minds become activated and aware, and our brains have biological alert systems to direct our attention. This process of monitoring sensory stimulation is described by Bernard Baars as "spotlight attentiveness."[7] It is when our mind's attention is drawn to a particular stimulus, such as when we notice a movement in a peripheral vision and swing our heads around to see what caused the movement. Our spotlight is triggered in the moments in theatrical reception where we notice transitions and become attendant to smell, taste, touch, vision, and sound in relation to theatrical interpretation. It is at this moment that we can begin to become conscious of the ways in which our body filters sensory-data from the ways which an artist has stimulated our senses.

Shaping attention

Paying attention to those first stimuli and how they begin to enter into our consciousness helps us attend to how theatre exploits the sensory world. If a director shapes the pacing of the play and directs the attendant's focus, these techniques will keep the attendant involved with the performance. The director, designers, and actors draw focus, create suspense, and create patterns for us to watch. How do attentive spectators experience sensory stimulation? Endel Tulving suggests that "large parts of the brain, such as the hippocampus, have a primary function of mismatch-detection: spotting events that violate our expectations, and triggering attentional mechanisms to direct the surprising events to consciousness."[8] When we encounter unexpected stimuli, we are forced to pay attention and that attention generates a large amount of brain activity. For example, if Robert Wilson changes the color of Hamlet's doublet in front of the eyes of attendants, then he has violated their notion of what is possible and captivates their attention.

The power of novelty to capture our spotlight of attention is useful to theatre practitioners. For example, we expect to see a man's chest when Robert Lepage removes his shirt during *Elsinore* (1997); however he has breasts. This disjunction can help guide the attendant's interpretation when we break established patterns to call attention to a significant detail that will help with understanding the performance. Gregory Berns believes that novelty is a universal desire. He describes an experiment where:

> subjects were rigged up to receive alternating drops of regular water and a sweetness-spiked liquid, brain scans showed more evidence of experiencing pleasure when the sweet stuff was delivered at unpredictable intervals—underscoring the importance of surprise. He goes on to separate pleasure (which can be worn down by familiarity, as when you eat a favorite food over and over) from a more lasting sense of well-being that depends in part on acquiring new knowledge and new experiences or even on tackling new challenges.[9]

By harnessing this pleasure we are able to shape the ways that attendants notice significant details during performance. If we set up a pattern where blocking is fairly predictable, then when we vary that pattern attendants will note the change and question what significance it has in relation to what was seen previously. It is a physical manifestation of foreshadowing. As we watch, we predict what will happen next. While we derive a certain pleasure from predicting accurately, it can be mundane. Thus when the violations occur, like a sudden twist in a murder mystery, the frustration is pleasurable.

An amazing aspect of how we see the world is that vision can deceive our own brains. Our control over what we think that we see is immense; we see what we think we ought to see. Gustav Kuhn has been studying magic tricks as a means to understanding how the mind perceives illusion. He states, "Magicians really have this ability to distort your perceptions, to get people to perceive things that never happened, just like a visual illusion."[10] He charts a slight-of-hand trick called the "vanishing ball," in which a ball apparently disappears in mid-air. When we look at the world we assume that what we see is real. The trick demonstrates that our reality "is more strongly dominated by how we perceive it to be rather than what it actually is. . . . Even though the ball never left the hand, the reason people saw it leave is because they expected the ball to leave the hand. It's the beliefs about what should happen that override the actual visual input."[11] Even though attendants did not see the ball, they perceived it because the clues from where they were watching suggested that the ball would be tossed in the air. Their prediction system was tricked. Kuhn interprets this, "Even though people claimed they were looking at the ball, what you find is that they spend a lot of time looking at the face. While their eye movements weren't fooled by where the ball was, their perception was. It reveals how important social cues are in influencing perception."[12] Not only does the eye detect the raw stimulus of the object's movement, but also it interprets the data according to lived experience. Similarly, in *Elsinore* LePage used theatrical tricks that fool perception to metamorphose a rotating platform into a dining table, a playing card, a trap door, and a ship.

How does this fooling of the brain happen? According to Mark Changizi, "Illusions occur when our brains attempt to perceive the future, and those perceptions don't match reality."[13] Our brains only work on a few second time-lapse. Think of the way a progressive DVD works, going a bit ahead of where it is being projected to adjust if there is a skip. Our brain needs to piece together the different bits of neural information for our consciousness to perceive it. Jeanna Bryner explains:

> Humans can see into the future. . . . We do get a glimpse of events one-tenth of a second before they occur. . . . It starts with a neural lag

that most everyone experiences while awake. When a light hits your retina, about one-tenth of a second goes by before the brain translates the signal into a visual perception of the world. . . . Foresight keeps our view of the world in the present. It gives you enough heads up to catch a ball (instead of getting socked in the face) and maneuver smoothly through a crowd.[14]

This time lag enables us to move smoothly through the world. Amusement park rides and three-dimensional movies make use of this neurological system to give us a thrill. These rides are able to trick our brains because it takes advantage of our propensity to predict what will happen in the next moment. As the illusion of the Borg assimilator in the "Star Trek Experience" dives toward our head and a chair mechanism prods us, we automatically shift our head to try and avoid the collision even though we know we are in a fictional setting. Changizi explains the brain function that enables this response, "The converging lines toward a vanishing point (the spokes) are cues that trick our brains into thinking we are moving forward—as we would in the real world, where the door frame (a pair of vertical lines) seems to bow out as we move through it—and we try to perceive what the world will look like in the next instant."[15] In this way, we can predict and respond accordingly to the world as we travel down a hallway.

Helping attendants empathize

The discovery of mirror neurons is important to theatre practice. Mirror neurons are a class of neurons that fire sympathetically when we see others performing an action such as bringing a banana to their lips. Our brains perceive the action as being performed itself. The human brain has multiple mirror-neuron systems that specialize in carrying out and understanding not just the actions of others but their intentions, the social meaning of their behavior, and their emotions. This sympathetic response enables us to be empathetic. Giacomo Rizzolatti discovered that mirror neurons fired in monkey brains when researchers were eating in the lab. Each time scientists brought food to their mouths it triggered a monitor hooked to the laboratory monkeys. When a monkey saw or heard an action, the same neurons fired as when the animal carried out the same action on its own. Michael Gazzaniga explains that this occurs on a broader basis in us: "In humans, however, the mirror system fires even when there is no goal. A hand randomly waving in the air will cause the system to activate."[16] We are able to empathize and take pleasure in other's actions because we too experience what others are doing even at a distance. Thus we are able to learn through watching as well as doing. Rizzolatti explains that, "Mirror neurons allow us to grasp the minds of others not through conceptual reasoning but through direct simulation. By feeling, not by thinking."[17] Art practice directly stimulates the attendant's brain, and as such, composition exploits the functional properties of mirror neurons. In LePage's *Needles and Opium* (1992) attendants were able to get a sense of an addict's drug induced "trip" when he mimicked the sensation of flight by suspending himself in front of moving images projected on a screen behind him. Close-up images of a needle sucking up a narcotic from a spoon made way for images of flying. Vittorio Gallese explains how our empathetic response is possible, "When you see the Baroque sculptor Gian Lorenzo Bernini's hand of divinity grasping marble, you see the hand as if it were grasping flesh. . . . Experiments show that when you read a novel, you memorize positions of objects from the narrator's point of view."[18] Our brain's ability to feel what someone else feels and understand that experience points to the inherently social nature of human existence. The live theatrical event stimulates that social behavior and shapes our experience of the world.

Whether we are watching Jean and Miss Julie taste wine or flirt in Strindberg's *Miss Julie*, our brains are simulating those actions on a neuronal level. We can interpret each character's objective because we are experiencing their situations in the same way that they are. Gazzaniga speculates that the significance of mirror neurons on experience is their involvement with understanding why the action is being done: "I understand that a cup is being lifted to the mouth (the action understanding of the goal) to see how its contents taste (the intention behind the action). The same action is coded differently if it is associated with different intentions, thereby predicting the likely future unobserved action."[19] We understand the context of the situation so that we can understand that Jean is picking up a glass of cognac and whether he is going to drink it, pour it out, or going to offer it to Miss Julie. Our observations of other's behavior are tied to our most basic perceptual systems that act upon us even before consciousness triggers. If, as an actor, you enact seduction, you experience the act of seduction because your body is firing the same neurons as a real seduction. Acting and directing become the medium of directing the emotional and physical experience of the attendant. Mimesis creates a cathartic experience because it orchestrates the attendant's experience and provides resolution to that experience in a short time. Our brains are changed as a result of theatre because the experiences of the event become a part of our electrochemical experience.

Activating the senses

Focusing on the senses of touch and hearing in a theatrical event can also show us how the senses can be exploited to create authenticity and help attendants imagine the conditions that the characters are suffering within. Amiri Baraka's *Slave Ship: A Historical Pageant* (1967) used the setting as a means of triggering discomfort within the audience. He describes the play's setting with the term "atmos-feeling," which denotes a multi-sensory approach to establishing a stage space. Eugene Lee's set placed attendants on benches within the bowels of the slave ship and the actors performed the action of the play in close proximity, thus making the attendants part of the play. They could feel the vibrations of the drums in their seats, and they were crammed together shoulder to shoulder giving them an impression of the cramped quarters. Henry Lacey describes:

> The set itself, a split-level wooden platform mounted on huge springs, was a brilliant conception and the play's chief metaphor, suggesting with its rhythmic rocking not simply the swell of the ocean as the slave ship sails across it, but also the structural insecurity of a black man both as a slave on his way to America and as a citizen once he has arrived and settled. . . . The lower level of the set, the dark hold . . . forced the audience to hunch over in order to see what was happening during the first part of the play.[20]

This, combined with music, made manifest the experience of the slave ship to the attendants, creating the physical reality of the ship for them, so in effect they became aware of their bodies or the state of their bodies in the uncertainty of confinement of the captive slaves. Types of sound production used in performance included sound generation by voice, environmental sound, and sound generation by musical instruments. The keening of the characters wore spectators down. The ambient noises of life aboard the slave ship created an atmosphere that conveyed the misery of the captive slaves. The consequence of this awareness by the attendants allowed them to make conscious the accumulation of sensations that enrich their conscious interpretation of the themes and actions presented during performance. As a means of mimetic realism, sound can transport the attendant to the time and place of the action and elicit an emotional response. The production was able to transcend showing action and make the attendants active participants in the experience of being on a slave ship.

Given the nature of the attendants' physiological response to the stimuli generated over the course of a theatrical event, directors have the opportunity to draw upon our learned social responses to intensify theatrical reception. When we are blocking scenes and shaping a play's action, we make use of conventionalized social patterns that are a result of biological needs. After all, cultural habits such as preferences to sweet food over acids developed holistically out of the constraints of our biology. Ellen Dissanayake, after studying interactions between infants and mothers from many different cultures, developed a hypothesis that the visual, gestural, and vocal cues that arise spontaneously and unconsciously between mothers and infants adhere to a formalized process similar to that used in artistic composition. These patterns are:

> the calls and responses, the swooping bell tones of motherese, the widening of the eyes, the exaggerated smile, the repetitions and variations, the laughter of the baby met by the mother's emphatic refrain. The rules of engagement have a pace and a set of expected responses, and should the rules be violated, the pitch prove too jarring, the delays between coos and head waggles too long or too short, mother or baby may grow fretful or bored.[21]

As directors manipulate an audience's expectations or repeat themes and motifs, they are engaging in the mechanics of stimulating, keeping attention, and passing on experience. Dissanayake "suggests that many of the basic phonemes of art, the stylistic conventions and tonal patterns, the mental clay, staples and pauses with which even the loftiest creative works are constructed, can be traced back to the most primal of collusions—the intimate interplay between mother and child."[22] In this way, theatrical performance is a form of intimate bodily communication that transforms who we are. Theatre has the power to condition our bodies and brains to respond to new types of experiences and thereby influence our future interactions with the world.

The power of theatrical expression

As our ever-changing and plastic brain becomes stimulated and begins to modify itself, not only does the brain shape culture, but culture also shapes the brain.[23] Norman Doidge explains, "Neuroplastic research has shown us that every sustained activity ever mapped—including physical activities, sensory activities, leaning, thinking, and imagining—changes the brain as well as the mind."[24] There are implications for virtual reality and other forms of mediated experience. As the brain does not discriminate between sensations and all stimuli are real, the body can experience a mediated experience and fire off neurons to the brain in the same way as a normal experience, depending on whether it is triggered in the same way that it is from proximate stimulation. Thus the virtual experience can become real, because mirror neurons and empathy neurons fire off sympathetic responses. The difference in how this occurs comes in between the ways that media stimulate the brain. The hypnotizing qualities of television come from its constantly changing flashes of light. Our eyes are attracted and cannot make sense of the stimulation. Ultimately, we respond like a deer in the headlights: frozen, staring. Movies are a series of still images that do not blend together in a manner that fires the neurons as if we are moving through space. These mediums are capable of triggering mirror and empathy responses from attendants, but those activities that stimulate the regions of the brain tied to action stimulate us much more. As we watch a Wilson composition unfold in front of us, the colors and movements of the objects draw our attention and influence our emotions and feelings. They provide us with an in-between state of response; we are experiencing this as if it is real even though we are fully aware that it is fiction. Though we may not realize it consciously, when a giant cat's paw breaches the proscenium's frame in *King of Spain* (1969), we accept it and respond to this improbable sight naturally. Through this process, we are learning by exposure to unfamiliar experiences and our plastic brains are strengthening neural networks, making the pathways light up more brilliantly. Theatre allows us to practice and make experience familiar. As we gain exposure, we strengthen the plastic brain's neural pathways and what is familiar is most pleasurable. Art can literally pave the way for experience, strengthening the neural pathways that our brains use to experience, interpret, and conceive of the world around us. By speaking directly through the senses, we can cut through all of the conscious baggage that we carry with us as we try to understand theatrical performance. In that way, our perceptions can be shaped by our neural processes before our consciousness becomes infected with the social learning and habitual experiences of interacting with the world around us, thereby revealing unexpected insights.

Moving between disciplines can prompt us to generate a language to describe and identify the types of tools that are used to stimulate our brain and to begin to understand the potential richness of sensorial interpretation. The nerves and neurons cut across culture and enable us to predict a range of potential responses within the attendant. How we understand and respond to those stimuli will still be colored by the contingencies of our own personal plastic development. However, our physiology and brain make-up give us an indication of the potential stimulation available to artists when they make use of recurring patterns, changes, shadows, and shapes. As we become more conscious of attending to our sensations, we will become more proficient at interpreting and developing complex interpretations of these cultural and experiential events. Neurobiology is providing a guidebook on how to push the right buttons to create provocative theatrical experiences that may yield rich expression and interpretation. As practitioners begin to make use of production techniques that challenge spectators' expectations of what performance should be like and how it is meant to be understood, they face the challenge of how to lead attendants to reassess their means of perception. It is a feedback loop of training—a place where ideas and practice collide.

Notes

1. Arlette Steri, "Perception," in Oliver Houde, ed. *Dictionary of Cognitive Science: Neuroscience, Psychology, Artificial Intelligence, Linguistics, and Philosophy* (NY and Hove: Psychology Press, 2004), 274.
2. Norman Doidge, *The Brain that Changes Itself: Stories of Personal Triumph from the Frontiers of Brain Science* (New York: Penguin Books, 2007), 303.
3. Steri, "Perception," 274.
4. Ibid.
5. Antonio Damasio, *The Feeling of What Happens: Body and Emotion in the Making of Consciousness* (New York: Harcourt, 1999), 53.
6. Ibid., 54.
7. Bernard J. Baars, *In the Theatre of Consciousness* (New York: Oxford University Press, 1997).
8. Ibid., 107.
9. Rob Walker, "Imitation of Life," *New York Times*, January 13, 2008.
10. Charles Q. Choi, "Study Reveals How Magic Works," *Live Science*, 20 November 2006, http://www.liveScience.com/strangenews/061120_magic_brain.html (accessed September 28, 2008).
11. Ibid.
12. Ibid.
13. Jeanna Bryner, "Key to All Optical Illusions Discovered," *Live Science*, 2 June 2008, http://www.livescience.com/strangenews/080602-foresee-future.html (accessed September 29, 2008).
14. Ibid.
15. Ibid.

16. Michael S. Gazzaniga, *Human: The Science Behind What Makes Us Unique* (New York: Ecco, 2008), 178.
17. Sandra Blakeslee, "Cells That Read Minds," *New York Times* (January 10, 2006).
18. Ibid.
19. Gazzaniga, *Human: The Science behind What Makes Us Unique*, 179.
20. Henry C. Lacey, *To Raise, Destroy and Create: The Poetry, Drama and Function of Imamu Amiri Baraka* (Troy: Whitston, 1981), 153.
21. Natalie Angier, "The Dance of Evolution, or How Art Got its Start," *New York Times* (November 27, 2007).
22. Ibid.
23. Doidge, *The Brain that Changes*, 297.
24. Ibid., 288.

8
Active Dramaturgy: Using Research to Inspire Creative Thought

Lenora Inez Brown

Dramaturgy, like design, is an art and a process, a way of doing and a field of study. As such, dramaturgy's philosophy and practice are not just inextricably tied; they are, in fact, one and the same. The dramaturg's responsibility and art lie in discovering ways to enliven the dramatic action by posing questions and judiciously employing theories and other researched ideas to aid their artistic collaborators: directors, actors, designers, and playwrights.

Many dramaturgs and collaborators erroneously believe that a dramaturg's only responsibility is to identify ways to buttress a director's concept. In truth, a dramaturg, and especially an active dramaturg, explores ways to extend, expand, and enrich the play's themes in addition to supporting the director's concept. While the necessary thinking and research may lead the dramaturg to question the director's concept or approach, the goal is to achieve a balance between the artistic and theoretical ideas, and not to compete or assume creative control.

The researched ideas, philosophies, or theoretical approaches that a dramaturg encounters may shape intellectual debates and represent accepted schools of thought among scholars, but active dramaturgs look at these theories or philosophical ideas with skepticism. In particular, this chapter works from the premise that theory is not an untested idea, but rather a set of ideas or beliefs put forth as procedure, policy to be followed, or an accepted basis for action. Philosophy, like theory, is a way of thinking, of framing ideas, but unlike theory it does not prescribe what the actions or behavior should be, although philosophies do inspire action or a framework for exploration. Active dramaturgy, for example, is a philosophy rather than, theory, for although a mindset can be defined, the exact procedure that dramaturgs follow cannot be determined because, like any creative process, dramaturgy is fluid.

The global acceptance of theories such as feminism, post-feminism, multiculturalism, or Marxism isn't in question. However, the philosophy of active dramaturgy does question the practice of investing in a strict, letter-of-the-law approach to using ideologies for production. While these aforementioned intellectual pursuits have greatly altered how society examines itself and its art, these ideas alone rarely possess what is needed to produce an engaging dramatic production. When a dramaturg or creative team seeks to stage a philosophy or theory, the result is a staged idea of an experience rather than an artful realization of an experience, and the production often proves unengaging, if not highly problematic. Active dramaturgy looks to mine select dramatic aspects of theoretical ideas and incorporate those discoveries into the rehearsal process and stage production.

For example, while dramaturging an expressionistic interpretation of Tennessee Williams' *The Glass Menagerie*, I read numerous articles that discussed Amanda's fading beauty, and how this relates to the South's fading glory, or painted Amanda as a conniving, heartless nag. One article referred to Amanda's most cherished items, especially the candelabra. Within Roger B. Stein's exploration of narrative and religion, he considers the important role they play in defining personal past.

> We are told by Amanda that the candelabrum 'used to be on the alter at the church of the Heavenly Rest. It was melted a little out of shape when the church burnt down. Lightning struck it one spring.' Amanda's comment opens up another dimension of the drama and reminds us that Williams, inheritor of a Southern religious tradition . . . has persistently drawn upon the language of Christian symbolism to define his characters' human situations.[1]

This excerpt of critical text analysis offers a production team active choices; such criticism can sometimes prove more practical than the many theoretical writings regarding socialism, feminism, or research supporting other aspects of socio-economic realities confronting Tom's family. Highlighting the damaged candelabra reminds us that Amanda is also a scavenger—an active agent in taking from others and using them or their items for her personal gain. Stein's observation opens the play by providing insights that do more than inform how an actor thinks and demonstrates how objects and symbols reflect the themes that actively influence a character's behavior and choices in the past, present, and future.

The essence of active dramaturgy

Active dramaturgy casts the dramaturg as a vital participant throughout the pre-production, rehearsal, and preview processes. In addition, active dramaturgy seeks to quash the notion that a dramaturg is a solitary figure who executes the ideas of others, a librarian, or a master of the photocopier/printer. Philosophically, the active dramaturg identifies themes, metaphors, dramatic forms (the way events come together), and innovative uses of time and language within a dramatic text to initiate or further creative exploration. Most important, the active dramaturg poses questions that encourage collaboration and help all artists strengthen and clarify their ideas.

When considering research that is appropriate for the rehearsal hall, an active dramaturg seeks information that enhances understanding and/ or influences actable choices or events that a production can achieve or enact. The active dramaturg resists the temptation to distribute numerous unedited or notated articles to the creative team. To facilitate the consumption and use of research, whether is it theory, criticism, or analysis, an active dramaturg provides excerpts and appropriate summaries—that is, brief introductions that remind the reader why the article is included or summarize an author's main ideas preceding excerpted pages—to provide necessary contexts and to accelerate understanding.

Researching historical and era-defining information

While active dramaturgs remain cautious of over-using theory and criticism in the creative process, conducting research remains a primary dramaturgical function for set texts. When working on set texts penned by William Shakespeare or August Strindberg or more recent works such as Caryl Churchill's *Cloud Nine,* José Rivera's *Marisol*, or Suzan-Lori Parks' *The America Play*, a dramaturg may be responsible for researching the play's era to help the creative team better understand the play's many obvious and veiled references. However, much of the available information can overwhelm the artistic team with facts that, while explaining the relevant era or politics, fail to generate active choices or suggestions for unlocking the play's action. How, then, does an active dramaturg identify material that addresses the specific needs of a given production and translate it into the rehearsal/production process?

While dramaturgs should know what inspired the writing of *Hamlet* (these facts help place the play and certain issues in context so that adventurous interpretations are possible), it is nearly impossible to stage the context surrounding a play's evolution. Instead, theatre artists aim to stage a play's story, which is what actively shapes the themes, the plot, and ultimately the production. If research can make a story tangible, in a dynamic way, then active dramaturgy will follow. Contemplating what makes historical or performance research production-appropriate proves an important function of active dramaturgy.

For example, it may be important to acknowledge that *Hamlet* dates from 1604, but if the production is to be set in 2004 and in Washington DC, this context proves less than significant in shaping production choices. In fact, choosing to bring these and other similar facts to the rehearsal hall can position the dramaturg as more of a teacher than a collaborator on the artistic team. However, identifying the timeless themes concerning grief, succession (be it for the throne or a corporation), and struggles for independence within the family, may direct the dramaturg to find and present more production-appropriate information that is vital and relevant to the creative team's decision-making process.

Entering the critical conversation

In seeking out research materials for the production process, the active dramaturg is looking for ways to better understand the critical conversations surrounding the play so that the dramaturgical insights can guide the artistic team away from predictable solutions to age-old questions. A strong sense of the prevailing discourse will allow aberrant theses and facts to rise to the surface as one's research process progresses. Furthermore, these unusual ideas or rarely reported analyses or facts can inspire active explorations of the text in the rehearsal hall that also play well on stage.

To best exemplify how socio-political context can inform the artistic team but may not prove as vital in the rehearsal hall, consider J. Chris Westgate's article "Toward a Rhetoric of Sociospatial Theatre: José Rivera's *Marisol*."[2] Westgate uses *Marisol* as "a starting point for theorizing a discourse in theatre studies to consider sociospatial concerns in dramaturgy and performance, a discourse that makes fruitful connections among cultural and critical geography, urban theory, and semiotics."[3]

When Rivera wrote *Marisol*, New York and many large urban centers were overwhelmed by a financial crisis, a rapidly growing homeless population, and the emerging AIDS epidemic. America's future seemed

bleak and its woes inconsolable. These were dark times. And yet some had hope; the fictional Marisol became one such optimistic figure.

Westgate takes care to describe and document New York's financial distress during the 1980s and the ineffectual or hard-lined efforts of Mayors Ed Koch and Rudy Giuliani, respectively. The merits of the historical information mentioned in this article cannot be overstated, and an active dramaturg might distribute this article to document life or the New York urban environment in the 1980s. Westgate also uses performance theory and semiotics to dissect and shape a specific reading of the text and interpret the play's urban signs and symbols. However, the article's exploration of how the play should make the audience understand or respond to the urban references makes it less appealing for the rehearsal hall.

Certainly grounding the production in a play's original period or a bygone era has merit, as does reminding the creative team about the play's history and background. Referencing Bertolt Brecht, Westgate points out "that the incidents depicted in [a] play were always influenced or inhibited by its place and period."[4] But much of Westgate's article reflects a form of critical analysis that defines interpretations for the company, and distributing the entire article runs the risk of limiting rather than expanding choice. Also, background information rarely moves the production or the play forward by providing actable choices, although reference to specific eras, struggles, and tragedies can and *do* inform the play's atmosphere and setting. When identifying an article or portion thereof, an active dramaturg looks to distinguish between information that defines interpretations as it explains dramatic themes or metaphor, and information that clarifies and creates possibility.

An active dramaturg's individual artistry reveals itself when the dramaturg uses atypical triggers such as an article or image to liberate thematic ideas to help shape the production's world (and atmosphere). Using key facts regarding 1980s New York's urban decay or economic decline, might lead to a visual storyboard that unites current global stressors with the then financial impropriety to elicit more relevant social commentary from *Marisol*. This realization of environment may also lead the production to distance the audience further from the characters, realizing a key aspect of Epic theatre and using Westgate's following observation to the fullest, "In rendering homelessness as a problem of the city rather than for the city, *Marisol* attempts to shift audience engagement away from the characters and toward the circumstances experienced by those characters."[5] In this case the theory helps generate a new approach to character and underscore the piece's relevance today while honoring its original era.

As an active dramaturg continues to research and prepare for the rehearsal hall, the second question becomes: What is the difference between research that creates context and research that propels action? Ronald Knowles' article, entitled "Hamlet and Counter-Humanism", helps answer this question and locate the iconic play within its original context by focusing on the shifting perception of humanism throughout specific eras and philosophies or beliefs (e.g., Christianity and stoicism). Throughout, Knowles documents the entomology of select phrases and asserts references that learned Renaissance audiences would grasp. As fascinating as it is to know the roots of linguistic phrases, too few of these ideas can be executed on stage. The article clarifies the context for the play's creation and character biography that influences the internal monologue, but not the external performance and dialogue.

The compulsion to share Knowles' article in full with the production team seems understandable, as the essay helps explain the evolution of or impact that certain lines and references had on audiences and why Shakespeare wrote in this particular way. For example:

> If we turn from Pico's esoteric Cabbalism to something like Giannozzo Manetti's *On the Dignity of Man* (1452) and its context, this will provide the background for the understanding of Hamlet's argument, the materials for which Shakespeare probably got not so much from Montaigne, but from Montaigne's source in his library, Pierre Boaistuau whose work was available to Shakespeare in reprints of John Alday's translation.[6]

However, the question an active dramaturg must ask is: Do these references clarify how the actors and director play or shape the moment? If and when the answer is no, the research must remain outside of the rehearsal hall. But, if specific ideas suggest dynamic ways to revision a character, then select passages might be useful to a production team at various stages in their process.

Knowles' article, for example, does offer a provocative reading of Humanism and grief. "In the anguish of grief and loathing Hamlet's subjectivity is realized in a consciousness which rejects the wisdom of tradition for the unique selfhood of the individual."[7] The insights regarding grief within ancient texts and how those texts might shape Hamlet the character (a philosophy student after all) might actively shape the rehearsal process. The article may inspire the active dramaturg to question how to establish a ritual of grieving outside the Renaissance era or to investigate diverse rituals regarding grief to inform new interpretations of the text rather than a production that appropriates foreign rites. This process might lead to research or source material regarding mourning and burial practices, or it may help to identify moments in the play where the rituals may appear or be violated. Isolating these moments can magnify pre-existing moments of tension and conflict between the characters and lead to a unique production that avoids traditional solutions.

Active dramaturgy and 'isms'

If the director chooses to use the literary theories that end with "ism" such as new historicism or feminism, post-feminism or multicultural-ism to ground or largely influence the production, then an article that outlines the philosophy or approach would help the artistic team define key elements and thus facilitate clear communication. The active dram-aturg identifies a source that simply defines the topic with prose, avoids obtuse, convoluted language, and is not overly simplistic. However, the active dramaturg takes care to present such material as background information or as a starting point for crafting questions that may help shape character, highlight themes, or develop atmosphere. Whenever presenting research or background information, it's important to model how the material informs choice rather than prescribes choice. For exam-ple, if using multiculturalism as a possible lens for exploration, an active dramaturg might remind the artistic team that this approach invites them to explore how cultural difference enhances and inhibits under-standing within the play's world and often changes the meaning of some dialogue, but that it often addresses difference from the point of view of the dominant ethnicity and as such can perpetuate the cultural disenfranchisement multiculturalism purports to eliminate.

Multiculturalism like feminism has fueled thinking and staging choices that liberate characters from the periphery. A multicultural approach can encourage artists to look at the characters who shape the action, even if they are silent, and to explore ways to shift the audience's gaze, which is largely shaped by cultural familiarity. While these ideological tools help artists examine a play or set of characters, as well as present possible frames for production—such as a Kabuki or Voodoo frame for staging *Macbeth*, difficulties begin to arise when "isms" become the sole impetus for a production.

Take, for example, an extension of multiculturalism, namely non-traditional casting. When first introduced, this theory for produc-tion encouraged casting people of color in roles traditionally given to

Caucasian actors. The goal was to increase the performance opportunities for actors of color and those with apparent and non-apparent disabilities. However, some believe that non-traditional casting does not invite an actor or the production to acknowledge the performer's appearance or ethnicity because non-traditional casting expects the audience and actor to ignore difference and, in essence, to see everyone as the same or as the cast's dominant ethnicity, which in most cases is Caucasian. Color-conscious casting, however, encourages the performer and production to acknowledge the actor's culture or ethnicity or disability (if the performer chooses) and asks the production to explore when ethnicity alters the play's dramatic tension and obstacles. For example, an African-American cast as a captain or chief of police may mean a rise through very segregated ranks, which informs character portrayal and choices when delivering dialogue.

An active dramaturg carefully evaluates whether the critical ideas open a play or narrowly define its impact, a common concern with critical analysis focused on writers of color.[8] Adrienne Kennedy's early works such as *Funnyhouse of a Negro, An Owl Answers*, and *Movie Star Has to Star in Black and White* present clear examples of plays that when analyzed, critics and scholars seek to explain her uniquely African-American perspective and ignore the many references to Caucasians and overlook that the plays often explore Kennedy's (or her character's) thoughts on what it's like for an African-American to live within a Caucasian-defined world. However, a dramaturg who researches the play to gain an understanding of Kennedy's world often finds information that focuses on African-Americans or an historical or literary figure mentioned in her plays, but rarely a discussion of both. The writing, ironically, perpetuates the idea of living apart, thereby espousing the false notion that ethnic groups do not interact. The criticism, even when touted as an act of multiculturalism, often supports a single point of view, which restricts a full understanding of the play and in turn its reach.

In fact, if a dramaturg were to dissect Kennedy's plays as a pure exploration of race, one might misunderstand her work and consider her plays denigrating to the African-American race.

To determine whether essays critiquing African American, Latino, Asian, and other non-Caucasian playwrights are successful in addressing difference, an active dramaturg looks for limiting terms and works to liberate plays from prejudicial or stereotyped thinking and analysis. The ethnicity of the writer in question does not guarantee a balanced nor biased-free discussion. What's more, articles that reveal a dated way of discussing difference may still be useful; given a clear introduction and frame, they may help the creative team better understand the emotional world the characters inhabit.

Considering literary and production criticism

Applying literary criticism to the production process requires active dramaturgs to question freely whether information is appropriate for the rehearsal hall. Choosing to glean a single idea (or two) from source material allows for more varied research and can liberate a dramaturg from the need to become an undisputed expert in the few weeks before rehearsal begins. In addition, looking for source materials that speak to various aspects of a play can facilitate a complex artistic vision that stimulates multiple points of view. Quite simply, a single idea can inspire enough ideas to fuel an entire production, shape each act, or inform any character's journey. And an active dramaturg works to identify key ideas that will fuel the artistic team's discovery process rather than simply support known choices.

But at times a dramaturg wants to share an entire essay, chapter, or article that analyzes a dramatic text. Looking for thinkers/writers whose work mirrors the process of an active dramaturg can help reveal research that is useful for the rehearsal hall. Writers who use language to reveal the story and its tensions (dramatic moments) can help us locate places in the text that offer multiple and simultaneous possibilities for the stage. Theatre critics analyze texts to identify ways to perform language's ironies, contradictions, and truths through body and word.

Many articles, chapters, or books written by theatre scholars function as either close readings of the text or a single character. What sets these writings apart from literary criticism or performance theory (as opposed to theories of performance such as Brecht's Epic Theatre) is an emphasis on the entire text or the character's journey in relation to the play's entire world and its inhabitants. Also, dramatic criticism explores the story *and* the character and how character serves the story rather than emphasizing how the story impacts and is received by the audience. As such, dramatic criticism can read like a series of obvious insights or unchallenging thoughts. Nothing could be further from the truth. The simplicity and directness within many of these writings work to transform complicated approaches to production into clearly articulated concepts for the creative team.

Ruby Cohn, Richard Gilman, Erika Munk, and Hilton Als represent a small group of critics who write in this vein. The key to successful dramatic criticism for the rehearsal hall is writing that illuminates how the themes support or challenge characters or plot points. The writing often avoids fitting texts into philosophical or theoretical boxes, although the writer may use a critical approach as a lens. The play serves as the central source, not a view that may fade from literary or critical favor.

For example, throughout Rutter's article "Snatched Bodies: Ophelia in the Grave,"[9] she focuses on Ophelia's burial scene as it appears in the play and then in three specific film adaptations. Rutter concentrates on specific elements in various films and why specific choices work and what insights they offer. Rutter begins by asking whether she should even explore her topic, "Am I right to argue for the visibility of the woman's body as a crucial maker of meaning in the scene? What if Ophelia's corpse is shrouded, or 'played' by a dummy, or brought to the grave in a closed coffin?"[10] She establishes herself as a questioner rather than an authority who may be questioned. Her approach invites the reader, and in turn the artist, to consider options as they encounter the essay. The work isn't a challenge to artists but rather a series of questions to inspire the creative team's processes. This essay, and other articles similar in approach to play analysis, are inherently dramaturgical. As a result, the artist or reader can both evaluate the choice and its repercussions to develop a number of additional options to explore during rehearsal. Options exist because Rutter, Cohn, Gilman, and others specifically discuss the *why* and *how* surrounding a choice or scene. Too often literary criticism explores what happens when only certain conditions are at play.

The most significant observation fueling Rutter's writing and that of writers who subscribe to a similar form of criticism is that the dramatic text is, at its heart, a contradiction; for it is both static (the text) and ever-changing (the interpretation). Different truths are at play within each production. The truth for this play may change because of the specific interpretation, but nothing is lost as long as the expression remains rooted in the text and its entire story. Essentially, Rutter uses feminism to inform her reading, but does not impose the theories on the entire play. Rutter accepts that a feminist vision magnifies certain elements of the play's story, placing elements in high relief and others in *bas*-relief. However, Rutter avoids forcing the entire play (or film) into the feminist box. In Rutter's hands the play still breathes.

Conclusion

To embrace the art of dramaturgy, the art of thinking thematically, often means discovering ways to discuss ideas and insights through verbal or written notes. It is difficult work to weave researched facts and theoretical ideas into thematic evidence and to articulate moments where these new insights can clarify the story or character without appearing to direct the artistic team. An active dramaturg, however, has the opportunity to support a creative vision by stretching it through questions and through facts or analysis that offer more questions. Active dramaturgs successfully introduce research into the rehearsal hall by connecting theories to the play's facts, themes, and directorial vision to help the production push against expectations. When sharing these ideas through well-posed questions grounded in specific references that illuminate the elements of drama—metaphor, language, time, character, spectacle—the dramaturg becomes an active thinker, laying the groundwork for a creative environment and establishing dramaturgy as a vital and integral artistic element.

Notes

1. Roger B. Stein. "The Glass Menagerie Revisited: Catastrophe without Violence," *The Glass Menagerie: A Collection of Critical Essays*, ed. R. B. Parker. (Englewood Cliffs: Prentice-Hall, Inc., 1983), 135–43.
2. J. Chris Westgate. "Toward a Rhetoric of Sociospatial Theatre: José Rivera's *Marisol*," *Theatre Journal*, 59.1 (2007), 21–37.
3. Ibid., 21.
4. Ibid., 34.
5. Ibid.
6. Ronald Knowles, "Hamlet and Counter-Humanism," *Renaissance Quarterly*, 52.4 (1999), 1049.
7. Ibid., 1066.
8. Toni Morrison's *Playing in the Dark: Whiteness and the Literary Imagination* (Cambridge: Harvard University Press, 1992) takes great care to note the many silent and forgotten African-American characters in the American novel. Most noteworthy is the African-American male character in Hemmingway's *To Have and Have Not*. Readers ignore the black character, who remains nameless except for an epithet in part one; in part two, however, the perception of the black character changes when he is named. But since Harry fails to acknowledge the black man with him, so does Hemmingway and, in turn, the reader (70–1).
9. Carol Rutter, "Snatched Bodies: Ophelia in the Grave," *Shakespeare Quarterly*, 49.3 (1998), 299–319.
10. Ibid., 300.

9

Intuition in Practice: Emotion and Feeling in the Artistic Process

Harry Feiner

> . . . I live in a sort of haze, and I often don't under-
> stand what I'm writing.[1]

> . . . I am becoming more convinced that it isn't a
> matter of old or new forms—one must write without
> thinking about forms, and just because it pours freely
> from one's soul.[2]

The pre-eminence of intuition

Theory, the calculated schemes that we believe come to us abstractly, may have little to do with how creative ideas develop, which perhaps depends more on instinct for making forms than conscious intellectual deliberation. (I am defining *theory* as a set of guiding principles; a system to understand a particular phenomenon—in this case creativity—and the proposed methods to accomplish it.) While a great deal of cognitive evidence has emerged to support the notion of intuition in creative activity, can one argue that theoretical activity may still have an impact on the creative process?

Recent research points to a physical connection between mind and body that firmly anchors our mental processes in the body and its feelings.[3] In distinction to the Cartesian model that contrasts mind-body as a paradigm of separate entities, mind is dependent on the body it is physiologically tied to and its ongoing relationship to the space inhabited by it. There is no disassociated "cerebral" thought (though we mistakenly give ourselves credit for such incorporeal potential as an example of human beings' exceptionalism).[4] Creativity depends on engaging our physical core through "feeling," no matter how intellectually removed "ideas" seem to be. I propose that the engagement with the physical

125

is the primary action of effective forms (the shape and structure of art objects). Forms' structures evoke feelings, affecting us instinctively with powerfully intuitive constructions that account for the experience of art. This may be especially so in the theatre, which is intrinsically dependent on space, and therefore powerfully linked to our neuro-logical somatosensory imaging systems and the emotional instincts tied directly to those systems.[5]

There are two aspects of the word *intuition* that are important to this argument: the ability to understand something *immediately,* and that such understanding comes without *conscious reasoning.* Effective art must grab us at a gut level first because that is how our conscious minds work.[6] Our neurological "hardware" is based on a concrete tie to the mechanisms of the body, so there is no such thing as mind/body separation with an independent spiritual aspect. This is not to say that we never go beyond our instinctual levels. Such a leap is necessary to achieve the uniquely human levels of consciousness that art aspires to, but I am doubtful that we can "think" our way into it. Although I assert that artistic processes are primarily intuitive, I will also discuss how they can be enriched by intellectual reflection in later stages.

In an article on the creative process, Patricia Hampl states she "had precious few intentions, except . . . to filch whatever was loose on the table that suited my immediate purposes . . . [which were] vague, incon-sistent, reversible under pressure."[7] Hampl refers to similar sentiments from other writers, all suggesting that intrinsic to creative activity is a vagueness of clear intent; it comes in an irregular jumble of "fits and starts," fragments and hunches.[8] When we create, we seem to imitate the processes of consciousness; we take a vast array of disparate information generated subconsciously and intuitively, and, through some "trick" of unification, produce what appears to be an organically seamless whole.[9] Our mind fools us; because of its structure, it is difficult to determine what happens first when many strands and pieces are constantly com-ing together, rearranging and reuniting. Our rational "thinking" self may be trailing slightly behind the sub-conscious "feeling" mechanisms that are selecting the materials that consciously coalesce.[10]

The idea that life is fluid, chaotic, and random, reflecting a fragmentary being that is uncertain, began to come into prominence in the nineteenth century as the notion of *modernity* developed with its increasing empha-sis on the individual and the psyche.[11] Charles Baudelaire described the confused underpinnings of life's reality as "the ephemeral, the fugitive, the contingent" ("whose other half is the eternal and the immutable").[12]

Such sentiments, however, were also marked by their dialectical opposite, a "will toward totalization."[13]

When I reflect back on my own personal work history, the best ideas have come obliquely, casually, almost unexpectedly. They seem to come when I am not engaged directly in "thinking" about the project at hand. Suddenly an idea is generated: "it pours freely"—from somewhere, and fools us by seeming purposeful. When I retrace the mental chain, I can no longer be certain that the string of ideas that felt to have such purposeful, rational coherence has any casual certainty in anything other than the fact that it has come into being. Even when a project begins with a clear scheme, such a method only serves as a departure point for the string of loose intuitive impressions that will follow.

Our neurological wiring is such that in order to "think," our primal emotional responses must be engaged, incorporating rudimentary biological processes, before an idea can be grasped by the mind.[14] It is by engaging the same neural mechanisms that create our sense of conscious being that art becomes "art," beginning with elemental emotions in order to generate the highest levels of consciousness. Art is effective because of its ability to amplify experiential qualities through our feelings and to make us "aware that we are aware."[15]

Theory, which is expressed through discursive thought, often diverts our focus toward the end details of an art form after the fact—what the particulars of a form look like, or how to construct it by following theoretical precepts. It is a discussion of describing something rather than wondering about the inherent qualities in a work that echo the experience of what life feels like. Theory is dependent on language for its articulation, which is a higher order means of communicating something that has already been experienced in a more elemental way.[16] Our sensory systems receive and transmit the "picture" of life we react to as neural patterns, electrical and chemical reactions, not as completed verbal thoughts.[17] Consciousness depends intrinsically on the process of feeling, which supplies qualities beyond literal significations that have to do with the ability of creative forms to invoke the texture of experience. Getting at the process of the non-verbal elements, before they are converted into discursive language and masked by the existence of that language, is crucial to understanding what makes art work and how art that works is made.

The notion that artists' perceptions are "ahead of their time" or precede scientific theory and experimental proofs, which later validate them, illuminates some sense of the importance of instinct and intuition in the practice of art. Jonah Lehrer characterizes artists as pursuing what consciousness feels like "from the inside," as opposed to science, which he describes as attempting to explain the same phenomena from observation and reductionism.[18] For example, a recipe for a food dish cannot communicate the experience of eating the dish. A similar sentiment is found in Leonard Shlain's *Art and Physics*: "Artists have mysteriously incorporated into their works features of a physical description of the world that science later discovers."[19] The artist attempts to describe what reality *feels* like, "reality as it [is] actually experienced."[20] This prescience is related to the instinctual nature of the artistic processes; a non-conscious, intuitive apprehension precedes the mind's intellectual understanding, and subsequent verbal explication. Though this may seem contradictory, it may be common to the nature of experience that ideas are originally intuited emotionally which are later explicated rationally with theory. We come to understand rationally what has already happened to us on a more primal level.

William Wordsworth's statement, "Poetry is the spontaneous overflow of powerful feelings: it takes its origin from emotion recollected in tranquility,"[21] is an example of how far-sighted some observations can seem. Crucial is the potential similarity of the creative process to what might be characterized as steps, or neurological "orders," as in a "first-order map-emotion."[22] Some experience (or an *emotionally competent stimulus*) speaks directly to the senses and initiates the neural process that sustains a feeling through emotion. Only when these neurological events are contemplated later ("recollected") is rational intellect engaged. Fundamental to our discussion here is that the initiating idea comes from an emotional response before the intellect is active.

First, our senses detect stimuli (either objects or situations) and transfer this information to the appropriate brain locations where a neural "map" of the event is made. The body reacts subconsciously with an appropriate emotional response that is also mapped.[23] The awareness of these (visible, exterior) emotions leads to (invisible, private) feelings. Consciousness is built on the ability to generate feelings; it is our "awareness of being aware," or the capacity to hold (in our memory) and reflect on our feelings that are reached through a give-and-take among neural images, emotions, and feelings, as they "speak" to each other in the mind.[24] The emotional-feeling reaction comes first, sometimes by the slimmest of margins, preceding conscious reflection with subliminal intuition. We may make up our minds about something instinctually before we later "agree" with ourselves rationally.[25] The margin of difference is so small that even conscious effort only allows us to grasp the intimation that it is so. To tap into the vitality of consciousness, forms should connect to our emotional lives.

Emotion, feeling, and form

A stimulus provokes an emotional reaction, unconsciously attracting attention at first. We are attracted to an idea before we understand it intellectually and have misconstrued how the mind functions because the true processes are all but invisible to us, occurring in milliseconds or seconds.[26]

Certainly all of us have had occasions when we felt ill at ease about a situation (like making a wrong turn in a strange area late at night); we react emotionally momentarily before we understand why. Because there are huge amounts of potential things, or "stories," coursing through our minds that we could be paying attention to at any moment, our neurological structures have to "flag" certain matters. Maybe that is what art does; it says "pay attention," commandeering the emotional structures already in place. Good artists instinctually sense how to create forms that use our sensory systems to say "pay attention!"

Art forms emotionally connect "back" through our memory to previous experiences and the feelings those experiences "carry." (This is similar to what Antonio Damasio calls the "as-if" loop.[27] Remembering can trigger the same emotions and feelings as a stimulus experienced physically outside the mind.) We need to work through the evolutionary ladder of neurological protocols from an emotional reaction (to sensory stimuli) where attention is grabbed, to feeling, to the higher states of conscious being. The successful work of art first gets our attention with its non-discursive compositional structure, or *form*.[28] Creative forms lead us through feelings to awareness, and thus to reflection and all the vibrancy connected to such interior life.[29] Form grabs the attention of the feelings that can later build intellectual thought through reflection. We follow nature's protocol, corresponding to our evolutionary development; primal emotions and feelings lead to later cerebral reactions.

Forms are vehicles for triggering feeling. They are objects our neurological systems richly "map," evoking emotions and feelings from connections to the symbolic worlds they construct.[30] "Consciousness feels like a feeling"[31] and that is something that cannot be directed intellectually; it cannot be expressed by "symbolization in the usual sense of conventional or assigned meaning, but a presentation of a highly articulated form wherein the beholder recognizes . . . human feeling."[32] Though art is driven by "objects" that are tangible constructions, the key aspect of the effect of the objects of experience is the palpable feeling evoked. "Assigned meaning" is not what life feels like as it streams by. That is what we struggle to employ so we can intellectually understand what has already happened to us emotionally.

Damasio states "Consciousness feels like some kind of pattern built with the nonverbal signs of body states."[33] The more proximate the vehicle of engendering feeling is to the nature of the feeling itself—the mechanism of consciousness—the greater the impact. Such vehicles conjure up primal sensibilities, like the sensation of life's pulse, our inkling of our being, and although we can translate our sense of what that feels like into language, it seems more immediate, closer to its visceral origin, when the medium is non-verbal. I do not mean to elevate other artistic disciplines at the expense of literature. The same criteria apply to literary forms; language-based arts have non-discursive qualities. Tone, atmosphere, imagery, and rhythm grab our attention before or in spite of discursive meaning. Walter Pater's assertion that "all art constantly aspires to the condition of music" is a reflection of music's emotional appeal and its difficulty in being described in literal, verbal characterizations corresponding to external experience.[34]

Art works constitute a special class of objects, *symbolic forms*. My use of this term comes through the philosopher Susanne Langer, whose book on aesthetics, *Feeling and Form,* personally feels like the most accurate description of the sense of the creative process familiar to my sensibility as a practicing artist.[35] Ideas such as the purpose of art being to "objectify the life of feeling" with forms "transformed" into sensual feelings, so intellect and emotion are unopposed to each other,[36] sound analogous to the present neuroscientific description of consciousness in that our sensory apprehension of objects eventually leads to our awareness of feeling. A successful artistic form works according to Damasio's paradigm of consciousness: spectators feel the emotion latent in an objectified structure of expression. The recall of the objects of memory leads to the experience of the feelings associated with that memory, so a potent art object, or form, can function similarly.[37] They are both made of neural maps intrinsically tied to memory.[38] The effective work of art can "objectify the life of feeling" because its form is able to integrate into the loops of consciousness (via sensory apprehension), and by intensifying those processes, the art object engages the same mental mechanisms that provoke our awareness of our lives as sentient beings. Just as the recall of a memory leads to the feelings experienced at the time, an art form can lead us back to the emotional stuff of its inception and the matrix of associated feelings.[39] This is not because meaning is assigned to it by intellectual process. That possibility can augment a work of art's power at a different level further up the neurological ladder, integrating the ability of the mind to hold fluidly objective and subjective states of mind.[40]

Organic unity

There are several problems associated with theories of consciousness that are important to the questions of creative process and the analysis of what helps us to understand how "invisible" intuitive mental actions create an organic whole from the chaos of the sense phenomena that surrounds us. "Binding," or the "unity of consciousness," looks at the phenomenon of the smooth, unified character of consciousness, though we perceive in fits and starts of fragments. Our intuitive "bites" must coalesce into something complete that seems plotted and planned (when it works). It is still a mystery how all the information from a simple visual observation, its line, contrast, color, and texture (as well as visual, audio, olfactory, taste, and tactile sensations), fuses in the mind when they are in multiple centers of the brain, traveling along different lengths of neurological trails arriving milliseconds apart, creating complete experiences out of ephemeral fragments. We also have no good way of verifying the correspondence of our various subjective experiences. Personal experience seems inaccessible to modern science, and the reality or validity of another's experience seems difficult to confirm or share. In both the unity of binding and subjectivity, the arts may have some advantages because their processes are tied to the same feeling-creating processes of consciousness that make our fragmented existence seem completely integrated.

How might the emotional aspects of our minds' processes create the dense consciousness of the artistic experience? If the objective correspondence of our experience is not the key point, but rather its authenticity in provoking a sense of what life *feels* like, we have a compelling hallmark for the affect of the phenomenon of art. What the work of art does is seem to be "organic," to have its own internal "sense" that does not (and perhaps should not) need to correspond to external empiric correspondences.[41] The "organic" form seems like consciousness because consciousness is organic, stemming from its own sense of the genuine—formed in the mind—not compared to an outside sense of objectivity. An art form need only have the sense of its own interior fidelity, interweaving with the same mental processes that allow us to build our own conscious reality.

The organic nature of individual subjective consciousness gives the creations of the mind their intrinsic reality no matter how abstract.

Although art is made of objects, whether the notes of a score, the words of a story, or the more concretized stuff of a sculpture, the "objective reality" of objects themselves, or *verisimilitude*, is not necessary for believability. Truthfulness is in the feelings a form generates, not its physical correspondence to an "outside" shape.

The notion that our minds have many fungible versions, that can become parts of our own reality, is the *multiple-drafts*[42] model. If we don't know that we are all seeing the same "picture" of the world, how do we pursue truth? We "overwrite" our own experience, fabricating various "drafts" into our version of things. When we remember experiences, we sometimes combine aspects of the recall and, therefore, "build" a slightly different narrative that seems no less convincing to us. Though potentially a fiction of sorts, it is autobiographical; it did happen in the mind.[43] It can't be broadly real in the minutiae of the details, because different people's minds may focus on different aspects of details and incorporate them in diverse ways, but it is actually happening in a particular mind and has the organic structure of mind-things that makes it compelling and convincing, and, therefore, truthful.

We are all symbol makers in the sense that our neurological processes depend on the creation of maps and patterns to put the world into a form that we can grasp. We do this naturally, invisibly, organically, without forethought. If our minds owe so much to intuitive operations, it is hard to imagine how we could create effectively by following the pre-determined precepts of a rationally structured theory. Perhaps such a theoretical prejudice could focus thought in a particular direction from which instincts can launch, but it might be just as likely that such predetermination as following a particular school's precepts could stymie the intuition's ability to make connections to its base in the realm of feeling. Consciousness is an instinctual image-making process; our survival depends on being able to make rational forms—"actionable intelligence"—out of sensa. Art forms parallel this process, which is why they augment consciousness, especially in their demand for awareness, focus, and concentration. But art forms allow us also to go further and ponder theoretical connections.

The unity we feel in art, with its seeming organic being and continuity, is real, bred by the congruence of the art-making process to the consciousness-making process. Ernst Cassirer (who greatly influenced Langer's ideas) presciently stated:

> [We] . . . remain in a world of 'images' . . . [T]hey are [whole] image-worlds where principles and origins are to be sought in an autonomous

creation of the spirit. Through them alone we see what we call 'reality,' and in them alone we possess it: for the highest objective truth that is accessible to the spirit is ultimately the form of its own activity. . . . [I]n all this, the human spirit now perceives itself and reality.[44]

Though we may not all feel the same thing from a blue stage, we have a similar experience *in experiencing it*. Consciousness generates the feeling of unity we all share.

Because the mind processes the chaos and fragments of perceptions into a unified whole through "top-down" organization,[45] we can visualize that reality is constructed by our own neurological processes. Works of art, which go through the same process of being given form in our mind, have a compelling truthfulness because they are formed through the same processes that give us consciousness. The process of creating art imposes a structure on the disparate elements of experience by taking the elements brought into focus by intuition from the disorder of our stream of consciousness and connecting them into a unified whole. That this process echoes how the mind unifies or "binds" together our own being accounts for the believability of any degree of abstraction art has that can meet the criteria of engaging our attention and making "organic" sense.

The contribution of theoretical richness

Thus far, I have emphasized the influence of intuition in the creative process; it initiates instinctual, momentary focus on one of the myriad things in the vast plenum of our conscious potential and thereby brings "things" into being in our consciousness. But we also have the ability to hold the images and ideas we create in our mind, pause and reflect on them, and incorporate new insights as we build upon ever-higher levels of mental acuity.[46] That ability, to engage the many levels of consciousness in a kind of discourse, accounts for much of the complexity of the arts. We have the ability to isolate and hold ideas as thoughts, developing richly contrasted collages of mental fragments into integrated totalities. Damasio speaks of the mind's ability to move from the largely instinctual and automatic process of registering responses to stimuli (as emotions), "mapping" those responses, leading to sentience of them (as feelings), and then responding with new stimuli from our experiences and memory that repeat the process, back and forth, adding layer upon layer of abundantly nuanced dimensions to an initially simple response.[47] This brings us back to a question I identified at the beginning of this essay: though intuition leads to imaginative invention, intellectual reflection (like theoretical speculation) can bring invention to a richer level. Such a progression corresponds to how we like to see the essence of human character, perpetually struggling between dualisms like the rational and emotional, or the sensuous and intellectual. The ambivalence of such an "endless dance and clash" of juxtaposed concepts may be a necessity of our cognitive structure, reflecting the variety of potential in our *multiple-streams* as well as an epistemic need for contrast.[48] Culture is enriched by our proclivity to reify the belief that we are such binary beings. The idea itself, of our rational, theoretical selves, may be another instance of the organic truth making of the mind. We are disposed to see experience through a cognitive "template" that divides the world into opposing categories. Perhaps there is an evolutionary reason for this: is it advantageous for survival that we see things with such antithetical clarity, like the distinction between predators and prey? At some point, this endurance mechanism morphed into argument, disagreement, and the tendency to "understand" as the juxtaposition of ideas (just as visual contrast propels form).

Humans' unique ability to transform cultural creations into concepts that have the power of biologically inherited characteristics was posited by Richard Dawkins as *memes*, units of cultural rather than genetic inheritance that describe our ability to transmit the associations of a classic work like *Macbeth* (or the image of "red" as bloody).[49] *Memes* could act as potential future associations, planted in our mind, waiting to be used in the processes of consciousness. This theory may also explain why the structure of antithetical thinking and the interplay of such ideas as *theory and practice* have become identified with what we think of as characteristically human. Adversarial thinking may not just be part of our cognitive processes, but also ingrained in a cultural make-up that provides for a persistent system of thesis and anti-thesis, as well as belief and doubt,[50] embracing the contradictions of theory and practice.

Conclusion: an example of intuition and theory

I began this essay by advocating the primacy of intuition and expanded to how theory and intellectual exercises might contribute to creative processes. Theory may also create reservoirs of information in our memory that can be accessed intuitively at a later time. In this way, intellectual discussions can become part of our experience, available to be tapped into at moments of insight. Take as an example *Waiting for Godot,* which has an abundant cultural history with a dense nexus of associations.

A designer would know Beckett's spare stage descriptions and habitu-ally stark imagery: the spare-ness, the bare tree, repetition, loneliness, darkness and light, and *time*. The designer would probably be familiar with notions of *absurdism* and its grounding in the anti-realistic concep-tion of post-World War II apocalyptic imagery. Additionally a designer has his own memories from education and personal experience, all the Godot-like impressions floating in the dark pools of the unconscious that might rise to the surface momentarily, to be grabbed by attention, and fitted to a progressing solution.

In a production I designed, the "road" became a diagonal cutting through the space, into the audience on the downstage side, and curving into forced perspective on the upstage—disappearing into the distance and blending off into nothing on its edges (see Figure 1). In addition to the tree, there was a broken road sign, with only " . . . 0 KM" still visible.

I could explain what the design "means"—how the great distance of the road and the bleeding off from painfully realized detail into noth-ingness and darkness give a spatial sense of time's unrelenting infinity and humanity's isolation in it. I could make an observation of how the broken distance marker balances the tree and points to the futility of man's attempting to understand the vastness of eternity with measure-ment. All these observations are valid, but I could not have explained

Figure 1: Waiting for Godot. Production Photo. Two River Theater Company. Photo by Harry Feiner.

them until months after the production was over, and I know I was causally unaware of them while I was working on the piece. If the design's form gets our attention, and connects disparate elements into a whole, then it has been animated in the consciousness of mind, and all that happened with an unintentional quality, except in the structure of its finished form.

The dialogue between instinctual emotion, conscious feeling, and intellectual ideas depends on an initial step of the intuition of a viable form, moving to feeling and reflection. The process is capable of generating increasingly more complex "ideas of ideas," and "ideas of ideas of ideas," as the body is modified by the relationships between neural maps, concepts, and the body interacting with the mind.[51] Perhaps this type of activity accounts for the high degree of value we assign to such concepts as conflict, contrast, ambiguity, and ambivalence in communicating the truth of experience in art. It is the unlimited wealth of the mind, capable of being accessed through the forms of its own creation.

Notes

1. Trigorin in *The Seagull* by Anton Chekhov.
2. Konstantin in *The Seagull*.
3. Antonio Damasio, *Looking for Spinoza* (Orlando: Harcourt Books, 2003), 6–14.
4. Antonio Damasio, *Descarte's Error* (London: Penguin Books, 1994), 248–50.
5. Ibid., 65. The *somatosensory* system is responsible for external and internal senses.
6. Ibid., 191.
7. Patricia Hampl, "The Lax Habits of the Free Imagination," *New York Times,* March 5, 1989.
8. Ibid. *Hampl* states, "The obviously genuine reports of writers make it clear that the process that brings finished stories into being does not look like the stories themselves. The story is fluid; the process is given to fits and starts . . . the process must fight fevers and fidgets." See also Daniel C. Dennett, *Consciousness Explained* (Boston: Little, Brown & Co., 1991), 212. Dennett seems to deny many fundamental beliefs of what most people would consider the existence of consciousness. [See: John R. Searle, *The Mystery of Consciousness* (New York; The New York Review of Books, 1997), 95–115.] While I also find many of Dennett's ultimate claims contrary to my own beliefs, his descriptions of some of the basic problems of consciousness, including the difficulties of what he calls "the Cartesian theatre," are helpful.
9. Dennett, *Consciousness Explained*, 366–7.
10. Ibid., 163–5.
11. Linda Nochlin, *The Body in Pieces: The Fragment as a Metaphor for Modernity* (New York: Thames and Hudson, 1994), 23–5.
12. Charles Baudelaire, *The Painter of Modern Life and Other Essays*, trans. and ed. Jonathan Mayne (London: Phaidon Press, 1964), 12.

13. Nochlin, *The Body in Pieces*, 53.

14. Damasio, *Descarte's Error*, 191.

15. Damasio, *The Feeling of What Happens* (San Diego: Harcourt, 2000), 15–6. Eric R. Kandel also uses the same phrase. See *In Search of Memory: The Emergence of a New Science of Mind* (London: W. W. Norton, 2006), 376.

16. Ibid., 107–11.

17. Ibid., 79–80.

18. Jonah Lehrer, *Proust was a Neuroscientist* (Boston: Houghton Mifflin, 2007), *xi–xii*.

19. Leonard Shlain, *Art & Physics: Parallel Visions in Space, Time and Light* (New York: Harper Collins, 2001), 18.

20. Lehrer, *Proust was a Neuroscientist*, 77.

21. William Wordsworth, *Famous Prefaces: Preface to The Lyrical Ballads* (Cambridge: The Harvard Classics, 1909), http://www.bartleby.com/39/36.html (accessed August 14, 2008); *ll* 151.

22. Damasio, *The Feeling of What Happens*, 68. See also *Looking for Spinoza*, 215.

23. Ibid., 169–170. See also, Kandel, *In Search of Memory*, 298.

24. Ibid., 170–7.

25. Lehrer, *Proust was a Neuroscientist*, 21–2.

26. Kandel, *In Search of Memory*, 389–90.

27. Damasio, *The Feeling of What Happens*, 79–80.

28. Susanne Langer, *Philosophy in a New Key* (Cambridge, MA: Harvard University Press, 1957), 100–1. Langer states, " . . . *feelings have definite forms*. . . . Their development is effected through their 'interplay with other the other aspects of experience.'" [*Italics*, the author's.]

29. Damasio, *The Feeling of What Happens*, 170.

30. Susanne Langer, *Feeling and Form: A Theory of Art* (New York: Scribner, 1953), 18.

31. Damasio, *The Feeling of What Happens*, 312.

32. Langer, *Feeling and Form*, 82.

33. Damasio, *The Feeling of What Happens*, 312.

34. Walter Pater, *The Renaissance: Studies in Art and Poetry: The School of Giorgione* (Authorama, Public Domain Books from Project Gutenberg), 135–6. http://www.authorama.com/renaissance-8.html (accessed December 9, 2008). To go beyond this often quoted phrase, Pater credited the power of this quality (in terms of lyrical poetry) because " . . . the very perfection of such poetry often appears to depend . . . on a certain suppression or vagueness of mere subject, so that the meaning reaches us through ways not distinctly traceable by the understanding" (137–8).

35. Langer, *Feeling and Form*, 392–4.

36. Ibid., 400–2.

37. Lehrer, *Proust was a Neuroscientist*, 81.

38. Damasio, *Looking for Spinoza*, 199.

39. Damasio, *The Feeling of What Happens*, 161.

40. Ibid., 168.

41. Kandel, *In Search of Memory*, 375–9.

42. Dennett, *Consciousness Explained*, 111–14.

43. Ibid., 98.

44. Ernst Cassirer, *The Philosophy of Symbolic Forms,* vol. 1, *Language,* trans. Ralph Manheim (New Haven: Yale University Press 1955), 58.
45. Lehrer, *Proust was a Neuroscientist,* 108–9.
46. Damasio, *The Feeling of What Happens,* 217–19.
47. Damasio, *Looking for Spinoza,* 55; 65.
48. Barbara H. Smith, *Belief and Resistance: Dynamics of Contemporary Intellectual Controversy* (Cambridge, MA: Harvard University Press, 1997), 123; 138–9. Smith posits that the human tendency to frame debate in ambivalent and conflicting concepts is a cognitive necessity "central to intellectual history, and . . . the dynamics of all living systems" (138–9).
49. Richard Dawkins, *The Selfish Gene,* 30th Anniversary Edition (Oxford: Oxford University Press, 2006), 192–201.
50. Smith, *Belief and Resistance,* xxvi.
51. Damasio, *Looking for Spinoza,* 214.

10
Resisting Binaries: Theory and Acting

John Lutterbie

People tend to think in binaries, such as mind/body, good/bad, and emotion/reason. This mode of thought is valuable in a crisis, because it reduces options and allows for direct and quick responses. It loses its usefulness, however, when a richer and more nuanced understanding is needed. It might be assumed that in acting, with the need to develop complex interpersonal and fictional relationships, the seduction of binary thinking would be resisted. Instead discussions about acting are rife with dualisms. Actors are categorized by the way they work—from the "inside out" or the "outside in," through the "emotions" or the "intellect," and depend on "technique" or creative "impulses." Initially these concepts were used for the sake of efficiency and served as short-hand for more complex concepts. But over time the connection to that complexity has been lost and they have become empty signs, accepted as true and rarely questioned. Theory can open these concepts and move the profession beyond the blinkered reductionism of binary thinking. By thinking beyond the terms traditionally used in discussions of acting and developing a new frame through which to perceive the actor, the creative process can be understood better, and more holistic ways of training actors imagined.

The three theories presented here question the value of binary thinking and encourage the use of a supple and flexible language that reflects more accurately the complex process of acting. Phenomenology, the philosophy of first-person experience, challenges the inside/outside dualism; while cognitive theory continues this argument, it also calls into question the separation of thought and emotion. Deconstruction is used to build on these two discussions by demonstrating how an understanding of metaphors can expand creative possibilities. In combination, they provide a robust way of thinking about and engaging the actor's process.

The phenomenological gesture: perception and action

The way actors approach a role is commonly differentiated between those who work from the "outside in" (Barba, Lecoq, Chekhov) and those who operate from the "inside out" (Stanislavski, Meisner, Hagen). Phenomenology questions the validity of this distinction. Acting is a special means of engaging the world that is both distinct from and a continuation of everyday life. For actors, performing is how they live day-to-day; at the same time, acting requires using "extra daily" energy.[1] Nevertheless, actors use the same life processes whether on stage or not. Phenomenology, a branch of philosophy that analyzes first-person experience, provides a frame for understanding this relationship.

In the phenomenology of Maurice Merleau-Ponty the individual is intertwined with the world. We both perceive it and are perceived by it.[2] This reciprocity provides each person with necessary information about the world and the confidence to act in it. As the basis of experience, perception is fundamental in defining a relationship with the world—not as an immutable form but as a dynamic process. New experiences give rise to new understandings, and to a continually emerging and shifting sense of self. Central to Merleau-Ponty's theory is the concept of the flesh, which he understands as the full extension of the senses. It reaches beyond the limits of touch to include the farthest reaches of seeing, smelling, and hearing.

Actors, on stage and off, continually engage the world, responding to changing dynamics, from variations in the weather to psychological relationships. This information is not gathered passively. They actively process data from other actors, and temper their own performance accordingly. Feedback loops of reciprocal exchange—receiving and expressing—makes communication between actors possible. This interdependence renders the distinction between acting "inside out" or "outside in" meaningless. "Internal" research draws on what other actors give, and working from the "outside" brings emotions and memories into play. Phenomenology opens the way to understanding each actor as a dynamic system that is responsive to the demands of perceiving and doing; and from the unstable boundary between self and other emerges a performance.

The yin yang of the body/mind

A dynamic system, like all other systems, consists of parts that have defined functions and operate according to principles, but is different because what emerges from it is changeable. Rather than producing predictable outcomes, dynamic systems continually respond to new information derived from the environment and feedback loops within the constituent parts. Viewing minds as dynamic systems has significant implications for understanding acting and creativity.

This understanding of cognitive processes challenges some basic and long-held assumptions about acting, particularly some of the primary binaries on which discussions are based. One of the most persistent of these dualisms is the mind/body split. René Descartes' maxim, "*Cogito, ergo sum*" ("I think, therefore I am"), has been parodied in the theatre: "You think, therefore you cannot act." The assumptions are that emotions are distinct from intellectual processes, and that reason gets in the way of good acting. Constantin Stanislavski's early emphasis on emotional recall and Lee Strasberg's method for actor training suggest that accessing emotional memories is both necessary and sufficient to creating the feeling on stage. Another binary is the distinction between technique and creativity. The need for technique is recognized, but dependence on it hinders creative, emotional expression. Similarly, creativity is necessary, but without technique it can become formless. Cognitive studies values emotion and conscious thought equally in ways that are positive and liberating, and that provide a more nuanced understanding of the complex relationship between technique and creativity.[3]

Cognitive theory asks us to redefine some of the basic concepts of acting theory: emotion, memory, technique, and improvisation. They are generally used metaphorically, lacking clear definition. Prudent use of science can clarify these concepts, enriching our understanding of acting. Some may question applying science to theatre studies but an actor studying voice benefits from knowledge of how each part of the physical instrument functions in developing a strong and supple instrument. Similarly a more precise understanding of these four concepts can clarify the acting process.

To ground this claim, emotions have three sources: perceptual information, memory, and thinking. There are two kinds of perceptions: exteroceptive (from the outside) such as feeling cold, and interoceptive (from the inside) such as hunger. Both activate neural networks, releasing neurotransmitters (such as serotonin and dopamine). The influx of these chemicals disrupts the current state of the brain as emotions are generated. If sufficiently intense, they become conscious and bring attention (thought) to the inciting event, leading to reactions based on previous experiences (memory). As a response evolves, the cognitive processes link back to the emotional centers of the brain, which in turn reiterate in modified form the initial emotions. The feedback loops among perceptual excitation, thinking, and memory leads, as quickly as possible (measured in milliseconds), to an action (which may be doing nothing) that responds to the disturbance, helping the organism achieve a stable, if temporary, state that accommodates the disturbance. The mind/brain is never at rest. Instead it is continually adjusting to dynamic fluctuations.

Emotions arise from the ongoing activation of neural networks, the release of neurotransmitters, and their pervasive impact on the system. The prevalence of emotions indicates that they are not only linked to "base" instincts but are found in every aspect of the cognitive process.

> The lower levels in the neural edifice of reason are the same that regulate the processing of emotions and feelings, along with global functions of the body proper such that the organism can survive. These lower levels maintain direct and mutual relationships with the body proper, thus placing the body within the chain of operations that permit the highest reaches of reason and creativity. Rationality is probably shaped and modulated by body signals, even as it performs the most sublime distinctions and acts accordingly.[4]

Emotions are not distinct from rational thought, but necessary to the process. If Antonio Damasio is right, when actors say that they do not want to be intellectual, but to trust their emotions, they cannot be speaking literally.

The belief that emotion is separate from thought arises from the experiences to which we pay attention. As I write, my focus is on the meaning of words, individually and in syntactic combinations: do they say what I want them to say? The emotional contents of the process only come to consciousness when there is a feeling of frustration at not finding, or relief at finally finding, the right words. Similarly, in an emotional situation, I am more aware of the joy or sorrow I am feeling, and less aware of the cognitive processes seeking to address the situation. Not all aspects of an experience will ever be fully conscious. Indeed, only a small portion of the activity in the brain ever reaches consciousness. This selectivity is a survival mechanism. If we were to be aware of everything that happens in the decision-making process, we would be overwhelmed and unable to focus on the situation. "[E]motional and cognitive processes influence each other continuously during an emotional episode, from the first neural changes induced by a triggering event to the synchronization of the entire nervous system in a coherent mode of thinking, feeling and acting."[5]

The "triggering event" of which Marc Lewis writes may mark the difference between what we perceive to be cold, rational thought and hot, emotional impulse. While "thinking, feeling, and acting" are part of the same coherence that arises during cognition, there are distinctions in brain activity. Functional Magnetic Response Imaging (MRI) indicates that more oxygen is present in areas of the prefrontal cortex during events that require analysis, while more is present in the corticolimbic system during moments of passion. The kind of perception, thought, and memory that initiates an event will engage a certain kind of response and, therefore, determine where it is processed. The type of input is not the only determining factor, however.

The frame of mind with which we engage the experience may be instrumental in privileging one kind of response over another. As I argue elsewhere, improvisation utilizes predominantly cognitive processes of association that *blend together* different kinds of information to generate novel images.[6] Analysis, on the other hand, emphasizes *discriminating between* different types of data. Indeed, data suggests that the stimuli and where they are processed depends on the questions we ask—how we frame our expectations and not only the information available in the world. How attention is focused on perceptual data either promotes the combination of perceptions in unexpected associations or differentiation to obtain a specific answer. This does not mean that one type of question appeals to the prefrontal cortex and another to the corticolimbic system: "results emphasize the cooperative nature of brain activity, where areas rapidly exchange information when engaged in mental operations."[7] The involvement of the neural axis may be global in nature, but the outcomes will indicate a privileging of the associative or the analytical, the intellectual or the emotional.

The presence of a frame with which perceptual information is processed indicates that technique is involved—in this instance the ability to determine quickly the kind of question most useful in obtaining a desired result. A technique is a learned practice gained through repetition, making certain activities more efficient, requiring less effort. Whether riding a bike, swimming, or training in stage combat, sets of skills are learned that provide a degree of mastery.[8] However, technique has a checkered reputation in the theatre. On the one hand, it is a valuable tool in constructing a performance score that is repeatable; and, on the other, it can be seen as a deadening obstacle to the expression of emotion. In its most positive form, it can open the way to new and exciting forms of expression. It is impossible to ride with no hands, if you don't first know how to ride a bike. Similarly, it is unlikely that a significant discovery will be made through improvisation if the rules are not known and followed—go with what is given, always say "yes" and be open to what the partner offers. The more frequently improvisation is practiced, the quicker the participants can get past easy answers to new depths of investigation.

Expertise in a technique also depends on improvisation. Reaching the point of mastery where the performer does not need to think about each aspect of the skill frees the mind to explore new possibilities. X-sports such as skateboarding require confidence in the basic techniques of negotiating on land before the skater can hazard aerial stunts, but, once mastered, new combinations of moves can be imagined and attempted based on existing techniques. Technique allows for the emergence of creativity; and the imagination paves the way for gaining new techniques. This is only possible because the neural networks in the brain work cooperatively by blending different memories and new images into fresh combinations. Riding a bike on new terrain requires a degree of improvisation to go with the established techniques of biking. Similarly, rehearsing and performing a play draws on technique and improvisation in the creation of a role and in responding to the changing nuances of performance.

Phenomenally in the world, actors utilize a body/mind whose identity is defined by an intricately intertwined and inseparable combination of emotion, reason, perception, and memory. In responding to and acting on the environment, they depend on the free play of improvisation and habitual structures of technique. The final theoretical model—deconstruction—defines a way of freeing this creativity in performance.

Deconstructing metaphors

Deconstruction is an abused term. It has been used to argue that all meaning is relative and therefore, for instance, a play can mean whatever a director wants. It has also been used to justify "concept" productions, such as Peter Sellar's production of *The Merchant of Venice*, which make choices without sufficiently considering the ramifications.[9] Deconstruction, in its most basic form, is an approach to recognizing and analyzing metaphors, particularly when they are accepted as substantive concepts, such as space and time. Jacques Derrida, the progenitor of the theory, argues that concrete terms are frequently used as metaphors, where a word or phrase is used to conceal values that are not readily apparent. If these figures of speech are taken apart, unexpected meanings can appear. Time is generally conceived as a constant that can be subdivided into intervals: seconds, minutes, years. Yet the experience of time changes with different contexts: "the time flew by" or "I thought that play would never end." In a recent issue of *Scientific American*, Paul Davies argues that in some branches of physics, time does not "flow" but is defined as a sequence of discrete instances.[10] Historians break time into periods, eras or ages, knowing that on closer inspection these divisions are arbitrary because some planes of experience change incrementally and others rapidly.[11] For cognitive theorists, time is the dynamic integration of data, combining past memories (long and short-term, explicit and implicit), anticipations of future events, and the immediate flow of perceptual information. So rather than being simply linear, time is a continually transforming consolidation of neural information identified with the past, present, and future. When applying deconstructive methodologies, denotative meanings give way to a plethora of connotations, all of which use the same term for different ends within different contexts.

Identifying different meanings associated with the same idea is the first step in using deconstruction. Derrida argues that metaphors and their associated meanings are not mere byproducts of language but reflect unspoken values. The preoccupation in discussions about acting with unlocking the internal emotions of the actor (found most notably in Strasberg's Method and in Sanford Meisner's approach to training) parallel an interest in realistic plays that explore the human condition from the perspective of character psychology. This fascination with the internal dynamics of relationships comes at a cost. The external or social conditions that give rise to the crises in plays are marginalized, serving only to influence character motivation. Nowhere is this bias more evident than in productions of Bertolt Brecht in the US, where focus on the private anguish of Mother Courage at the loss of her children negates Brecht's expressed interest in the political and economic determinants of her choices. The values implicit in these choices resonate with American individualism, which values personal well-being over social welfare. These ideological values are reflected in dominant modes of actor training, affecting definitions of good acting and limiting tolerance for alternative means of expression.

Deconstruction, when used with rigor, provides triggers for opening texts, allows for new associations, and engages a wider range of an actor's cognitive abilities. In a recent production of *The Seagull*, a relationship was developed between the servants and Constantine.[12] A look, a touch, and a relationship were established, adding depth and human caring to the young artist's character, revealing conflicts between avant-garde and traditional approaches to art, as well as between classes. Deconstruction is not a soft methodology that condones relativism. Rather, it is a means for revealing values that allows new understandings to emerge. Training actors by enhancing their ability to work with associations through the analysis of metaphors can release their creative energies by increasing the pool of images from which to draw. This work also has the potential for improving their sensitivity to the environment, including other actors.

Conclusion

We cannot avoid using binaries. They serve a useful purpose in everyday life. In acting, however, they promote prejudices and interfere with the creative process. The actor is a dynamic system that continually processes perceptions, thoughts, emotions, and memories in the simultaneous activity of analysis and association—each dependent on the other, each informing the other. From this interaction of actor and environment emerges a performance. What is at stake is the shape and force of that performance. Creative processes depend on the emergence of what is new and unexpected. Thinking about acting as emotion-based psychological realism limits the actor's potential. We need, instead, approaches that open possibilities and new horizons. The pervasive call for new and more vital forms of theatre cannot be answered unless the existing paradigms are challenged and, through theory, we allow what is truly unexpected to emerge.

Notes

1. Eugenio Barba, *Beyond the Floating Islands*, trans. Judy Barba, Richard Fowler, Jerrold C. Rodesch, and Saul Shapiro (New York: PAJ Publications, 1986), 71–2.
2. Maurice Merleau-Ponty, *The Visible and the Invisible*, trans. Alphonso Lingis (Evanston: Northwestern University Press, 1968), 139.
3. See Antonio Damasio, *The Feeling of What Happens: Body and Emotion in the Making of Consciousness* (New York: Harcourt Brace & Company: 1999), and Bruce McConachie, *Engaging Audiences: A Cognitive Approach to Spectating in the Theatre* (New York: Palgrave Macmillan, 2008).
4. Antonio Damasio, *Descartes' Error: Emotion, Reason, and the Human Brain* (New York: Avon Books, 1994), 200.
5. Marc D. Lewis, "Bridging Emotion Theory and Neurobiology through Dynamic Systems Modeling," *Behavioral and Brain Sciences*, 28 (2005), 169–245.
6. See John Lutterbie, "Neuroscience and Creativity in the Rehearsal Process," in *Performance and Cognition: Theatre Studies and the Cognitive Turn*, eds Bruce McConachie and F. Elizabeth Hart (New York: Routledge, 2006).
7. A. R. McIntosh and N. J. Lobaugh, "When Is a Word Not a Word?," *Science*, 301 (July 2003), 322–3.

8. See Robert Crease and John Lutterbie, "Technique," in *Staging Philosophy: Intersections of Theater, Performance, and Philosophy*, eds David Krasner and David Z. Saltz (Ann Arbor: University of Michigan Press, 2006), 160–79.

9. See Richard Pettengill, "Peter Sellar's *The Merchant of Venice*," *Theatre Research International*, 31.3 (2006), 298–314.

10. Paul Davies, "That Mysterious Flow," *Scientific American Magazine*, 287.3 (September 2002), 40–7.

11. Fernand Braudel, *On History*, trans. Sarah Matthews (Chicago: University of Chicago Press, 1982), 31.

12. This performance of Anton Chekhov's *The Seagull*, in a version by Christopher Hampton and directed by Ian Rickson was seen at the Walter Kerr Theatre, December 17, 2008.

11
Moving Spectators Toward Progressive Politics by Combining Brechtian Theory with Cognitive Science

Bruce McConachie

> Bad as it may sound, I have to admit that I cannot get along as an artist without the use of one or two sciences.[1]

Many theatre and performance scholars today continue to look to the theories of Bertolt Brecht as a guide to creating and critiquing politically progressive theatre. Brecht's name and his ideas figure prominently in current surveys of valid theoretical approaches in theatre and performance studies, including *Theory/Theatre: An Introduction*, by Mark Fortier and *Critical Theory and Performance*, edited by Janelle G. Reinelt and Joseph R. Roach.[2] When Brecht wrote most of his theoretical work in the 1930s, 1940s, and early 1950s, he could assume that his ideas were generally congruent with the science of the day, especially the psychological and social sciences dealing with behavior, crowds, and economics. His *Galileo* and the revisions he made to the play text after Hiroshima in 1945 indicate that he kept himself informed about the physical sciences as well, and willingly changed his mind in the face of new scientific evidence. The citation above, plus copious other evidence, suggests that Brecht believed that he was creating a theatre that could intervene scientifically into the political and economic problems of the twentieth century.

Brecht died in 1956. Since then, new sciences have emerged to study cognition and emotion and many of these scientists have questioned the validity of the premises upon which Brecht constructed most of his theories. Now, more than 50 years later, following wide-ranging empirical tests in the cognitive sciences, several valid theories undermine and, in some cases, contradict the earlier scientific basis of Brecht's ideas.[3]

In particular, recent insights into conceptual blending, empathy, emotion, and natural behavior are often at odds with Brecht's theories of acting and audience response. I think it is worthwhile asking how the savvy Marxist theatre artist might respond to this new science, were he alive today. Would he reject the new science out of hand and hold tight to his old theories? Or would he embrace the insights of the new cognitive sciences and try to understand how he might use this knowledge to advance his goals for progressive, revolutionary theatre? This essay is based on the assumption that Brecht would take the latter path. Science—indeed, Brecht's entire body of theatrical theory—was a means to an end for him. If better science could have assisted Brecht in creating a kind of theatre that could help spectators to move toward a socialist utopia, I believe he would have embraced it.

In this chapter, I contrast the ideas underlying Brecht's epic theatre to new insights from cognitive science that offer alternative ways of arriving at Brecht's theatrical goals. My aim is not to debunk Brechtian ideas, but to amend them so that they might better achieve their political purposes. In doing so, I will rely on well-known examples from Brecht's theories and plays to close the gap between a cognitive perspective on theatre and the dialectical theatre of the playwright-director.[4]

Updating Brecht with cognitive science may initially appear to be a daunting challenge. To begin with, Brecht altered several of his theories during his career. I will primarily focus on his theoretical concerns in the ten years or so after he turned to Marxism, in part because his rationalism during this period contrasts sharply with present cognitive ideas. Where Brecht believed that theatrical illusionism could trap spectators in unreal fantasies, the science of conceptual blending posits a notion of theatrical performance and enjoyment that integrates the make believe and the material components of dramatic theatre; the human ability to do conceptual blending renders moot many of Brecht's concerns about illusionism. Similarly, Brecht feared that empathy could lead to spectator passivity, but recent investigations into the capabilities of our mirror neurons challenge Brecht's notion of empathy to recognize the educational potential of empathetic engagement. Although Brecht's *Verfremdungseffekt* posits a three-stage transformation of his spectators, leading them toward the revolutionary Marxian insights of his dialectical theatre, the cognitive operation of meta-response suggests that Brecht underestimated the importance of the emotions in this process. Finally, while Brecht understood the roles of nature and history in shaping human identity, he did not give enough credit to evolution and the potentials that it offers for progressive change. As we will see, however,

Brechtian theatre often succeeded in its political goals despite Brecht's theories to explain his theatrical strategies. A cognitive perspective on Brecht's dialectics allows us to amend his theories as a preface to applying them for potentially progressive purposes in the theatre.

Illusionism and conceptual blending

Brecht believed that the pleasurable illusions of dramatic fiction on stage were both necessary and dangerous. Fiction played a significant role in his "epic" theatre to animate spectators to change their social reality. In some of his later theoretical writing, Brecht decided that the term "dialectical" better suited his theatre than "epic." For Brecht, theatrical fictions should present the contradictions—the conflicts between theses and antitheses in the real world of Marxian history—to enable spectators to grasp the dialectical truth of their situation and change the world.[5] Nonetheless, the separation of illusion and reality that underlies dialectical theatre carried dangerous political implications for Brecht.[6] Because theatrical illusions are often convincing, Brecht was concerned that spectators might become so entranced by the events on stage that they would mistake them for reality. If that occurred, spectators might not distance themselves from what they saw and heard, and might refuse to imagine alternatives to the apparently "real" effects on the stage. Led to accept the illusory for the real, spectators would turn passive and lose agency; at its worst, theatrical illusionism could objectify and naturalize spectators.

This possibility caused Brecht to break with unified, realist scenic conventions for his productions at the Berliner Ensemble. Applied to the production of *Mother Courage* in 1949, for instance, his concern with illusionism led Brecht to adopt an aesthetic of minimalism that avoided realist effects as much as possible. By emphasizing the designed, constructed nature of the set and the general artistry of his theatrical conventions for *Mother Courage*, Brecht sought to counter possible audience passivity and keep the spectator aware of her or his potential agency in history. As critic-historian John Rouse notes, Brecht hoped to instill in his audience a desire to "swap a contradictory world [i.e., the nascent capitalism that powered the Thirty Years War] for a consistent one, one that they scarcely know of for one of which they can dream."[7]

Likewise, Brechtian theory advised actors to remain at the edge of their characters and to emphasize the constructed nature of their performances. Spectators, said Brecht, should never believe that actors are actually the characters they are performing. To counter actorly illusionism, Brecht tried a variety of strategies, including writing roles like Azdak in *The Caucasian Chalk Circle*, whose contradictory behavior keeps emotional identification at a distance. Perhaps his most effective strategy was directing his actors at the Berliner Ensemble to emphasize the *gestus* of their characters. More than gestures, the *gestus* was everything an actor presented to the audience. It was meant to clarify the role's socio-economic class and encourage spectators to understand how the character's class position shaped his/her behavior.[8] On the basis of an actor/character's *gestus*, spectators should be able to formulate "an attitude or opinion" about that person and rationally determine the character's role in the Marxist unfolding of history.[9]

Brecht's assumption that theatre presents dramatic illusions that can somehow entrap spectators, however, is contradicted by recent developments in cognitive science.

Conceptual blending theory, as outlined in *The Way We Think* by neuroscientist Gilles Fauconnier and literary critic turned cognitive psychologist Mark Turner, underlines the foundational reality of all theatrical production and representation for actors and spectators. Actors, of course, are real people on a stage in the present and they are also the roles they represent in the make-believe space and time of the dramatic fiction. Turner and Fauconnier demonstrate that actors can engage in this theatrical doubleness and spectators can understand it because of human beings' ability to do "conceptual blending," the mental synthesizing of concepts from different areas of cognition. This operation, ubiquitous in human imagination, occurs nearly automatically and mostly below the level of consciousness. One consequence of this cognitive process is that audience members do not "willingly suspend their disbelief" when they enjoy an actor's doubleness.[10] Instead, actors and spectators unconsciously create a mental fourth space, distinct from the perception of themselves in real time-space and the knowledge that they are playing a game of make believe. In this fourth space, information from both of those prior domains, plus the general domain of "identity" taken from memory, can be "blended" together to create perceptions that are distinct from the other three mental spaces. For acting, this means that the actor takes aspects of him or herself (that he can move and speak, for instance) and blends them with parts of the character (the character's past, her present circumstances and intentions, and so on) and mixes them with the general concept of identity to create, in effect, the identity of a blended actor/character. In experiencing a dramatic performance, spectators and actors mostly "live in their blends," according to Turner and Fauconnier:

> The spectator will live in the blend only by selective projection: Many aspects of her existence (such as sitting in a seat, next to other people, in the dark), although independently available to her, are not to be projected to the blend. . . . The actor, meanwhile, is engaged in a different kind of blend, one in which his motor patterns and power of speech come directly into play, but not his free will or his foreknowledge of the [dramatic] outcome. In the blend, he says just what the character says and is surprised night after night by the same events.[11]

Our ability to project and compress information into a blend is a necessity for acting and spectating; without it, theatre would be cognitively impossible. According to Turner, this ability emerged in *Homo sapiens* about 50,000 years ago and is uniquely human; the brains of other higher mammals do not allow for it.

What the human mind blends together, it can also pull apart. The spectator above hears something amusing on stage, slips out of the blend to perceive others laughing, and begins to laugh herself. The actor hears the laughter, momentarily suspends his own blend to accommodate it, and then plunges back in to the behavior of the actor/character. Actors and spectators drop in and out of their blends throughout every performance, interacting to sustain and/or modify their enjoyment of theatrical doubleness. According to Turner and Fauconnier, cognitive blending structures enable all games of make believe, from playing with dolls to professional football.

Deriving theatrical doubleness from cognitive blending may seem innocuous and even commonsensical, but it undermines several conceptions of performance, Brechtian theory among them. The linkage between theatricality and blending complicates the usual distinctions dividing realist from overtly theatrical productions and so-called passive from active spectators. Given cognitive blending, it is clear that all plays on stage (not just Brecht's) involve spectator recognition of theatrical framing. Spectators do not need to be reminded of the split between the theatrical and the dramatic (i.e., the material and the make-believe aspects of viewing), as Brecht believed. In performance, some productions may invite spectators to move in and out of various blended frames more than others, but these are differences in degree, not in kind. Consequently, it is unlikely that formal differences in the degree of dialectical theatricality will have much to do with the political efficacy of a specific production.

Formal differences aside, however, a production that uses various theatrical frames to draw attention to controversial political content might have more of an affect on viewers than one that does not. In *The Measures Taken* (1930), for example, two dramatic frames intersect throughout—a present frame involving the report of four Communist agitators to a chorus of judges in Moscow and a past frame in which the four agitators act out their reasons for killing a fifth, a Young Comrade who bungled their attempt to incite revolution in China. By using both frames, Brecht sharpened his attack on colonialism and heightened his call for Communist party discipline. *The Measures Taken* invites the audience to imagine the actors in several different kinds of blended actor/characters and the fission among these blended frames probably increased the play's political impact at performances in Germany in the early 1930s. There is no cognitive reason to believe, however, that the framing alone would have made much of a difference in the politics of the play for its spectators.

Einfühlung and imaginary transposition

Believing that the theatre could enfold unwary spectators in illusions, Brecht was especially critical of what he called empathy. In the nineteenth century, German romantics used the term "empathy" (*Einfühlung*) and its cognates to denote the ability of humans to project themselves into nature. Early in the twentieth century, phenomenologist Edith Stein continued this tradition in Germany by discussing empathy as a means of losing oneself in a different reality and then proceeding to act on the basis of a perspective offered by that reality.[12] Rejecting romantic mystifications for what he took to be Marxist science, Brecht opposed this notion of empathy and sought to build his theatre on the basis of rational, rather than empathetic response. Assuming a dualism between reasoned response and empathy, Brecht argued that empathy would "wear down the capacity for action" in his auditors. Under the spell of empathy, said Brecht, "nobody will learn any lessons."[13] Brecht brought to bear all of the techniques of his dialectical theatre to counter the empathetic involvement of his spectators.

If empathy were what Brecht believed it to be, his strategies to counter empathetic identification (like his general goal of dispelling dramatic illusionism) would probably have been effective. Cognitive scientists now propose a very different notion of empathy, however—one that does not entail the loss of agency in a mystical merging with some Other and actually holds the promise of enhancing a person's rationality in social situations like the theatre. Recent psychological and philosophical investigations centered on cognitive science have established an emerging consensus about empathy. From this point of view, empathy is a cognitive operation that provides a non-symbolic way of "reading the minds" of other people.

Citing several empirical studies, philosopher and scientist Evan Thompson usefully distinguishes between three different levels of empathy, the first two of which are important for Brechtian theatre. The first level, which is based on the recent discovery of the mirror-neuron system in our minds, Thompson calls "sensorimotor coupling."[14] In brief, groups of neurons in the brain are equipped to "mirror" intentional motor activity produced by other humans. When one person watches another grasp a coffee cup, for instance, the same group of neurons is activated in the observer as if the observer had grabbed the cup for him or herself. In this way, by mirroring the muscles of another, we can begin to know "intuitively" what that other person is experiencing. As Vittorio Gallese, one of the first to investigate mirror-neuron systems in monkeys, notes, "When we observe actions performed by other individuals, our motor system 'resonates' along with that of the observed agent."[15] The classic example is two crying babies in the same room; when one starts to wail, the other one will too, in empathy with the first. In a good theatrical production, too, spectators "resonate" with actors for much of the performance; their stage movements alone prompt the activation of our mirror systems, putting us "in tune" with their basic emotions and intentions. For this reason, Gallese and his co-workers have identified the mirror system as "the basis of social cognition."[16] This makes sensorimotor coupling, the lowest level of empathy, the physiological basis for the other levels noted by Thompson.

"The second type of empathy is the imaginary transposition of oneself to the other's place," states Thompson.[17] This is much the same as the common-sense notion of empathy as "putting yourself in another person's shoes." On the basis of sensorimotor coupling, humans can recall what it is like to experience the thoughts of others and, through memory and imagination, can attempt to see the world through another's eyes, even when that other person is not present. Thompson emphasizes that this form of empathy can range from simple emotional agitation to a rich understanding of another's situation. Imaginary transposition, which develops in children from between about nine and 12 months of age, requires more active cognition than sensorimotor coupling.

At both levels, however, empathy is natural, easy, ubiquitous, and mostly unconscious. Within this new consensus, empathy is a simple cognitive process, not an emotion or feeling. Empathy may lead to such neurological and chemical responses, but the ability to simulate another's state of mind is prior to the kind of judgment that induces fear and lust or sympathy and antipathy.

From this new perspective, Brecht's concerns about empathy were misplaced. Most spectators at performances of *The Threepenny Opera* in 1928 probably empathized with the performer singing "The Ballad of Mack the Knife" at the top of the show to catch his attitude toward Mackie and his opinions about the criminal underworld of London around 1900. Few spectators likely sympathized with this cynical figure, but they needed to pay attention to his face, voice, and movements in order to read his mind. It is clear that Brecht would have understood and even welcomed this kind of response from audiences, but he did not call it empathy. Brecht enjoyed the physical exertion of sporting events and wanted his theatre spectators to watch a play in much the same manner that he observed a good boxing match. Cognitive scientists today would note that it is impossible to watch two boxers sparring in the ring without our mirror neurons moving us toward empathy. Had the definition of empathy changed to its present meaning while Brecht was alive, he would not have discarded empathy as a legitimate response in the theatre.

The *V-effekt* and emotions

In opposing what he called empathy, Brecht hoped to activate the agency of his audiences to work for progressive political change. His primary strategy to transform audiences into political agents was his much mis-understood *Verfremdungseffekt*. Often mistranslated as "alienation," the famous V-effect is better understood as a process rather than as a singular stimulus and response. According to critic Reinhold Grimm, Brecht envisioned *Verfremdungseffekt* as a triadic operation for audiences—from contentment with the normal, to bewilderment about its strangeness, to the insight that the normal must be transformed. During the course of watching *Galileo*, for example, Brecht believed that spectators should shift from accepting Galileo's actions as normal and natural, to bewilderment and even outrage as he sacrifices his integrity to save his skin, to a final determination to reject Galileo's cowardice for an enlightened socialism that would place science at the service of the people. Grimm points out that this was a Hegelian process for Brecht: "Our initial, both imperfect and incomplete, comprehension equals a Hegelian thesis; this gives way, if only temporarily, to a total incomprehension equaling a Hegelian antithesis; and this, in turn, provokes the final and genuine comprehension, which is tantamount to a Hegelian synthesis."[18]

The reversal process in Brecht's *Verfremdungseffekt* is similar to what cognitive critic Susan Feagin terms "meta-response." In brief, a meta-response involves audiences in a reversal of their feelings; a spectator first responds one way to a character or situation and then reacts against her/his first response when new information alters the spectator's judgment.[19] In Scene 13 of the Charles Laughton version of *Galileo*, to continue that example, most spectators will probably shift their judgment about the physicist from moderate antipathy to fervent sympathy when they discover, with Andrea, that Galileo has completed his *Discorsi* in secret and will allow Andrea to sneak it across the border to be published. For the audience, a situation that appeared to be bland and normal is revealed as intriguing and strange. The third step of Brecht's V-effect will likely occur for most spectators, if it occurs at all, at the end of the scene. When the scientist admits that he recanted because he was afraid of physical pain, Andrea objects that he is still a hero because he has contributed to science. "No," says Galileo, and Brecht has him launch into a long monologue explaining that the purpose of science is to ease human existence, not to serve the needs of power. In 1947, Laughton and Brecht understood that they were taking on the collusion of science and government that had created the atom bomb and the vast array of scientists, generals, and defense contractors that would soon be called "the military-industrial complex." Brecht was eager that his audience understand that Galileo had sold out. If the spectator does arrive at this conclusion, s/he will have undergone another meta-response, probably shifting from heightened sympathy to mild antipathy for the scientist.

While cognitive scientists hold different definitions and conceptions about human emotions, most recognize that our emotional lives are closely tied to our interest in survival.[20] In this sense, the general goal of all spectators is the same as the goal of every human being: to maximize pleasure and minimize pain, the two foundational values of our biological lives. While these goals are often complicated by other purposes, sympathetic and antipathetic investments can be understood as general orientations to a spectator's pleasure and pain experienced vicariously through actors/characters during a performance. Actors/characters that bring mostly pleasure to themselves and others in their fictional worlds and to empathizing spectators are candidates for sympathetic engagement, while those that cause repeated pain are usually discarded with varying degrees of antipathy. Further, it appears that some appraisal of a person or situation generally precedes feelings of sympathy and antipathy, the kind of feelings that Brecht tried to evoke for his Galileo and Mother Courage. Psychologist Keith Oatley's widely accepted theory of emotional response emphasizes the importance of appraisal: ". . . [E]motions are elicited not by events as such but by evaluations of events relevant to goals," he states.[21] From Oatley's perspective, spectatorial evaluation will hinge on appraising the plans, as well as the desires and interests, of actor/characters.

If this account of spectatorial response is accurate, how might spectators respond to Courage and Galileo at the end of their plays? Brecht supplies audiences with logical reasons to reject the moral position of his two protagonists, but both have complicated personal and social situations that most spectators will take into account in their appraisal of each. Courage has just lost her daughter. Given the strong link between emotions and survival, most spectators will sympathize with her for this reason alone. On the other hand, Courage herself has caused repeated pain to others (and to the audience) during the course of the play and spectators will likely draw back from her for this reason. Galileo, too, has caused some pain to others, especially to his daughter and to those who believed in him. But his actions have not directly caused the death of anyone (even though Brecht wants to blame him at a distance for the atomic bomb) and his plans include giving the *Discorsi* to Andrea, an action that will destabilize an oppressive status quo. Further, neither Courage nor Galileo gives in to despair; both will survive and persevere, despite old age and poor prospects. In short, when spectators appraise the intentions, actions, and plans of both protagonists, they will likely arrive at complex conclusions that admit different degrees of sympathy and antipathy. Without a firm emotional rejection of their response to the previous position of Courage and Galileo, spectators are unlikely to experience another meta-response.

For this reason, the third stage of Brecht's *Verfremdungseffekt* may not occur for spectators as they watch the endings of *Life of Galileo* and *Mother Courage*. For the first two steps of the V-effect in most scenes of both plays, logic and emotion are mutually supportive. In the case of Galileo and Courage at the ends of their plays, however, Brecht supplies audiences with logical reasons to reject the moral position of his protagonists without pushing his spectators to reject them as people. Lacking an empathetic emotional reversal, spectators might not reach Brecht's conclusion that history must be transformed so that the normal lives of people like Courage and Galileo may be transformed through utopian possibility. Auditors may understand the desirability of a Hegelian synthesis that could overcome the contradictions of capitalism and support a Marxian classless society, but without the emotions to support it, audience members may draw back from pursuing revolutionary activity.

From a cognitive perspective, the likely complex emotional response of the audience to the final scenes of *Galileo* and *Mother Courage* may compromise the fulfillment of the process of *Verfremdungseffekt* for many spectators. I would suggest, though, that this response need not compromise the progressive political promise of either play. Brecht wrote most of his theoretical essays under the shadow of Nazism, the bleak years of World War II, the rise of McCarthyism in the US, and the triumph of Stalinism in Eastern Europe after the war. As a political realist and a utopian revolutionary, he affirmed both the difficulty of transformation and its ultimate necessity. If revolution seems a long way off at the end of both plays, a good production of either one will point out the contradictions of both dramatic situations and provide enough glimpses of utopian possibility so that spectators need not retreat to cynicism and passivity.

Of course a cognitive approach to Brechtian theory and practice cannot guarantee a progressive response from an audience watching *Galileo* or *Mother Courage*. But neither can an approach based on orthodox Brechtian aesthetics. The primary reason to prefer one to the other is that today's science is more likely to produce better results than the outmoded science of Brecht's time. While good science can never claim objective truth, the cumulative efforts of scientific research during the past 50 years have been able to narrow the range of possible explanations in a variety of fields, including cognition and the arts. Brechtian theory has been central to our understandings of the possibilities of progressive theatre and performance since the 1960s. I hope the insights of cognitive science not only destabilize conventional approaches to Brecht's plays, but also open the way for a reconsideration of all politically ambitious performances. We still need to change the world and good performances can help us to do it.

Notes

1. Bertolt Brecht, *Brecht on Theater*, trans. John Willett (New York: Hill and Wang, 1964), 73.
2. See Mark Fortier, *Theory/Theatre: An Introduction*, 2nd edn (London: Routledge, 2002), 4, 5, 29–33, 166–8 and *Critical Theory and Performance*, eds Janelle G. Reinelt and Joseph R. Roach, revised and enlarged edition (Ann Arbor: University of Michigan Press, 2007), 4, 22, 29, 33, 38, 48, 268–72, 275–7, 296–308, 536–37.

3. My 2008 book, *Engaging Audiences: A Cognitive Approach to Spectating in the Theatre* (New York: Palgrave Macmillan) introduces several of these theories and specifically comments on their relationship to Brechtian theatre on 3, 17, 20, 34, 76–7, 138, 146, 171–3, 210, 216, 226.

4. By relying on the generally accepted elements of Brechtian theory from the middle period of his career, I recognize that I will be ignoring instances in which Brecht changed his mind. Regarding these changes, see Lauren Kruger (*Post-Imperial Brecht: Politics and Performance, East and South* [Cambridge: Cambridge University Press, 2004]) and John J. White (*Bertolt Brecht's Dramatic Theory* [Rochester, New York: Camden House, 2004]).

5. On the importance of dialectics in Brecht's theatre, see Douglas Kellner, "Brecht's Marxist Aesthetic," in *A Bertolt Brecht Reference Companion*, ed. Siegfried Mews (Westport, CT: Greenwood Press, 1997), 281–95.

6. See, for example, Brecht's model book for *Mother Courage and Her Children* ("The Mother Courage Model [1956]," in *Bertolt Brecht: Collected Plays*, vol. 5, eds Ralph Manheim and John Willett [New York: Random House, 1972], 338).

7. John Rouse, *Brecht and the West German Theatre* (Ann Arbor, MI: UMI Research Press, 1989), 29. See also Elin Diamond's comments on Brechtian theatre in her *Unmaking Mimesis* (London: Routledge, 1997), *passim*.

8. As Brecht scholar Carl Weber notes, Brecht's notion of *gestus* included much more than an actor's gestures: "It is an ensemble of the body and its movements and gestures, the face and its mimetic expressions, the voice and its sounds and inflections, speech with its patterns or rhythms, costume, make-up, props, and whatever else the actor employs to achieve the complete image of the role s/he is performing." Quotation from Carl Weber, "Brecht's Concept of *Gestus* and the American Performance Tradition," in *Brecht Sourcebook*, eds Carol Martin and Henry Bial (London and New York: Routledge, 2000), 43.

9. Ibid., 44. On Brecht's work with actors, see also Margaret Eddershaw, "Actors on Brecht," in *The Cambridge Companion to Brecht*, eds Peter Thompson and Glendyr Sacks (Cambridge: Cambridge University Press, 1994), 271.

10. Gilles Fauconnier and Mark Turner, *The Way We Think: Conceptual Blending and The Mind's Hidden Complexities* (New York: Basic Books), 217–67.

11. Ibid., 267.

12. See Karsten R. Steuber, *Rediscovering Empathy: Agency, Folk Psychology, and the Human Sciences* (Cambridge, MA: MIT Press, 2006), 6–9, for a discussion of various historical understandings of empathy. Also relevant is C. Daniel Batson, "These Things Called Empathy: Eight Related but Distinct Phenomena," in *The Social Neuroscience of Empathy*, eds Jean Decety and William Ickes (Cambridge, MA: MIT Press, 2009), 3–15.

13. Bertolt Brecht, "The Modern Theatre is the Epic Theatre," in *Brecht on Theatre: The Development of an Aesthetic*, trans. John Willet (New York: Hill and Wang, 1964), 37; and Brecht, "A Dialogue About Acting," in *Brecht on Theatre*, 26.

14. Evan Thompson, *Mind in Life: Biology, Phenomenology, and the Sciences of Mind* (Cambridge, MA: Harvard University Press, 2007), 393–5.

15. Vittorio Gallese, "The 'Shared Manifold' Hypothesis: From Mirror Neurons to Empathy," in *Between Ourselves: Second Person Issues in the Study of*

Consciousness, ed. Evan Thompson (Thorverton, UK: Imprint Academic, 2001), 38. See also Gallese, "Of Goals and Intentions: A Neuroscientific Account of Basic Aspects of Intersubjectivity," in *Naturalizing Intention in Action*, ed. Franck Grammont, Dorthee Legrand, and Pierre Livet (Cambridge, MA: MIT Press, 2010), 201–25.

16. See Vittorio Gallese, Christian Keysers, and Giacomo Rizzolatti, "A Unifying View of the Basis of Social Cognition," *Trends in Cognitive Sciences* 20 (2004; rpt. *www.sciencedirect.com*): 1–8. Interestingly for theatre studies, the authors speak of empathy as an "as if" performance: "Side by side with the sensory description of the observed social stimuli, internal representations of the state associated with these actions or emotions are evoked in the observer, 'as if' they were performing a similar action or experiencing a similar emotion" (5).

17. Thompson, *Mind in Life*, 395.

18. Reinhold Grimm, "Alienation in Context: On the Theory and Practice of Brechtian Theatre," in *A Bertolt Brecht Reference Companion*, 42.

19. Susan L. Feagin, *Reading With Feeling: The Aesthetics of Appreciation* (Ithaca: Cornell University Press, 1996), 130–1.

20. See, for example, Antonio Damasio, *The Feeling of What Happens: Body and Emotion in the Making of Consciousness* (New York: Harcourt, 1999), 37–8, 54–6, 136–9.

21. Keith Oatley, *Best Laid Schemes: The Psychology of Emotions* (Cambridge: Cambridge University Press, 1992), 98.

Part III
Case Studies: Activating Theory within and through the Production Process

Introduction: Part III

Megan Alrutz and Julia Listengarten

Part III, "Case Studies: Activating Theory within and through the Production Process," includes case studies by practicing theatre artists from a variety of areas; these chapters qualitatively describe and analyze the intentional role that theory plays in each artists' theatre-making process, exploring the function(s) of theory within the decision-making process for directing, devising, choreographing, designing, performing, dramaturging, and voice coaching. Through case studies that articulate experiments in and methodologies for applying theory to creative production practices, this section contextualizes and exemplifies different models for the relationship(s) between theory/practice, and artistry/scholarship. Rather than present solidified or static approaches to production, the models discussed in this part remain fluid and seemingly incomplete in any given moment. Together, the authors offer inspiration and ideas for applying, staging, and developing theory through one's own work.

The first two chapters in Part III examine the relationship between theory and methodology, highlighting an inherent reciprocity between theory and theatre practice. In the opening chapter, acclaimed theorist and practitioner Herbert Blau discusses how the KRAKEN group employed *Hamlet* (the text, the characters, and its surrounding contexts) as theory, methodology, and ultimately a multi-layered vocabulary to form and inform all aspects of *Elsinore*, a devised performance project that he co-created with the group of actors in the 1970s. His chapter includes a small excerpt of the *Elsinore* text, illustrating how *Hamlet* can "act" as both theory and theatre, as well as a new introduction and conclusion, specifically written for this book, which push us to consider how theatre is theory and how theory is theatre—rather than simply a set of ideas, systems, and questions.

In the following chapter, director Donald C. McManus continues to ponder the inherent reciprocity between theatre and theory, encouraging us to consider whether a production itself is, or can be, a theoretical idea—not unlike Blau, or rather, if it helps us negotiate theoretical ideas, tensions, and contradictions. McManus reflects on the theoretical problems of intercultural performance by self-consciously examining his own direction of *Cyrano on the Moon*, an original piece performed in India, and inviting us to approach this production as a theoretical statement, as well as a site to test theoretical ideas and navigate multiple challenges of interculturalism in performance. Furthermore, his chapter foregrounds how theoretical questions that drive a creative process will ultimately reveal new tensions and areas of exploration that might otherwise have been missed or ignored. This case study points to the transformative nature of theoretical criteria and the potential of theory to emerge from, within, and through the creative process.

The theatre practitioners in Part III also examine theory as a tool to complicate performance texts, highlight intersections between historical and contemporary contexts in a given production, and ultimately encourage viewers to re-imagine their relationship to culture and identity. In the next two case studies, the authors discuss theory as a framework that enabled them to discover, illuminate, and perform subtext; theory in these chapters also functions as a political tool for challenging systems of power and presenting and/or repositioning voices of the "other." Director Julia Listengarten and choreographer Christopher Niess, for example, discuss the influence of landscape theory on their approach to representing marginalized voices in a production of José Rivera's *Marisol*. Their case study examines the impact of landscape theory on their artistic choices specifically in the creation of physical terrains and vocal topographies that perform absence and/or silence. Presenting a theoretical framework as a site of possibility that can offer new ways of seeing, imagining, and ultimately staging, this study of theoretically engaged directing and choreography examines how landscape theory itself was performed through acting, movement, and scenic elements and how theory inspired the staging/performing of the text's less explicit meanings and relationships.

Similarly highlighting the political nature of theory and performance, Laura R. Dougherty, uses post-colonial theory to question the performative power of appropriated stories and bodies. In this case study, Dougherty discusses her work as the voice coach on a production of Suzan-Lori Parks' *Venus*, interrogating the direct and indirect impact of theory on her choices in working with the actors on "performing language." Emphasizing the importance of "the theoretical intervention" in how and why we make artistic decisions, her chapter suggests that theory can help us complicate the performance of identity as marked through voice and language in efforts to de-colonize the stage.

In debating the role of theory and its influence on the overall vision of the production, Dougherty echoes Lenora Inez Brown's previously discussed claims about active dramaturgy in a creative process, and further introduces additional case studies in this section in which theatre makers rely on theory as an impetus to gain perspective and necessary dramaturgical inspiration for shaping narrative and developing characters. Actor and director Brook Hanemann, for instance, offers another study of landscape theory in theatre practice, but unlike Listengarten and Niess, she reflects on how theory inspired a new methodology for approaching acting, voice, and movement, ultimately offering her a platform for theorizing the process of character development. Using theory as a guide for developing dialect, as well as shaping and framing body in a rehearsal process, she engages in a broader theoretical question about what constitutes character. In doing so, she contemplates practical implications of moving away from a traditional Stanislavski-based approach to character development toward the creation of physical, emotional, and temporal landscapes specific to each character. Theatre artist Alissa Mello, too, explores the ways in which a hybrid of theories—specifically "an ideological grab bag" of theory, analysis, and literary criticism—affects, guides, and influences character development, as well as production narrative, as she devises a puppetry performance that re-imagines women's stories from *The Odyssey*, *The Arabian Nights*, and *Ramayana*. Suggesting that in her own process she is both playing with and being played by theory, Mello echoes several contributors to this part who discuss theory as an inspiration and a filter for developing content for performance. Furthermore, Mello investigates how theory can become a tool for developing a constructive dialogue in the rehearsal process, helping to articulate one's ideas, prompting new questions for further exploration, and ultimately unifying an artistic vision.

In a case study that examines how music theatre practice has shaped current trends in music theory, music theatre director John Bell broadens the earlier discussion about the dialectic nature of theatre/theory and methodology to engage the subject of music theory in music theatre training. But unlike Blau's notion that theatre/practice is both theory and methodology, Bell's more traditional understanding of the theory/methodology/practice triad is grounded in his approach to theory as a set of principles that shape a particular method, suggesting that the birth of new theories is often precipitated by the necessity to dispose of and/or transform accepted notions of practice in music theatre. Specifically, this case study examines the recent shift in music theory away from the emphasis on literary principles as a guide for studying and performing music theatre material toward the language of music itself as a key for analyzing musical properties. Bell's chapter suggests that in practice this new music theory expands the director and performer's interpretive process, and ultimately enriches dramatic expression in musical theatre.

The final two case studies in Part III explore the role of theory in the developing area of practice-as-research, or PaR, prompting us to consider our production work as research that both engages existing, and produces new, knowledge and/or theoretical frameworks. Approaching practice as "a means for embodied investigations," choreographer Carol Brown and designer Dorita Hannah employ a PaR methodology to expose the stage as a "machine of transformation" or an "altering place." Playing with dynamic interactions between memory and mythology, body, space, and architecture, their research/performance acts as a means for destabilizing our relationship to mediated representations of acts of terror, such as recent suicide bombings. Through reflective descriptions of their site-specific devised performance project, *Tongues of Stone*, which continues to be (re)created in new spaces/places, the authors highlight the dialectic nature of this long-term collaboration; each additional phase of this project becomes a new theatrical/theoretical iteration of the same fractured narratives coupled with the unique and specific contexts of the sites themselves, as well as the memories and histories of the collaborators. Exploring the ways these performances were influenced by multiple unpredictable contexts, Brown and Hannah intentionally avoid relying on a single theoretical model to create situational encounters/performances that can "deal with complex constructions of terror." Writing in a playfully poetic style, the authors interweave the multiple theoretical threads that informed their devising process and challenge the binary between theory and practice. Brown and Hannah situate their own reflective discourse in a cycle of engagement, resistance, and revision, dancing—rather elusively—with theoretical paradigms and embodied practices.

Collaborators Michael Rohd and Shannon Scrofano, makers of new site-specific performance, consider ways to "situate work in process, to intersect [their] inquiries with the work of other artists or social researchers" that support, challenge, and contribute to artistic choices that produce civically engaged and dialogic theatre practices. Presenting a dialogue around *BUILT*, an interactive, site-specific production that explored the changing nature of cities in the US, the authors draw on theories from site- and context-specific performance and architecture, as well as Paulo Freire and Augusto Boal's theories around dialogic education and theatre respectively, to reflect on intersections between the personal and political in performance. Like Brown and Hannah, Rohd and Scrofano acknowledge the challenges of articulating a separation between idea and choice, theory and practice, and rather offer their use of theory as a way to situate performance in a greater cultural dialogue, to gain/offer access to intersections and inquiries with the work of others, and to develop what they call "responsible output." This case study also draws on Anna Pakes' discussion of embodied knowledge in PaR to interrogate where new knowledge resides: does the practice itself, or the reflection on the practice, embody new knowledge? Approaching theory as a muscle, a useful outsider, an established situation, a mobile hypothesis, and ultimately a methodology for a site-specific performance, Rohd and Scrofano converse about creating new modes of dialogue through and within theatre in which the viewer-participant and the actor occupy the same space of imagination and reflection in a "a sustained moment of coexistence."

Individually, and placed in dialogue with one another, the authors in this section suggest ways that specific theories can bridge various contexts embedded in a play/production process with contemporary perspectives and experiences of the production team. In the opening chapter of *Playing With Theory*, Mark Fortier compares theory to a marriage that both productively, if not frustratingly, offers support and inspiration, coupled with increased responsibility. In various ways, each of the case studies in Part III tap into this sentiment, articulating how theory makes us pause, pushes us to question or reconsider our practices/choices, and ultimately offers frameworks for intentional, responsible representational practices. Part III invites us to consider multiple ways in which theory and practice converge and diverge in theatre. How do theoretical frameworks shape where and what knowledge is created and meaning is made? In what ways does theory function as theatre, theatre as theory, and practice as research? Finally, how do these chapters, coupled with those in Parts I and II, inspire us to experiment with theory in our own production processes, and what questions remain elusive as we strive to consciously consider the activation of theory in our creative practices?

12
Theatre is Theory: A Case Study of Ghosting

Herbert Blau

Whither wilt thou lead me? Speak. I'll go no further.[1]

Prefatory note

With the advent of deconstruction, we had an extensive discourse about theatre as specularity, derived from the etymological affinity between theatre and theory. What seemed inevitable then (or so it was for me) were reflections on its vanishing, the appearance of disappearance, now you see it now you don't, the materialization of theatre from whatever it is it is it is not. And so it has been, too, through the history of drama, which has always distrusted theatre, that site of mere appearance, from the awakening of the Watchman (that character perfectly named), as if from barbaric darkness, in Aeschylus' *Oresteia*, through the "seeming, seeming" of Shakespeare's *Measure for Measure*, to the mirror stage of the Grand Brothel in *The Balcony* by Genet—an apparatus of surveillance that is, as the Madame says, always being watched. As I think these ideas, they are not applied to practice, but intrinsic to the theatre, engrailed, as in the play-within-the-play, that Hamletic conception, with the watchers watching the watchers watch. This view of (the) theatre emerged from the last work I did, with the KRAKEN group, which in the elision of theatre and theory—as with writing as performance—became a habit of mind.

The KRAKEN group and the conception of *Elsinore*

In the fall of 1975, my KRAKEN group started on a project that gathered momentum from the work already in progress, wholly improvisational, but with words, empty words, playing upon the surface of memory

169

like the sediment of a text, ghostly, metonymic, words displacing words, and endlessly so—like the data of prehistory or the half-forgotten substance of dreams. There was something about it like symbolist poetry, approaching the condition of music; yet for all the cadenced imaginings, inquisitive, psychophysical, what we were doing, like a mission, was not progressing very far. It was rich and strange but tautological, circling back upon itself—not really an impasse, but a proliferation of questions at the unnerving ends of thought, precisely where thought escapes us, compelling us to pursue it, not coming to a conclusion, but driving us to distraction. Or "distracted from distraction by distraction" (making a heuristic virtue of what T. S. Eliot deplored), we were closing in on a subject, as months of rehearsal seemed to collect in a state of mind that caused us to turn to *Hamlet*, not because we wanted to do that play in any conventional sense, but because the play, we thought, was somehow rehearsing us. When we defined the state of mind, asking ourselves where we were, we said we were in Elsinore (see Figure 2).

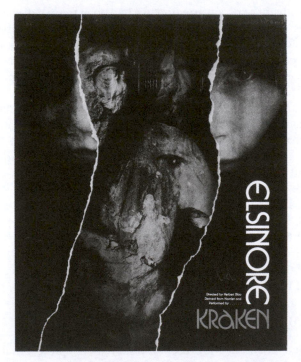

Figure 2: Elsinore: Production Poster. From the "Analytical Scenario" to the Mind's Eye. Poster image provided by Herbert Blau.

When we described the way we worked, we called it *ghosting*. We found ourselves thinking through *Hamlet* as if *Hamlet* were thinking us, and as if without the play we could not think at all. The play had become a language pre-empting what we thought.

The actors were never assigned roles in the Shakespearean text, but they knew it in its entirety, having memorized it all, all the words words words (and variants too, from competing editions). Whatever it was we explored, or with any bodily image, each actor might speak lines, phrases, fragments, from any scene or sequence, any character, in any order whatever, splitting syllables, spastically, or in whatever soundings, as a verbal collage, with one restriction only: they could speak no words but *Hamlet*. In the self-reflexive investigations that continued for about a year, the *whole play* was always present at any moment of thought like the whole structure of language in every single act of speech. If, as the work came into performance, you looked around for Hamlet, he seemed to have disappeared into the structure, or into something beyond or prior to structure, as if between word and breath. You could not identify him with any one (or more) of the actors at any given moment, but only as a transformational presence in a gravitational field, with other characters from the play as pulsations or emanations. Hamlet was there in all seeming appearance as an energizing source, identifiable only as a skein of vanishings, or the principle of indeterminacy in the spoor of thought.

The actors in KRAKEN were, for all this emphasis on thought, extremely adept with their bodies. They could act, literally, standing on their heads, or in every conceivable corporeal style, mimetic or ideographic, laid back, ribald, wild, as if out of nightmare or in eye-opening figurations that, in the recombinant seeming, approached the "miraculated" schizophrenia of a "body without organs." There was in performance, thus, a volatility in the verbal, charged in body and mind, like an ideographic charting of the fever in the brain. That charting will be charted here in an extract from *"Elsinore: An Analytic Scenario"*—but before we come to that, somewhat more about the ghosting, and how we went about it, which I've written of extensively in *Take Up the Bodies: Theater at the Vanishing Point*. "Theater is theory," I also wrote there, "or a shadow of it." As for the ghostings of the Ghost, and the power behind it, only the shadow knows, as it returns us everywhere to the overwhelming question: "Is there a divinity that shapes our ends?" Speaking of theory—what incited deconstruction, Derrida on Husserl—we are back to the question of origins, which in the ghostings also had to be thought.

So, too, with the awful burden that the dying Hamlet places on Horatio: "If thou didst ever hold me in thy heart, / Absent thee from felicity a while, / And in this harsh world draw thy breath in pain, / To tell my story." *What* story, and *how*? One can imagine Horatio like another ghost, that graybeard loon, the Ancient Mariner, with glittering eye, telling and retelling to no avail, just words words words, as the images proliferate in the stream, including the dispersed image of the teller. The work was done nearing 40 years ago, but I'll be speaking here in the present tense. Thus, each actor carries with him his version(s) of the story, or hers, each with its own compulsive life and course, intersecting and colliding, surging, some of it lost, all of them with rights of memory in this kingdom, forming the one structure of *Elsinore*. In the process, what's lost is lost. At the moment we start each night, the rehearsal as research, it's as if the source, history, or text, all copies or versions, fair and foul, are lost. There is nothing to go on except what's remembered, though over a long period of rehearsal, memory can be unreliable. Or capricious. What's there is all there is. The acting is a reconstruction, or remonstrance, done collectively, in perception and performance, one thought inciting, shaping, correcting the other, animadversions, enactment pressing back on thought, raising the immanent shaping question: "Who's there?"—that challenge on the ramparts, and the self-reflective response: "Nay, answer me. Stand and unfold yourself." The actors do just that, one or another, or more, moving into the space.

And what about the director? I circle the area around the observers, asking sharply and repeatedly—at the intensity of the performer's emotion or pitched to an incipient criticism or out of an intuition of the observing actor's desire to know (perhaps my own)—what eventually (my voice and presence subsiding, another ghost) they ask themselves: *What do you see? What do you think? What does it mean?* (the words more conjectural, often metaphoric, less literal). *Speak!* Solo, duo, syncopated, a whole chorus—the murmur of inwardness outwardly projected, in an animated system of cross-reflection. In the act of acting, observing; in the most estranging watchfulness, performing. *Describe that. Analyze this.* DO IT. *Tell the story.* One response guides another, shocks it, deflects it, bevels the edge of an intuition, speaks your thought (even of the acting), makes it *responsible as performance,* observed of all observers. The reflection surrounding the specific enactment becomes, *as spoken,* a kind of conceptual music, throwing the anonymous body of the actor back, like the mysterious hebona, into the porches of the ear, where concept forms.

As the actors contemplate the space of performance, they are speaking an inward speech, like the interminable story out of the rottenness of Denmark, that almost dirty silence, if unspeakable, what they feel

compelled to speak. Then, substitutions and displacement with no res-
pite, like the compulsiveness of dream, one actor moving from the discursive level of thought right into the condition of the other actor, being
where-the-other-*is*, un-silenced, spontaneous, almost without transition
from perceiver to perceived, seeing what is seen there in the actual body
of thought. The specific qualities of each actor produce qualifications of
what is *being-seen*, male/female codifications, through the substitutions
proceeding at various levels of perception, intuitive and framed—and
including, if partially repressed or explicit, attitudes within the group,
what they think of each other, affections, doubts, hostilities. Not abstract
but active, active when abstract, what it came to in performance, the
eventual visceral tension, was what I called "blooded thought."

It is the fine suddenness of the substitutions which is critical, the
unimpeded fluency of displacement, uncensored, like overlapping currents of the one stream. While the actors, within the closure of a finite
ensemble, replace each other at the same level of emotion—the glyphs
of reflection as identical as similar bodies can make them—the stress is
always on the collectively *shaped* emotion. It is not an ordinary kind
of improvisation; that is, within the auspices of a character or plot
or a situation or a game. There is much more explicit mental activity, including narrative, and split-second jumps between apparently
detached analysis (with no requirement that it be dispassionate) and
totally "involved" acting, to almost purely dissociated kinetic states,
as if hallucinating. The hardest thing for the actor to learn—once
the verbalizing of reflection begins—is to keep speaking, *not to stop*, the
temptation being at first to withdraw into internalizing thought. The
actor will justify it with the conventional rationalization about not
being "prepared" yet to speak. But in this work, that preparation is not
only a hindrance, but an irrelevance.

Two arbitrary rules: one, told to go into the space or to leave the
space, the actor does so instantly, often with doubt, or resentment,
which simmers in observance; two, told to speak, the actor speaks,
keeps speaking—and under the pressure of cross-reflection is compelled
to speak with greater accuracy of abundance. Asked to describe what
s/he sees, for instance, the actor may want to associate away. But the
insistence may be—by reflection or indirection—that s/he *detail*, with
no interfering judgment or deflection, what is *out there* in the space.
Or the suggestion may be more open and deliberately ambiguous, a cue
for turning what is out there back upon the self, associatively, calibrat-
ing the inside against the outside in the other meaning of the word
seeing. In the earliest training for the work—with all the accent upon

the resources of the body—words are, indeed, a seminal aspect of the method. As Gerard Manley Hopkins wrote of the forged verbal life of his poems, the instressed fastened flesh that bursts and darts, "it is the rehearsal / of own, of abrúpt sélf there so thrusts on, so throngs the ear"—until the words are second nature, reflexive.

But let's look now at the words which became *Elsinore*. The "Analytic Scenario" emerged from the long period of improvisational studies. The images were recorded during rehearsals, analyzed, and sorted out, but none of the writing was done until after about six months of work, by which time, too, as if breaking the sound barrier of *Hamlet,* other words came into play. I have left the scenario pretty much as it was, a dialectical incitement to the actors. What they encountered on the page mirrored and deflected what they had been doing, questioned or provoked it further, abraded the edge of an image, changed its contours. Sometimes they could barely recognize what they had done, which became an issue in the work; sometimes what one actor did was assigned to another; sometimes they wanted desperately to repossess it against the "authority" of the text, or the seemingly arbitrary placement of a personal image in a seemingly impersonal structure. They continued, however, to work through these and related images (which seem to have disappeared but are still subliminally there) over an additional period of five months, and then through the final *scoring* of the performance. There were further improvisations around the early versions of this material, which was always meant to be provisional, an ongoing aspect of the work-in-progress, not a script to be performed. If the rehearsals, as already suggested, were associational, allusive, cryptic, and open-ended, the eventual work was never meant to be anything but impeccably performed, unalterably *there,* legible if difficult, with the desire for the impossible perfection of the circle of accomplishment that is mentioned in the text.

What follows is not the entire text of the scenario, but rather the opening sequences. The initials designate the actors, and since the scenario was originally addressed to them, I have tried to clarify things by additional comments in brackets. The words actually spoken in performance are, as another increment of textuality, placed here in italics, and the words on tape in another typeface.

Elsinore

Each major image is separated into its elements, with commentary on themes and motives. The text is either specified or suggested. The outside reflections and the political mapping will be developed in rehearsal as a further aspect of the thinking through. The sequences are named:

T'have Seen What I Have Seen

Actors standing at the walls: neutral to will and matter; observed of all observers. The audience, entering, is also observed. A tape is heard when they are seated:

> KAR: I saw a player rise from a group of players and walk
>   slowly out to the center of the circle.

The actors are reimagining at some time in the past what they have done at some time in the past to tell the story that, known, comes obscured through history. What was being seen, told now in the present, is motive and cue of its own future, since it is being heard now by the actors who are about to act, already acting in the act of fear. (What was seen may later, after being played, be told again, playing and telling no longer the same. The retrospective may be taped or told right there.) The actors move toward the playing space. Action of describing a perfect circle. The circle has traditional connotations of unity, order, perfection, truth in the center, unhidden. Its edge is a smooth body. The actors shift ground in respect to each other, always an imperfection: in nature? a particular fault? They gaze at the space, which invites and unfolding. They contemplate each other. "Who's there?" Always: otherness, double-ness, strangeness, rue. The watching are being watched. "I'll have grounds more relative than this."

[Actually, the tape—which continues through the circling and seating of the actors and the rising of the actor, below—started with my voice, recorded while giving directions to the actors during the taping of the following sequence. What I said—partly audible, partly not—was about the cadence of perceiving, seeing and being seen. It just happened to be on one of the many recordings we made and was spliced into the front of the tape during the final rehearsals. Karen's voice continues:]

>   I saw each step he took, each foot raised, fearfully.
>   At the center I saw the player softer:
> DEN: Saw shoulders, chest, arms, hips, thighs.
> JAC: The player saw—
> KAR: I saw the player's knees lock.
> JAC: —and turned away.

Figure 3:   Elsinore: "I Saw the Player Arch Back, Eyes Open, Face Whiten." Photo by Chris Thomas.

DEN: I saw what he did not want to see.

KAR: I saw the player arch back, eyes open, face whiten (see Figure 3)

JAC: Running running, saw—

PET: —saw the forms, moods, shapes of grief.

KAR: —mouth open, flailed from side to side, I saw him
          wrenched back.

PET: I saw a near perfect circle.

KAR: I saw him wrenched back again,
          Then I saw him dip down and come up with an older face,
          a monster face.

MAR: I saw a circle made and made again.

KAR: I saw the player turn.

MAR: I saw the King.
          And saw in his hands the power that wields my life.
          And saw the strength in that body and what it meant.
          I saw I was afraid.

TOM: I saw two woman; two woman. I could see no more,
          I saw one woman, I looked at her face. It was drawn and tight.

```
         I saw many others. I felt, felt, felt they would turn
             against me.
         Certainly I saw my pride,
KAR:     I saw a woman on her knees, She tried
             reaching forward with her knees, but as if she were
             unstrung inside—
JAC:     I thought I saw the ground move,
KAR:     —kept falling forward.
         I saw her face was a great rock.
PET:     I saw the unseen wall.
KAR:     I saw her trying to form the sound and pointing.
         She would smash that rock!
PET:     I saw a tongue flicking and flashing inside her mouth!
         I saw teeth closing. In the beginning, I saw the Word.
JUL:     I saw silence.
MAR:     I saw venom.
KAR:     With her fallen limbs rising I saw her accuse.
TOM:     I saw the circle, inscrutable—the thing run from, foolish.
         I saw a crab going backwards.
DEN:     I saw myself making a mouth of my eyes.
JUL:     A woman examined herself in front of me quite nakedly.
         I saw it really meant nothing,
MAR:     I saw a knavish speech sleep in a foolish ear.
JAC:     I saw a blade of many faces.
         I saw it mirror the poison I must defeat
             and the poison I must become.
DEN:     In my dream I saw the body of my father,
             full and fat and black from the waist down.
         Layer on layer, I saw his flesh hang.
PET:     I saw one enter, entered, transformed, transform
             again, hesitate, and leave.
```

[The others have already come from the walls into the playing space.
Peter is only now in the corner, about to enter the forming circle.]

```
JAC:     I saw how quickly the flesh grows old.
DEN:     I saw the blackness my mouth drew out of this man.
         With every bite, I saw his sores are my grief:
             they break my skin.
         I saw this body enter my body.
         I saw too much.
```

[Each of the lines exists in several dimensions: relative to the source-play, as an act of confessional self-consciousness, as an intimation of what is to be performed, and as a reflection upon the actors' relationships with each other—here, for instance, Denise shifting the image to Jack, Jack reflecting on play, self, image, and Denise:]

JAC: I saw a grave too narrow for my mind.

KAR: I saw Hamlet in grief, I saw Hamlet caring,
          passionate and foaming.

PET: I saw nakedness clad with distance.

MAR: I saw the voice wears masks.

[The actors are by now seated in the circle, and during the following lines Tom rises for the sequence described below.]

DEN: I saw the ghost of the Ghost, rising.

KAR: I saw my body—

TOM: —the hollow skull, the wind.

KAR: —and saw how I couldn't get out of it:
          my father was at my back!

JAC: I saw the beauteous majesty of Denmark.

KAR: Following the blood to my heart, circling, I saw it beat there,
          walking slowly to the center of the circle, backwards.

TOM: Two heartbeats, wrapped in a single coil:
          I saw an almost smooth body.

JUL: I saw a very futile attempt.

DEN: I saw the sponge of my weakness take up those sores
          and drop them on everyone around me.

TOM: I saw myself choke back my pain, harden against
          the softening and lose my will.

JUL: I think I'm afraid there were times, I'm afraid there were
          times when I was too busy to see.

PET: I saw a wheel whose rim is in the center, and
          the head on top took turns being crushed.

DEN: At the innermost point of my brain I saw a Court.

MAR: I saw dirt, soil
          I saw I was fascinated by it.

TOM: I saw a Crown.

JAC: I saw for a fleeting moment two players seeing:
          It was painful to see.

My Offense Is Rank

1) Tom moves to the center, infolded in thought. He does not take on "character"; he is "himself":

TOM: *My offense is rank:*
       It hath the primal eldest curse upon't—

He reverses the key words:

       It hath the eldest primal curse . . .

Jack ghosts the words.

       Bow, stubborn knees.

The stubborn knees which won't bend, buckle through sheer force of will. The prayer which won't go up, goes down. The body is virtually torn apart in resistance to an atonement which, wanted, cannot in principle be grounded. The reversal of words already indicates that there will be an analytical tendency in the performance, with a short circuit from head to gut. The "O" before "My offense" [in the text of *Hamlet*] is eliminated because there is the explicit personal assumption of fault, the particular fault (*My* offense) and the fault in nature—inherited, inherent, first and agèd cause, before time ageless, primal. The action is a symptom of the act of fear and a raging denial of it; it is also a demonstration (active/passive? torn apart, tearing itself apart). The actor (Claudius? Hamlet? nephew/uncle) withdraws from the space [after the ideograph of tearing-himself-the self-apart] and returns to the edge, sitting.

2) As Tom moves center [above], Jack pivots out, squatting. He sees in the mind's eye the knees buckle and the body torn. He breaks into a run circling the audience, after ghosting Tom's words and crying "Lights! Lights!" As he runs, Tom sings out wildly, when still in the center:

      Why, let the stricken deer go weep,
        The hart ungallèd play.
     For some must watch, while some must sleep;
        Thus runs the world away.

There is a contrast, conceptual and personal, between Tom's broken willfulness and Jack's obsessive flight, which is both an avoidance and a response. The running (pursuing the Ghost? delirious to the closet? a figure of the figure of the stricken deer?) is an act of fear which, paradoxically, stabilizes visually the strange eruption in the state: Tom's tearing-the-self-apart. The circle is adhered to even though it's been broken. There is a declension of energy as he runs, entropic, a leak in the universe. Maimèd rites. Mortal coil.

3) On Tom's buckling, all except Jack speak these lines from the soliloquy:

> *O that this too too solid (sullied?) flesh would melt,*
> *Thaw, and resolve itself into a dew;*
> *Or that the Everlasting had not fix'd*
> *His canon 'gainst self-slaughter. O god, god.*

The words are just audible. ["Solid" and "sullied" were variables.] This is one side of the dialectic of which Julie's response is the antithesis. Extinguish the Self or murder the Other? It is the verbal cognate of the diminished energy in Jack's circling: melt, thaw, resolve into a dew; regressive. Dynamics: actions which are hard, willed, *yang*, contrasted to those which are soft, yielding, wanting to go inert, *yin*. [An important discipline of the group, with an intrinsic figuring of the yin and yang, was the Tai Chi Ch'uan.]

4) Julie has watched with horror but insists on naming the truth hid in the center. The word seems to draw her voice from its bowels: *MURDER!* As Tom leaves the space, she builds to a scream enveloping the nothingness at its center, first naming, then demanding: *MURDER!* It is a response, the opposite of the soliloquy's, to the primal eldest curse; it *is* the eldest primal curse. Whether born to it or victimized by it, it can drive you mad.

5) Peter, in response to Julie's *MURDER!* exclaims: "Long live the King!" (After the second or third *MURDER!* depending on how that is developed by Julie. Repeat??) The tone is indeterminate. The words signify a desire for continuity, as in Jack's run. But what does one mean by King? And who is that? Peter's (own) sense of irony is relevant here.

A Grass-Green Turf

1) *"Murder! Muurrder! Muuuurrrderr!"* Within the structure of Julie's image—vocally, then her movement—a continuum, hard/soft, yin/yang, thus: T'have seen what I have seen is to go mad. The brain splits in the

scream. Whoever it was, that voice, Julie is now suggesting Ophelia, crossing the empty space. She is singing:

> *He is dead and gone, lady,*
> *He is dead and gone;*
> *At his head a grass-green turf,*
> *At his heels a stone.*

(Sing first stanza too?—"*How should I your true-love know ...* ") As she crosses, she raises her hands and focuses on the imagined center through a cross-hatch web of fingers, her body oscillating in the crossing.

2) Denise gives a pure empirical description of the crossing, as Julie goes, thus: "Left foot, right foot ... to the edge of the circle etc."

3) In the transition from *Murder!* to "*How should your true-love know,*" Peter narrates, his lines orchestrated with the song and Denise's descriptive following:

> *The King, elected, assumes the throne.*
> *The mourning Queen undoes her hair.*
> *The Prince is summoned from Wittenberg.*
> *Ophelia is asleep in her chamber.*
> *Laertes, the brother, sails from France.*
> *The old man floats in the ground headdown.*
> *Fortinbras shouts his orders.*
> *An unnamed captain lies bleeding.*
> *Two friends of Hamlet arrive in Court.*
> *Horatio calculates his next move.*
> *The King calculates.*
> *The Queen weaves.*
> *Fortinbras rides off.*

4) The slight tone of mockery in Julie's song becomes more grieving. Lowers hands as she reaches the other side of the circle, turns and speaks into the space:

JUL: *Why look you now, how unworthy a thing you make of me! You would play upon me, you would seem to know my stops, you would pluck out the heart of my mystery.*

DEN: *Seems, madam? Nay, it is. I know not "seems."*

Julie's tone changes again, a green thought in a green shade:

> JUL: *Lord, we know what we are, but know not what we may be.*

5) Karen has risen and is moving center. Julie sits in Karen's place. Karen lies down, motionless. Julie's full image shows the implications of the curse. The terminals of psychic transformation—as an acting process—illuminate and frame each other: fresh death, fresh madness. A grass-green turf: Karen's bald fulfillment [below] of the requirement for a dead body focuses again on the act of acting. It establishes, too, the cross-sexual technique of the piece. *He* is dead and gone but he's a *she*. Julie's closing line, above, transcends and comments on the murder/ madness. It anticipates themes to come: divinity shaping ends; providential sparrow; ignorance of final things: *do* we know what we are? Julie foreshadows a later shift, on one structural emotion, from Ophelia to Gertrude—the self (mad) telling its story through the Other.

6) " . . . *we know what we are* . . . ." To Julie's line, Denise's *"Seems, madam? Nay, it is. I know not 'seems.'"* That determination is represented, first, in the plain insistence of her phenomenological description of Julie's crossing. How do we know what we are if we can't see what we see? Counterpoint of Denise's description and Peter's narrative: what's *there* (the eye is the law) and the mythicizing of what's there (the mind's eye). Giving audience to the act: to see in both dimensions, out-there, in-here. In the act of observing, of all observers, Denise's "nature" is relevant [she always bristled at the idea of having a nature]. Her concern for the "truth" in a realm of seeming, seeming. The sequence of images, disjunct but thematically joined, is a congealing and conjuring of the dreamscape of *Elsinore*. Forms, moods, shapes: Julie is after all shamelessly *acting* in her grief. To her shame. A passing show. We shall presently see Denise passing, reaching for the truth hid in the center, beyond the center, all the way out there: Is there a divinity that shapes our ends? She will ask that question explicitly, later.

So Like the King

1) Before she lies down after moving center, Karen stands there and removes her jersey, baring her body. In the manner of a demonstration, she runs her fingers along the side of her rib cage and over her chest. *"No marks of abuse, she is innocent."* She does the same on the other side. *"No signs of struggle, she is guilty."* She says these lines to the audience as dispassionately as possible. She then sits, center. *"Out of this soil,"* she

says, *"violence will spring."* She lies down, ceremoniously placing the jersey over her bare chest.

2) Peter calls across the space of the dead body: *"Who's there?"* Jack, who has stopped abruptly on Julie's song: *"Nay, answer me. Stand, and unfold yourself."* The exchange returns us, "dramatically," to the "actual" ramparts. It is also, as compared to Karen's dispassionateness, a motive and cue for passion. (Add another: *"Long live the King!"*)

3) To which, in "a figure like your father," Karen responds. From supine lifelessness, neutral to will and matter, she gradually materializes the Ghost, breathing harshly, growing louder, larger, hyperventilated, spasms of limbs infused by some daimonic force. The magnitude of the materialization in Karen's very small body, an issue. At the crest, outcry of the sheeted dead (which did "squeak and gibber in the Roman streets") transposed to: *"I—am—thy—father's—spirit."* Which, as related to the process of acting, makes sense. *She* is. An act of unfolding, fearful, impelled by the primal eldest curse. The line squeaks and gibbers. As she rises, Margaret tolls: *Be now be now be now be now etc....* Karen's action, a conceptual piece (overall), starts by further estranging the view of Ophelia we have had with Julie. We have seen the murder infuse the conventional madness (Julie's crossing should be composed of the "remembered" Ophelia). Now we are asked to understand it by seeing it askew. In Karen's observations on her body, *presented*, the issue is brought forward, too, by the suggestion of rape and the distressing question of how the woman is supposed to respond to it or how she is judged in terms of her response. Hamlet's abuse of Ophelia is a kind of rape, as her serving as an instrument of Polonius is a betrayal. The dead body, motionless, is both material and immaterial (in the realm of evidence); that is Hamlet's "machine." But it also becomes, "this soil," sullied, the grass-green turf. The sweater marks the sheeted dead. When she rises, the breasts will be bared again, and to the degree the Ghost is oracular there should be suggestions of the breasted prophet (cf. Tiresias), giving as eerier cast to *"I am thy father's spirit."* It emphasizes, too, the motherliness of the Ghost ("Father and Mother are one flesh"), as well as providing a maenadic image for the weaving in Purgatory [below], contributing to the Walpurgisnacht. The whole image, from the conceptual presentation on Ophelia to the ideographic resurrection of the Ghost, contributes to the graded perception of the acting process, the varieties of play within the play. One final thing: the cool impersonal presentation of the evidence will, most probably, deepen the felt presence of Ophelia's madness (it's weirder than the "real" thing as usually performed) and contrast with

the hyperventilated passion of the Ghost's rising. He has come from her grave, in the maimèd rites.

In the Blossoms of My Sin

1) Karen moves to the periphery, "fasting in fires." Jack crosses diagonally, Ophelia's ghost. Hand on loins ("o'erteemed"), hand on breast, spiraling. His tongue flickers, Eve and Serpent at once (lascivious source of the words words words); suggestion of the Garden, the primal space, site of the curse. He coils off. The surround is Purgatory.

2) Denise follows an impeccable line, extruded, in the opposite direction, arm stretched taut and reaching into the abyss, a distended and hallowed sound, like some desperate sounding of the distance from nature to eternity. In the tension between these passings, the undiscovered country from whose bourn. . . .

3) Karen, having risen from the dead, weaves on the circumference [behind the audience] the sound of Purgatory. Her voice moves from the low loud notes of the grave to the top of her compass, a high pure shriek, but controlled. A sound-abstraction forms around Karen, all the actors; then a tonal allusion to the ramparts, snatches of "rampart calls": frightened, lyric, frantic, baffled, singsong, fierce, birdlike. *"Stay illusion."* Cockcrow and bird of dawning. Come, bird, come. A text for Purgatory:

> KAR: *I—am—thy—fath-er's—spi-rit.*

She moves to the periphery on a shrill crest of Hamlet's name, weaving through the circumference. Margaret, crouched and sibylline, has been tolling: *Be now be now be now etc.*—"the bell then beating one!"—on Karen's ascension. Jack and Denise are crossing on the same diameter: expulsion from the Garden in a mortal coil; a reaching from nature to eternity, the undiscovered country between them fusing with the purgatorial image. As his tongue flickers, her mouth is wide open, calling from some bourn in the body, as if tongueless.

The sequence that follows is rapid and rhythmic, distant and cadenced, a kind of singsong. The cockcrows, bird of dawning, and the braying out are developed between lines and sustained with variations, which means that each actor must score an almost continuous line of words and sounds. As if in one breath:

> MAR: *Be now*
> PET: *Stay*

TOM: *Speak*
JUL: *Looks he not like the king?*
PET: *Most like*
MAR: *Not now*
TOM: *Like the king that's dead*
JUL: *Speak*
PET: *The king is a thing*
TOM: *Staayyy*
PET: *Illusion*
MAR: *If it be not now*
PET: *Stay*
JUL: *Like the king that was*
TOM: *Most like*
MAR: *Yet*
TOM: *Like the king that's dead*
JUL: *Come, bird, come!*
PET: *Speak*
MAR: *If it be not to come*
TOM: *Come*
PET: *Like the king*
JUL: *Stay*

(together)

TOM: *Illo*
MAR: *Be not now*
PET: *Like the king that's dead*
JUL: *Illusion*

(ghosting)

TOM: *Illusion*

(Peter with Julie, but a distant echo:)

PET: *Illuuuuuuuu*
MAR: *It will come*
PET: *Stay*
TOM: *Illo illo*
JUL: *Illu*
MAR: *Hic, et ubique*
TOM: *Come, bird, come*
JUL: *The king is a thing*
PET: *Boy!*

MAR:	*If it be not now*
JUL:	*Illo illu*

(together)

PET:	*illu*
TOM:	*Boy!*
JUL:	*Speak*
PET:	*Like the king that was*
JUL:	*Was*

(together, but differently pitched)

TOM:	*And is*
JUL:	*Most like*
MAR:	*'Tis not*
TOM:	*Illuusionnn (tolling)*
MAR:	*Yet it will come*

They have been crouching, turning this way and that. They now rise and move abruptly, here and there, chasing the Ghost, Karen alone holding the circle.

PET:	*Come?*
JUL:	*Illo illu*

(together)

TOM:	*Illoouuuu*
ALL:	*Stay*
JUL:	*'Tis here*
TOM:	*'Tis here*
PET:	*Like the king that's dead*
JUL:	*Illo illo illu*

(together, Tom's voice distant)

TOM:	*Illu illu illo*
PET:	*'Tis gone (brays)*
MAR:	*Now*

4) Karen is still weaving, like fate. The other women are now huddling together, a ghosting chorus, coming out of the purgatorial fires, as Jack—who has passed to the other side—spirals backward to "removèd ground." There is a scurrying over the playing space, Tom moving swiftly, Peter crossing: pursuit of the Ghost.

5) As Denise is passing off, Peter is alone in the center, confounded, looking into the dark, after calling, *"O, answer me!"* He stops. His hand moves into the light, as if disembodied, not his. He sees it. Suddenly, it slaps him, hard. Then again and again and again. He slaps himself to the periphery, braying, crossing Tom, Jack recoiling, the women gathering. The following chorus is an extension of the previous sound texture, still playing with the paradoxes, another weaving, the Fates, be now be now, come come come etc. receiving stress, as their faces assume masks of the elementary figures of the Great Mother, watching Jack perform, as if in an instant of time, the forms, moods, shapes of Hamlet. In the whole sequence leading up through Jack's performance, there is something like a Walpurgisnacht, a wassailing, a braying out around the permutations of providence. The readiness is not yet. The swaggering upspring reels. The ground is constantly shifting in the center, as in the rhythms of this chorus. On the outside, from the actors, reflections (narrative, political, etc.) keeping madness in reason.

[Each word of the chorus comes exactly in the spacing indicated, the whole composition being a unity and yet each voice maintaining its own line and inflection:]

```
JUL:    If          If                      If it bé not to come
MAR: If it be now                           If it be nót to come
DEN:      If                  tis not to come    If it be not to cóme


JUL:  If         It will be now    If it be not now       It will come
MAR: If    It will be now          If it be not now    yet
DEN: If          It will be now    If it be not now       It will come


JUL:      If         now               If it be
MAR: If it be now                   come            If it be not
DEN:        If         'tis not to come         If


JUL: If    not         come     it will be now      If       yet
MAR:                      come             If it be not now
DEN: If it be not to come              now      If       yet


JUL:  it will come      yet         now If         yet      now
MAR:            If        If it be     If it be now     if
DEN: it will come     now     yet         If      now    'tis not


JUL:       come     if it be not to come      it will be now           yet
MAR: yet        not                 now it will              come
DEN:    to come    if     not    come    it will be              now
```

```
JUL:              not                    if it will come    if it be
MAR: if it be          not now yet                  if                      if it be not
DEN:            yet              if it will come              if


JUL: yet      If     now            come not      if          If it be now
MAR:    if                it will come          now    If it be
DEN:    if it be now             come yet      if          If it be now


JUL:                     come              if it be not now
MAR: 'tis not to come     it will be now                      yet it will
DEN:                     come          if it be not now


JUL:
MAR: come If it be now, 'tis not to come; if it be not to come, it will be
DEN:


MAR: now; if it be not now, yet it will come.
```

[In the first three lines, above, I have indicated the kind of permutated stress that occurs throughout the piece, which is itself a reflection of the thought process of the entire structure of *Elsinore*.]

Afterword

The analytic in the scenario, though only a partial text, should suggest, too, what also became for the actors, even in body language, ideographically so, also a habit of mind. About this, one final word: if playing with theory in theatre practice assumes that theory is there in advance, then *Elsinore* is, if not a non sequitur, no exemplary instance of it, since the assumption of the work with KRAKEN was that there is no theory without practice—and it might take months of practice, as it did when we turned to *Hamlet*, to acquire some sense of theory at all.

Note

1. Hamlet to the Ghost in William Shakespeare's *Hamlet*.

13
Cyrano's Intercultural Voyages in India

Donald C. McManus

In an effort to examine the theoretical implications of intercultural the-atre, PAJ: A Journal of Performance and Art published *Interculturalism & Performance* in 1991, while Routledge published *Imperialism and Theater* in 1995 and *The Intercultural Performance Reader* in 1996.[1] This initial phase of critical reaction collected a variety of responses that focused on the political and social problems implied by the self-conscious combining of cultural modes. Many critics identified a tension between the dynamic nature of the work itself and the prob-lem of negotiating social power structures while combining artistic traditions. Since the late 1990s however, interest in critically exam-ining the complexities of power dynamics has been replaced with efforts to solve these theoretical problems by developing a perform-ance method that stresses points of connection between the tech-niques of disparate cultures. *The Intercultural Performance Handbook* by John Martin, published in 2004, draws on actor training from many different cultures, but it is designed to create a holistic, expres-sive performer, not an actor who will bring out disjuncture.[2] An even more extreme case is *Psychophysical Acting: An Intercultural Approach After Stanislavski,* published in 2009.[3] In this volume, author Phillip Zarrilli attempts to create an intercultural methodology that helps actors achieve the kind of psychological realism associated with the Stanislavski system. Both Zarrilli and Martin seem to view intercultural performance as a path to greater truth. Where these recent scholars have sought to harmonize interculturalism, stressing commonalities between East and West, my approach has been the opposite: the disjuncture created by the clash of cultures is where the interest lies.

Cyrano on the Moon: can interculturalism be satire?

This chapter takes as its starting point the theoretical position that interculturalism is most exciting when the artists self-consciously agree to create a recognizably new mode of performance that explores the "play" between one or more traditions or sets of cultural referents. In 2002, I produced my original play *Cyrano on the Moon* at the India Habitat Center in New Delhi as a self-conscious test case for the theoretical problems of interculturalism. The goal was to make theatre that the audience would recognize as formally distinct from other plays that they may have seen, even though most of the theatre the Delhi audience had experienced would qualify as intercultural by the standards used in *The Intercultural Performance Reader* simply because most of the theatre season is performed in English and derived from European and American models.

The inspiration for the project came from an essay by Italian author and literary theorist Italo Calvino (1923–85). *Cyrano on the Moon* was the title of one of Calvino's essays in which he argued that the obscure seventeenth-century literary figure, Cyrano de Bergerac (1619–55), was a prescient theorist who provided a model for post-structuralist thinking long before Roland Barthes and Jacques Derrida were born. I borrowed the title of Calvino's essay for the title of a new play based on Cyrano's satirical novel *Histoire Comique des États et Empires de la Lune*.

Cyrano de Bergerac is a familiar character to most people because of the play by Edmond Rostand (1868–1918) written in 1897 in an antiquated style of rhymed couplets. Rostand's expert swordsman with the big nose and broken heart was the prototypical heroic figure of the late-Romantic era. While Rostand's creation immortalized the name of Cyrano, the historical character became overshadowed forever by his theatrical Doppelgänger. My play *Cyrano on the Moon* was designed to recover some of the irreverence of the genuine Cyrano de Bergerac that had been "sicklied o'er" with the pale cast of sentiment by Rostand. In Calvino's words "Rostand's bellicose swordsman was in fact an adept at 'making love, not war' although still sharing a procreative urge that in our contraceptive age we cannot avoid thinking of as obsolete."[4]

The real Cyrano was a gifted writer of pamphlets, plays, verse, and a picaresque fantasy in which he travels through space to meet with philosophers, scientists, and moralists from other cultures. The *Histoire Comique* was written around 1655, ten years before the birth of Jonathan Swift, who was one of many authors who borrowed freely from it.[5] Like Gulliver,

Cyrano tells a tale of outrageous travel and otherworldly philosophy that is broadly comic, but seriously satirical. Religion, science, art, culture, sex, violence, language, and political philosophy are all irreverently explored through the conceit of interplanetary exploration.

I freely adapted Cyrano's *Histoire Comique* for the stage by combining physical theatre with pre-recorded narrative to create an original play entitled *Cyrano on the Moon*. The protagonist was presented as a sophisticated clown, cerebral by nature, whose experience in each episode allowed the audience to share his naïve yet cynical point of view. The nature of the satire was bifocal. Certain timeless foolishness was true to the seventeenth century. Other foci changed as the production moved to a new location, with different collaborators and cultural milieu. This flexibility was considered to be key to the performance as both new content and new performance styles were added when the production moved between cultural worlds.

I staged three separate productions of *Cyrano on the Moon*. The initial American version used actors from Pakistan, Saudi Arabia, England, the US, and India. Lighting and sound designer Viraj Mohan and actor Alex Lubar worked on both the American production and the Indian version, so there was consistency in the team, although the two productions were executed quite differently. In India, a well-known radio personality, Yuri, and three theatre and film students were added to the cast, and a team of Indian dancers was recruited to create a filmed projection of the creatures of the moon. A third version of *Cyrano on the Moon* was produced at Theater Emory in Atlanta, Georgia as part of the Brave New Works festival of plays in 2007.

The source material for *Cyrano on the Moon* foreshadows several core ideas in contemporary theory including the idea of play between cultural traditions. New York-based multimedia artist and critic Daryl Chin has said that the idea of interculturalism is "duplicitous" because one culture usually has greater power, and the presumptions of the dominant power make intercultural exchange work to the detriment of the weaker culture.[6] Chin's own work is largely dedicated to playing with the complexities of this duplicitous relationship. Clive Barker uses the rhetoric of international relations and world-market economics to champion cross-fertilization wholeheartedly in the arts without concerning himself with the problem of dominant and subdominant power positions.[7] Cyrano's *Histoire Comique* is extraordinarily modern in the way it acknowledges the vicissitudes of power. As Cyrano moves from culture to culture and region to region, he is forced to adjust his understanding of the nature of power and his position in the overall structure. This celebration of entropy made the *Histoire Comique* an ideal source to explore the play of cultural exchange in modern theatre.

Critiques of interculturalism: was Brook's *Mahabharata* Orientalist?

Peter Brook and Jean-Claude Carrière's theatrical adaptation of *The Mahabharata* in 1985 was a seminal event in establishing interculturalism as a vibrant style of theatre. But it also came under scrutiny as an example of how Western high art can raid Asian culture and, by reframing it, create a kind of cultural colonization. One of the most eloquent critics of the work, Gautam Dasgupta, concedes that the Brook epic is no less accurate a representation of the over 90,000 stanzas of *The Mahabharata* than kathakali and jatra performances based on the same material. He never insists that the epic should be the sole possession of Asian peoples, but he claims that it is "indisputably true" that Indian stagings of the traditional texts "address, implicitly or explicitly, a deeply-ingrained structure of ritual beliefs and ethical codes of conduct intrinsic to its audience." *The Mahabharata* becomes an "empty shell" if it is read "merely as a compendium of martial legends, of revenge, valor and bravura."[8]

Dasgupta's criticism of the Brook-Carrière project illustrates a legitimate problem with all cultural fusions that deal with separate philosophical creeds and traditions. Whether his criticism of Brook and Carrière is "indisputable" or not is debatable. I'm not convinced that a production of Indian myths that honors the "ritual beliefs and ethical codes of conduct of its audience" is necessarily better theatre than what Dasgupta dismisses as an "empty shell."[9] Referring to his approach to *The Mahabharata*, Brook said: "we are not presuming to present the symbolism of Hindu philosophy."[10]

I purposely set out to avoid the kind of Orientalist spirituality and supposed ethical lessons that Dasgupta argues are inescapable in a work like *The Mahabharata*. *Cyrano on the Moon* was dedicated to heterodoxy rather than any search for essential truth. What was missing from Brook and Carrière's adaptation of *The Mahabharata*? According to Dasgupta the "coterminous philosophical precepts" of the epic were not adequately emphasized.[11] "Coterminous philosophical precepts" were exactly what we set out to satirize in *Cyrano on the Moon*.

Chin has suggested that the colonial history of East and West cannot be avoided when Western and Eastern modes mix; my strategy was to embrace this unavoidable tension by compounding the levels of colonial reference. The historical Cyrano was the product of an arrogant,

European state with colonial aspirations, but his writings were essentially anti-authoritarian. After having fought in the French army and having been wounded twice, Cyrano became a Parisian gadfly whose plays, verses, and letters satirized the state, the army, the French education system, and the church. Satire was the primary device in the *Histoire Comique* and informed all my choices while creating *Cyrano on the Moon*. The primacy of one culture over another is redundant in this theoretical approach because the satire of cultural norms is the locus of attack.

Cyrano's *Histoire Comique* challenged European assumptions about the nature of global expansion and his critique transferred effectively to a contemporary Indian context. Early in Cyrano's novella, his hero fails to reach the moon and lands, instead, halfway around the world in New France. The first person he meets in Quebec is an "Indian" from the Huron nation. In our production, of course, an Indian played the "Indian." The French Governor manipulates the Huron and Iroquois into war with each other, paralleling India's colonial past in which the British divided and conquered the subcontinent in a similar way. These points of historical interconnection dominated any effort to project cultural distinctions and similarities between Indian and Western performance traditions, making Chin and Dasgupta's critique of intercultural praxis irrelevant. The French Colonial war machine becomes the means by which Cyrano actually achieves his goal of landing on the moon. He is blown into outer space by a cannon meant to explode the natives of Quebec.

Cyrano lands literally in the tree of life in Eden and is met by the prophet Elijah. He eats the fruit of the tree of knowledge despite a warning from Elijah and stumbles away from Eden. Lost on the moon, he is attracted to beautiful, multi-legged women who lure him into slavery. He is forced to perform as a circus animal until he is rescued by a shape-shifting Daemon, who then becomes his guide through a series of adventures eventually leading him to the Sun. The stage version ended with Cyrano and the Daemon reaching out for the blazing Sun. The Daemon was an amalgam of several different characters in the source material. The idea of shape-shifting is implied in the original, but the creation of a consistent entity from scene to scene was an innovation of our adaptation. This decision resonated in unforeseen ways in the Indian production although it originally stemmed from pure dramaturgical expediency (to create a character that would serve as a consistent foil). Our modern re-fashioning of seventeenth-century French fantasy had resonance with Indian concepts of divided spirits and transmogrification.

Interculturalism and overlapping content: was Cyrano practicing *ahimsa*?

One of the key differences between Cyrano's novella and Rostand's stage character is the protagonist's sword and his heroic status as a soldier. Calvino points out that the soldier's weapon was replaced by the phallus in Cyrano's narrative, while Rostand's hero remained violently valiant until the end.[12] A career soldier who had been seriously wounded in battle and had killed many men, the historical Cyrano had no romance for battle.

Cyrano's expression of revulsion for war and violence had special resonance in the Indian context and related directly to the post-colonial consciousness of our company and audience. Non-violence in India is synonymous with the country's founder Mohandas Gandhi. Gandhi had been an enthusiastic supporter of the troops during the Boer War in South Africa and might have been describing Cyrano when he said "you cannot teach *Ahimsa* (non-violence) to a man who cannot kill."[13] Gandhism was overtly addressed in the production of *Cyrano on the Moon*, especially during the sequence where Cyrano is enslaved and tortured by his captors. The Daemon echoes Gandhi's principle of *ahimsa* when he tells Cyrano to rejoice even as he is being tortured because he has an excellent opportunity to explore the philosophical proposition that captivity is a state of mind and that captors are as imprisoned as their captives. In the first American production, the Daemon actually wore a mask with Gandhi's image on it in this scene. We dispensed with masks in the Indian production because we wanted to avoid superficial, anachronistic cultural signs. I wanted any potential commonalities between Eastern and Western experience to remain open and in play rather than dictated to the audience. What points of connection would they respond to? The Asian audience needed to be free to interpret Cyrano's experience without directorial dictation on culture. The implicit connection was clear to the actors and apparently in performance, as the audience laughed at the oblique reference even though the hero was being tortured at that point.

Although the hero of our play and the founder of India shared a pacifist philosophy, Cyrano's sensual impulses and boundless skepticism make him the inversion of Gandhi's asceticism and moral certainty. When confronted with Elijah in Eden, who in our production looked very much like Gandhi in a dhoti, Cyrano couldn't resist making a vulgar joke comparing the serpent to the male organ. The impetus for this scene was satirical but it also had resonance with the concept of kundalini in

Indian tantric lore: "By that the sleeping kundalini is agitated and awakened, and straightens up just as a she-serpent straightens up with a hiss when beaten by a stick."[14]

Modern India's attitude to the place of sexuality in its cultural history, like its reverence for Gandhi, is mixed with political ambivalence, if not bitterness, in some sectors of the population. Our production made no claim to rectify these contradictions, but rather to draw parallels between internally inconsistent cultural markers in both East and West.

Interculturalism and dramatic form: is tragedy a Eurocentric concept?

In addition to the content-driven satire of these cultural correlations, *Cyrano on the Moon* also explored formal elements that raise questions about cross-cultural theatrical traditions and performance practice. According to Dasgupta, intercultural experiments that merge Western and Hindu culture tend to valorize the Eurocentric concept of tragedy. Tragedy is irreversible and definite and therefore has "no place in the endless cycle of birth and rebirth, the crux of Hindu thought."[15] If Dasgupta's theory that tragedy is a Western mode is true, then my version of *Cyrano* was guilty of cultural colonialism because it had a tragic ending.

The ending of the play was entirely of my own conception. Cyrano's *Histoire Comique* begins on earth, travels to the moon, and eventually reaches the sun. I used the voyage to the sun as the ending of my stage adaptation, but only after inserting the character from Rostand's play to kill Cyrano in a duel. While voyaging from the moon to the sun, Cyrano and his guide, the Daemon, stop at the "isthmus of intertextuality" where they are accosted by Cyrano's double. I stole Cyrano's first line in Rostand's *Cyrano de Bergerac* in which he challenges an incompetent actor in a theatre: "Coquin, ne t'ai pas interdit pour un mois?"(1.iii). Cyrano doesn't recognize his Doppelgänger because, being a seventeenth-century person, he doesn't know that the nineteenth-century play about his life has been written. Once the Doppelgänger has been explained to him, he realizes that he is doomed to lose the duel, crying: "A fictional character! Then I haven't a chance in a fight with him!" Cyrano is given a tragic final speech and a classical death scene:

> Cyrano: Can it be that I must die when I am so close to my goal? I can feel the strength of the sun and all that its wonders have to offer, but I also feel the chill of death as my life slowly fades. Daemon! Don't leave me to die alone in this terrible place. What of the levels

of consciousness that were to protect my physical self? Has all my study of philosophy been fruitless? Have you only seemed my friend and companion all this time, but really been my tormentor? Tell me. I must know the truth before I die. (He dies.)[16]

This tragic ending raises the specter of Dasgupta's criticism of tragedy as a non-Indian mode. But is it true that tragedy is a Euro-centric concept? The respected Indian literary scholar C. D. Narasimhaiah has actually argued that the Greek view of tragedy, "based in sin bringing suffering and suffering leading to wisdom," is nearer to the Indian world view than the "Anglo-Saxon born of enthronement of, or over attention to, the self."[17] Indeed, it is the over-attention to the self that Cyrano most directly satirizes. Cyrano, like his descendent Candide, is in search of truth and understanding about the universe and ultimately his place in it. Where Candide had a guide in Dr Panglosse who encouraged him to view the universe as the best of all possible worlds, Cyrano's guide was a shape-shifting Daemon who pointed out that each destination was as bad as it possibly could be. In our version, Cyrano's tragic end was followed with a rebirth in a transcendental form of his previous physical body. Only this form could allow him to travel to the sun.

My intention with this faux tragedy was not to echo the cyclical Indian philosophy of birth-rebirth. The theoretical starting point for all the work in India was to eschew reverence for cultural norms. I was interested in satirizing philosophical postures, including contemporary literary theory and the received wisdom of the structuralist legacy. In keeping with this spirit, the Daemon leads Cyrano through "the graveyard of the author" and "the ozone of parenthetical prefixes and suffixes" before landing on the "isthmus of intertextuality" and the fateful meeting with his theatrical other. These tropes of literary theory were satirized even while they formed the theoretical foundation for the performance. Reincarnation and Indian spirituality were evoked and satirized in a comparable way.

The Indian audience: is interculturalism in the eye of the beholder?

The actors, filmmakers, and dancers who collaborated with me on the Indian *Cyrano* viewed the project primarily as a piece of modern theatre. Nevertheless, as the text developed in rehearsal, resonances with India's traditional philosophy came into focus. I slowly realized that my anti-philosophy bias, and my preference for satire, did not affect the reception of the play by Indian audiences. Many of the viewers read the performance as thoroughly Indian in conception and spirit. They were able to laugh at the comedy even as they absorbed the imagery as Indian. One elderly audience member, grandfather of our lighting director and a devout Hindu who spent half an hour a day in prayer, was clearly moved after a performance, with his eyes full of tears. He spoke little English. When I asked him to describe what he thought of the play, he told me through an interpreter that the show was a comic masterpiece. The contradiction of his reaction touched me. This man had come to New Delhi from the Punjab during the great migration of population that was partitioned in 1947. For him the satire was the significance.

Sita Raina, an Indian actress with whom I participated in a workshop at the Asian Academy of Film and Television, attended rehearsals of *Cyrano* and made suggestions on textual and performance choices. From her point of view, the play was a quotation of essential elements from the *Bhagavad Gita*. When Cyrano flies through space, he initially lands in the "tree of life." The tree of life is similar to the eternal sacred tree or *Asvattha* described in the *Gita*. The sacred tree has roots on top and branches below, and the *Vedas* are written on its leaves. The juxtaposition of content-ridden images was primarily comic, but this didn't seem to make it less relevant to our audience. The moment when Cyrano ridicules the serpent in Eden was interpreted as a reference to Kundalini. The audience laughed while recognizing the reference as strangely familiar.

The central relationship of Cyrano to his Daemon is the clearest example of the potential "Indian-ness" of de Bergerac's novella. Sita wanted me to insert direct quotes from the *Gita*, either at the end of the play or punctuating the action:

There are two kinds of beings in the world, the one divisible, the other indivisible; as I am above the divisible and also superior to the indivisible, therefore both in the world and in the *Vedas* am I known as the Supreme Spirit. He who being not deluded knoweth me thus as the Supreme Spirit, knoweth all things and worships me under every form and condition.[18]

I resisted the temptation to quote directly from the *Gita* as Sita suggested. I felt that such a direct code for the audience would betray my theoretical credo of irreverence and land the entire project back in the mire of Dasgupta's critique of Brook's *Mahabharata*. And yet the resonances between the text we had created and Hindu tradition were valid. The company discussed the resonances between our developing text, the source material, and Asian tradition, but collectively agreed to leave the commonalities to be read or ignored by the audience. Early in the play, Cyrano disputes his theory of physics with the governor of New France, who fancies himself a scientist.

> Cyrano: It is a matter of common sense to think that the sun is placed in the center of the Universe, since all bodies in nature need its life-giving heat. Nature placed genitals at the center of man, pits in the center of apples. It is as absurd to say that this great fireball revolves around our irrelevant planet as it would be to roast a lark by holding the bird still and carrying the oven around it.

These lines have a striking parallel in Hindu tantric lore:

> Just as an atom consists of a static center round which moving forces revolve, so in the human body *kundalini* in the "earth-*cakra*" is the static center round which She in kinetic aspect as the forces of the body works. . . . It is because She is in this state of latent activity that through Her all the outer, material-world functions of life are being performed by man.[19]

We made no overt effort to draw attention to similarities between Cyrano's novella and Asian tradition, leaving our audience to make such connections themselves. My Indian collaborators were anxious to create a recognizably modern performance at the expense of specific cultural traditions. In the New Delhi production, the moon world resembled India more directly than the earlier scenes. Four dance students from the University of Delhi created a many-legged, strangely seductive moon creature that drew Cyrano into their environment and enslaved him. The dance they created evoked traditional characters and gesture, but the performers (who created all of the choreography) thought of their contribution as modern dance. The music was contemporary Asian funk.

Lessons learned: can performance function as theoretical statement?

The starting point for the whole project had been to make theoretical problems the essence of performance in a play designed as a test case. In the final analysis, the reception seemed as much a key part of the project as the effort to create disjuncture by design. I believe that the Indian significance of what we did was put into focus precisely because our production was so clearly European in source and modern in execution. Brook attempted to stage an epic with spiritual implications in *The Mahabharata* and antagonized Dasgupta by presenting an "empty shell." We attempted to stage a satire on Indian and European culture, consciously respecting no creed, and accidentally put old ideas in relief. Intercultural performance has no special theoretical relevance if it doesn't make the audience recognize that cultural elements are at play and create a distinctive new form. My Indian collaborators were ultimately more interested in the tension between tradition and modernity than varying perceptions of Eastern and Western tradition and thought, and the play's reception in Delhi reflected this consensus. Although this particular understanding of intercultural theory was not what I had anticipated, the performance itself stands as an independent theoretical statement. When practitioners take a theoretical starting point for a specific project, they do so to create interesting art rather than to validate or disprove the theory. Often new questions and areas of inquiry supplant the theoretical questions that served as the impetus for creation. Bringing *Cyrano* to India with the expressed intention of exploring the theoretical problems of intercultural performance raised by Dasgupta, Chin, and others, unearthed unforeseen connections that we would have missed had we ignored theory in the first place.

The tension between modernity and tradition that rose to the surface in the Indian version of *Cyrano on the Moon* influenced my thinking on subsequent productions. I revisited the *Cyrano* material in 2007, rewriting the text extensively and inserting a woman as the manipulator/Daemon. The story was refocused on gender/identity issues (also present in the source material) with the intercultural element serving as an echo from the earlier production, commenting on the developing plot. Cyrano's death scene was played in the arms of the Daemon who served as Cyrano's guide, rescuer, double, executer, and lover. In many ways, this version was much less formally adventurous than its Indian predecessor. After three separate voyages with *Cyrano*, Rostand's Romanticism had crept back into our vision of the sword-fighting, irreverent adventurer. The change in emphasis was a direct result of an entirely new cast, Theater Emory's workshop environment, and its long association of interaction with its audience.

Philip Zarrilli's book *Psychophysical Acting* was named Association for Theatre in Higher Education's Outstanding Book of 2010, suggesting that intercultural performance remains vital in the twenty-first century. It may be that the longing for input from a diverse and challenging audience is what sustains interest in developing praxis for this constantly transforming mode of performance. The global audience, such as the audience I encountered in Delhi, does not view itself as marginalized or culturally inferior to the West. Audiences transform theoretical criteria by responding to a dynamic and interesting performance. It is ultimately the diverse and challenging audience in active discourse with artists that will dictate the future of intercultural theory.

Notes

1. Patrice Pavis, ed., *The Intercultural Performance Reader* (London: Routledge, 1996); Bonnie Marranca and Gautam Dasgupta, eds, *Interculturalism and Performance* (New York: PAJ, 1991); J. Ellen Gainor, ed., *Imperialism and Theatre: Essays on World Theatre, Drama and Performance* (London: Routledge, 1995).
2. John Martin, *The Intercultural Performance Handbook* (New York: Routledge, 2003).
3. Phillip B. Zarrilli, *Psychophysical Acting: An Intercultural Approach After Stanislavski* (London: Routledge, 2008).
4. Italo Calvino, *The Uses of Literature*, trans. Patrick Creagh (New York: Harcourt Brace Jovanovich, 1986), 338.
5. Cyrano de Bergerac, *Histoire Comique des États et Empires de la Lune* (Paris: Galic, 1655).
6. Daryl Chin, "Interculturalism, Postmodernism, Pluralism," in *Interculturalism and Performance*, 87.
7. Clive Barker, "The Possibilities and Politics of Intercultural Penetration and Exchange," in *The Intercultural Performance Reader*, 247–56.
8. Gautam Dasgupta, "*The Mahabharata:* Peter Brook's Orientalism," in *Interculturalism and Performance* (New York: PAJ, 1991), 78.
9. Ibid.
10. Peter Brook, "Foreword," *The Mahabharata* (New York: Harper & Row, 1987), xvi.
11. Dasgupta, "Peter Brook's Orientalism," 81.
12. Calvino, *The Uses of Literature*, 337.
13. Mahadev Desai, *Day to Day with Gandhi*, trans. Hemantkumar Nilkanth (Varanasi: Sarva Seva Sangh Prakashan, 1968), 172.
14. Arthur Avalon, *The Serpent Power* (New York: Dover Publications, 1974), 245.
15. Dasgupta, "Peter Brook's Orientalism," 82.
16. Donald McManus, *Cyrano on the Moon*, unpublished script, 2002.
17. C. D. Narasimhaiah, *Shakespeare in Indian Languages* (Shimla: Indian Institute of Advanced Study, 1999), 13.
18. W. Q. Judge, *Bhagavad Gita* (Pasadena: Theosophical University Press, 2008), xv.
19. Avalon, *The Serpent Power*, 48.

14

(Re)presenting Silenced Voices: Negotiating Multiple Landscapes Through Body, Voice, and Architecture

Julia Listengarten and Christopher Niess

Introduction

This chapter is a dialogic exploration of, and reflection on, a collaborative production project. The authors, Julia Listengarten (JL) and Christopher Niess (CN), directed and choreographed, respectively, a production of California-based, Puerto-Rican playwright José Rivera's *Marisol* at the University of Central Florida in 2008. The play's multifaceted world unearths hidden, forgotten lives of the diseased and oppressed voices often silenced by political powers and/or oppressive, inflexible social constructs. Representing these silenced voices through the negotiation of multiple landscapes embodied through movement and sound, as well as scenic architecture, became the ultimate goal of our production process. Landscape theory provided us with a sensibility and vocabulary to navigate the performance of silence by creating a complicated, ever-shifting physical terrain and polyphonic vocal topography. Through a dialogue in this chapter, we discuss the influence of landscape theory on our approach to creating a multi-temporal, multi-dimensional environment, in which the architectural and the performative blend or transform into one another, heightening the dynamic between the presence and absence of silenced voices. Our subsequent choices to make the traditionally unseen/hidden visible, and the silenced "unsilenced," was intended to upset power structures and ultimately challenge the status quo.

Theory/what theory?

(JL)

The purposeful application of the term "landscape" to theatre originated with Gertrude Stein's "landscape drama" rooted in the idea of

"continuous presence" in which various spatial environments and different temporal zones coexist on the same stage.[1] The "landscape" approach
to theatre thus resists the principles of traditional linear, logical progression
of time and events in favor of multi-layered patterns of inner and outer
space as the core organizing principal of performances. In their anthology
Land/Scape/Theater, Elinor Fuchs and Una Chaudhuri propose "landscape"
as a new paradigm for understanding "complex spatial mediations within
modern theatrical form and between modern theater and the world."[2] This
paradigm embraces a particular, "post-temporal" way of seeing, imagining,
and dreaming, in which the traditional relationship of space to time no
longer exists. "[W]e are interested in the entire *field*, the whole *terrain*, the
total *environment* of the performance, as performance, and as imaginative
construct,"[3] writes Fuchs, referring to the existence of multiple, and equally
important, focal points on stage, which affect the audience's perception
by encouraging it to view the entire stage at once. While experiencing the
total environment of the performance, viewers are, therefore, invited to
absorb juxtapositions, accumulate often repeated images in their mind,
and engage in constructing webs of associations and imaginary "scapes."

Rivera's play *Marisol* offers theatre makers an abundance of opportunities to engage the viewer's associative thinking: to weave together
contrasting, incongruous images, follow action in many temporal zones,
and connect the characters' various states of consciousness. In Rivera's
post-apocalyptic vision, as a warfare between God and his angels begins
to unravel, New York City loses its recognizable features, transforming
into a desolate landscape of violence, homelessness, and death.[4] The
nightmarish disintegration of the city experienced by the play's protagonist, Marisol, coincides with the collapse of her own constructed
identity as an educated, middle-class woman. Homeless and frightened,
she begins to uncover the layers of her consciousness, rediscovering her
ethnic roots and gaining insight into a universal spiritual turmoil and
its profound effect on humanity. As we embarked on the production
journey, we continued to ask ourselves how to capture this complexity
of meanings and images in the production/on stage while offering the
audience a non-linear way of perceiving the time and space in which
the presence of characters is often marked by their absence.

Moving theory into context

(CN)
Multiple planes and layers of time and space are embedded in the fabric
of *Marisol* (Marisol—the title character—of the present, Marisol as young

urbanite, Marisol as cultural model, Marisol as representative of capitalism). As movement choreographer/coach, my entry into negotiating the complexities of the production came midway in the design process. One of the basic challenges in revealing these multi-layered planes lay in creating a representation (though not exactly "realistic") of parts of New York inhabited by Marisol, her co-worker June, and June's half-wit brother Lenny in Act I, and then transitioning or positioning that world further from "reality" in Act II. Ultimately, in Act II, the audience sees a shifting landscape that eludes recognition. Marisol, at times, recognizes elements of the city, but focuses her recognition in odd locations and arrangements.

"The new spatial theater," Fuchs argues, "[is] marked by shifting and unstable lieux. . . . Time . . . has retreated, leaving behind such freshly interesting theatrical perspectives as landscape, territory, geography, and the map."[5] As JL conceptualized this "shifting landscape" ascribed by Rivera for *Marisol*, she shared pictorial images from contemporary opera and film with the creative team. The images are both intricate in their topography and grand in scale. One image in particular reflects a regular pattern of small hills with a smooth snow-like texture, repeated across an expansive stage.[6] The landscape is barren, yet at the same time energized. I associated this juxtaposition of a death-like wasteland, imbued with a kinetic force, with another image of a woman whose features are transfigured by a thin shroud stretched across her face.[7] The shroud creates both a human face frozen in a mournful expression and a sense of otherworldly, heightened struggle. Inspired by these images, we began to discuss the possibility of casting several actors to perform the shifting landscape; these movement-actors would shape the environment(s) from underneath the large "shroud"—a large piece of fabric draped over their bodies to mask the landscape of Act I and create the literal landscape on stage in Act II. We explored whether the movement-actors could alternately capture elements of the eerily vacant landscape, as well as its energy and transient nature. We also discussed the ways in which the movement-actors, in the process of literally molding the landscape, would have the opportunity to interact with the actual characters serving as both a background to these characters' action, and physical signs and symbols reflective of their memories, dreams, and emotions. We were excited by the possibility of the movement-actors' bodies, slowly moving and shifting shapes, to transform into an interactive, living landscape for Act II.

This idea for staging Act II provided an opportunity for transforming the landscape in a way that traditional scenography does not typically allow. By constructing a movable scenic element out of the actors' bodies, we intended to break up a static sense of location and, at the same time, to reinforce the "landscape" approach to the performance stage as "a complex whole of associative spaces."[8] It also provided a juncture for punctuating silenced voices, specifically the voices of the dead emerging from the graveyard under the city streets, and creating the background sound for the war between God and the angels. Growing out of landscape theory, this staging necessitated the construction of the "continuous presence"—for instance, human voice was coming from underneath the material while the same voice was being amplified in various locations on the stage—thus merging events/images/dreams/ voices from multiple temporal realities and ultimately pushing viewers to engage their associative thinking. This particular approach to staging *Marisol*, therefore, offered the opportunity to frame the absence of urban humanity and simultaneously highlight and amplify the presence of a few lonely, abandoned characters in the script, such as panic-stricken Woman with Furs and wheelchair dependent Man with Scar Tissue roaming the stage in search of clarity, both internal and external.

Once we had outlined the way in which a group of movement-actors would facilitate the world of the play presented in Act II, we began to discuss the movement dynamic implied in Act I. The challenges of negotiating this process concerned the ways in which the performance spaces—a subway train, city apartments, city offices, alleyways—had to be represented as somewhat recognizable structures, while potentially shifting size and shape along with the energy of the scene in order to embody our approach to the play's landscape(s) as "shifting and unstable lieux."[9] Furthermore, Act I contains additional figures whose presence is continually shifting as well. In the script, the Angel's presence is felt throughout the act: the Angel sometimes physically interacts with Marisol, though unseen by her, and sometimes drives the action on stage, thus occupying the foreground. At other times, the Angel peripherally observes in the background or merely punctuates the void created by her self-heralded absence. It is also implied in the script that homeless characters relentlessly dot the action of Marisol's city, moving outside of her apartment between the background and foreground, and creating chance encounters in the street. We explored the ways in which Act I, too, calls for the construction of the scenic and movement environments that break apart static place and time, alternating the characters' presence and absence, blending the epic and the local, and ultimately privileging marginalized voices.

Through associative thinking embedded in the "landscape" approach to theatre, inferences could be drawn between the shifting homeless characters, the fluctuating presence and absence of the Angel, and the moving landscape of Act II. The homeless figures in the production became a predominant image/symbol of humanity. Like the Angel, they seem to "float through" the opening tableau image in the play, unrecognized by Marisol. Marisol, while on the subway train, immediately assumes that Man with Golf Club is an insane homeless adversary; then she finds herself in a role reversal in Act II as she wanders the desolate landscape marked by the absence of a recognized city. The character of June interprets the homeless as violent, yet transforms in Act II into the very image she despises. Her brother Lenny, who is confused, obsessive, and ineffective while living in his sister's apartment, becomes empowered and aware when he is cast out and homeless in Act II. The homeless in Rivera's play continually traverse the physical and metaphysical lines between presence and absence, silenced by socio-economic borders and cultural boundaries, both frightened and frightening. In the design and production process, we pointed to the necessity of weaving the homeless figures into the fabric of the performance of Act I; we wanted this dynamic to be echoed by the movement-actors whose bodies (and voices) created the shifting landscape of Act II, serving as a metaphor for the entire play and marked by Marisol's shifting awareness and identity.

In order for the audience to maneuver through these ideas, it was crucial to create images strong enough to encourage their synergetic power, the ability of individual images to generate a large form/image/symbol. Multiple views in the play occur simultaneously. Characters are ignored and then framed. They shift rapidly between becoming foreground and background. We searched for ways to achieve this simultaneity of layers through the dynamic shifting of images on stage, believing that if the audience could be empowered to draw relationships between images, as in a contemporary dance performance, rather than being led through a monochronic, linear narrative, multiple meanings would be possible. Symphonic composition in the production of *Marisol* replaced linear narrative, propelling the audience to become active in developing its own responses to the multidimensional and multi-focal imagery.

Playing with theory in scenographic decisions

(JL)
For Fuchs, "the collapse of boundaries between human and world, between inside and outside, foreground and background"[10] characterizes the postmodern landscape theatre. In our design discussions,[11] similar ideas about collapsed spatial boundaries and disrupted spatio-temporal

relationships drove the process of creating scenographic/architectural landscapes. We were interested in presenting multiple focal points on stage, heightening the transformative ability and/or power of performance space as landscape and complicating the spatial dynamic between "inside" and "outside" spaces, and thus giving performers the opportunity to create a fluid movement on stage within and among various focal points. In Act I, Marisol travels through three distinct landscapes: the Bronx where she lives, the Manhattan where she works, and the Brooklyn where she escapes with June to hide from a devastating "fire on a massive scale" that slowly envelops the city. We wanted to highlight the simultaneous presence of these locations on stage to embrace the "entire" continuous landscape, as well as to hint at the treacherous terrain of the city with its many fire escapes dangerously lurking in the dark, graffitied walls, perilous pathways, and empty subways. The space transforms both physically and viscerally as Marisol traverses those different spaces. The danger is at times real, at times imagined—similar to the figure of the Angel who appears and disappears on a fire escape, often perceived rather than seen by the characters.

Working toward a set design that would offer a solid sculptural effect, as well as provide a fluidity of movement, we were inspired by the designs of George Tsypin, particularly by his sets for *West Side Story* and Sergei Prokofiev's opera *Fiery Angel*[12] in which architectural constructions of distorted steel skyscrapers create a feeling of a natural city environment transformed by a powerful destructive force. In our production, several fairly open architectural units signified simultaneously present locations—a run-down apartment building in the Bronx, a corner of a Manhattan building (reminiscent of the Chrysler building), and a seemingly more solid apartment building in Brooklyn—and offered the possibility of blurring the lines between inside and outside, the apartment and the street, the impermanent and the movable, the real and the magical (see Figure 4). The streets were marked by the "invisible" presence of the homeless, who blended in with the destructive city environment and became part of the set. Pieces of the set, specifically the Angel's platform, traveled across the stage as the homeless moved the platform to transfer the Angel or to create alleyways and pathways for the characters to cross the spaces. The performance space expanded and/or contracted: the streets turned into narrow, dangerous labyrinths; the walls became "transparent," the divine angelic presence intermingled with the earthly surroundings, the inside of the apartment space spilled into the outside, blurring the boundaries between safety and danger, dream and reality, the familiar and the unpredictable. Landscape

Figure 4: *Marisol*: Act I. University of Central Florida. Photo by Matthew Brandt.

theory with its attention to "the dispersed visual field" that retrains "the perspectival spectator"[13] contributed to our choices in making the invisible visible and foregrounding the background in designing and later directing and choreographing *Marisol*.

The morphing of the various landscapes became even more apparent in Act II of the production as the large piece of white fabric dropped onto stage, covering the set's sculptural units and creating an effect reminiscent of Christo's wrapped buildings (see Figure 5).[14] The white cloak completely disembodied various parts of the city and heightened the sense of disorientation and loss for both the characters and the viewers. The homeless in this open unrecognized space were no longer hidden, "invisible," and confined; the barren landscape unearthed their silenced voices and hidden bodies. The space under the fabric, however, created another layer of invisible bodies whose non-presence was marked by seven movement-actors. Hans-Thies Lehmann writes that in "postdramatic" theatre in which visual dramaturgy is rooted in associative, poetic, and sensory experiences, a "simultaneous and multi-perspectival form of perceiving" replaces "the linear-successive."[15] This approach to viewing/perceiving is fundamental to the principles of landscape performance and continued to guide our production choices. The act of viewing/perceiving, however, became even

Figure 5:   *Marisol*: Act II. University of Central Florida. Photo by Matthew Brandt.

further complicated and "multi-perspectival" in Act II by splitting the focus between the visible focal points and the invisible movement under the fabric that resulted in various imaginative shapes.

Physical terrain—actors' bodies

(CN)
One of the challenges of directing/choreographing the movement-actors lay in breaking a learned linear exchange in relationships on stage. Overall, the actors were accustomed to the pattern of "character A" expressing thought followed by an emotional/intellectual response by "character B," resulting in a reaction by "character B" toward "character A," and so on. For the actors, to create a shifting, dynamic terrain that would literally become a set, it was necessary to allow themselves to transform into an active background to the present action around them—at times becoming a past echo of an expression by a present character, at other times becoming the "voiced" anguish of the non-present homeless or victimized. The notion of collapsed/collapsing boundaries between character and environment in landscape theory informed our artistic choices in rehearsal, but our actors, too, had to accept an idea of shifting identity

that would "communicate" on multiple levels in order to create the intended performance landscape.

The difficulty the movement-actors had in literally seeing through the white lycra fabric chosen as the "shroud" for Act II proved helpful in facilitating the idea of shifting relationships between character and environment. Since there was a limited opportunity to actually see the actors (those playing scripted characters) through the cloth, the "concealed" movement-actors had to rely on marks on the floor, sound, contact with other bodies, and a sense of orientation in the entire space. This literally created a sense of shifting boundaries and added layers of physical communication and reaction to/with the actors above the cloth.

The "visible" actors who performed outside of/above the cloth, however, found themselves challenged in several ways by the blurring of the relationship between, and the presence of, character and environment that we desired to achieve in the production. The actor playing Marisol had a tendency at times to follow the pattern of linear interaction—applying a process of interaction to the physical landscape(s) as if it were a character. She realized the presence of the landscape, had an emotional response, and then reacted to the landscape, expecting a similar exchange. It was through explorations of multiple simultaneous layers—the actual physical topography, its connection to her current emotional state, its (the environment's) existence as a symbol of internal chaos, and so on—that the actors began to adapt to, and then utilize, the shifting landscape, acknowledging the changing dynamic between character and environment.

Likewise in Act I, it was necessary for the actors functioning in a more "realistic" world to release themselves from a similar linear exchange with the constructed environment. It was essential that they create and shape the nature of the playing space by their actions, rather than accepting a passive role of reacting to the environment—taking it at its physical "face value." Even as time shifts occurred and degrees of presence changed in the middle of a scene, it was problematic for the actors to allow themselves to alter what they had already established as physical boundaries for the environment. For example, the fight that erupted in an apartment between June and Lenny needed to expand physically as Lenny's obsession with June grew, even physically spilling into what had been established as "outside space." This choice was echoed in an escalated conflict between Lenny and Marisol later in Act I. Both fights expanded beyond the bounds of domestic argument, and the physical expansion into "outside space" created an epic quality, each with its own specific image. The first example evokes the monster within—a physical threat erupting from what we consider safe domestic space. The second example recalls a "gun battle" that spilled out onto the street. Both of these images erupted from previous action, were played out, and added to the audience's perception of the characters and what they symbolized. They echoed each other, and their violence was further echoed in various scenes in Act II, heightening marginalized voices of the homeless in the production and gradually achieving mythic proportions.

The ability to transition in and out of each of the images provided by these examples demands flexibility from the actors who, in our case, were accustomed to linear plot progression. It was not so important that each of these conflicts resulted from a progressive and logical build as it was for the actors to embrace the images and the physical space the conflicts encompassed. This required a trust in the audience. Rather than the actor relying on the "sense" of a linear escalation of action, s/he had to trust that through embracing a dynamic shifting of images, the audience would interpret and classify the material. The actor, therefore, had to believe that the spectator, as in Stein's proposed landscape theatre, would largely control "the method and organization of viewing and processing information," transforming this experience into "more contemplative or meditative than the rushing experience of linear drama."[16]

A more dramatic example of this shifting of images was Marisol's encounter with the Angel in Act I—a scene which moves freely from dream to reality, shifting temporally and redefining the playing space at will. Initial efforts by the actors to play at these different levels resulted in bipolar shifts between intimate physical space and public address. The actor playing the Angel fought the impulse to mimic balletic movement and to speak "Zeus-like" from the imagined heavens; the actor performing Marisol grappled with speaking uni-directionally to "the heavens" to communicate with the Angel. The more successful moments occurred when these actors could imagine the entire landscape of the scene— invoking memory, both individual and collective, allowing them to move beyond static archetypes. This awareness began to reveal the multiple layers at work in the play—the individual struggle of the characters in the present, as well as universally encompassing cultural and spiritual tensions and negotiations.

Vocal topography

(JL)
In the "interplay between the land and human adaptations to and indeed *of* it"[17] there is an implied shifting mode. This shifting mode also applied to creating vocal topography in the production.[18] The variety

of sound sources in the production, such as a combination of recorded voices—guns, battle noise, a commentary by newscasters—and live sound, was further complicated by the background/foreground vocal interaction that highlighted the landscape idea of multiple views. Specifically in Act I, Marisol was haunted by the voices and screams of the apartment building residents she did not see, but feared intensely; these voices then shifted from the background of her apartment building to invade the foreground of her imagination. The identification of the voices, however, was clear for the audience, who observed the residents on various levels of the stage and whose presence remained stable throughout the scene.

As the landscape—both physical and vocal—continued to shift, the question of vocal identification became complicated for the audience as well. The voices of the invisible enveloped the stage in Act II, mostly emerging from under the cloth. These live voices, created by the unseen movement-actors, comprised an intricate musical score: delicate angelic inflections, disturbing cries of babies, distant battle noise, celestial sounds signifying Marisol's final transfiguration. This multi-layered musical score was highly associative and required a "simultaneous and multi-perspectival form of perceiving," in Lehmann's words, by inviting viewers to connect (or disconnect) the invisible voices with the constructed/performed images and assign their own meaning. Moreover, a series of implied sounds such as buildings moving and morphing in front of Marisol, as well as imagined/perceived voices such as a silent scream—one of the images created by the movement-actors—added to the complexity of the production's vocal topography.

Blurring landscapes/merging performance and imaginative constructs

(JL & CN)
As the architectural and performative spaces interacted, conflicted, and/or blended together in our production, the lines between various landscapes continued to blur. For instance, in the graveyard scene in Act II, the sliding movement of the "concealed" movement-actors to create an architectural image of the tombstones under the cloth elicited a chilling vocal effect—an eerie whisper of the silenced, dead babies, thus blending the architectural with vocal topography. Furthermore, throughout Act II, the movement-actors constructed a range of shapes from underneath the fabric that interacted with the other images on stage. The figures could be assigned specific architectural functions or manifest different states of characters' memory or mind, such as the harrowing

Figure 6:   Marisol: Act II. University of Central Florida. Photo by Matthew Brandt.

moments of interrogation, the unsettling fantasies of childhood, or the sensation of physical pain caused by burning flesh (see Figure 6). The blurring of these landscapes ultimately heightened the stakes for the audience in navigating through the abundance of performed and perceived/contemplated images and voices and acknowledging/accepting tensions in the process of meaning making.

In viewing the "entire field, terrain and environment of the performance, as performance, and as imaginative construct"[19] to echo Fuchs once again, we opened the possibility for the audience to experience not only *present*, but also silenced, marginalized voices. Landscape theory, with its focus on collapsing boundaries, shifting environments, and blurring distinctions between humans and inanimate objects, offered us very specific ideas for creating an active, *continuous present* for the audience—one that encourages viewers to participate in re-imagining and/or re-constructing their approach to, and understanding of, culture, identity, and spirituality.

Notes

1. Gertrude Stein first applied the term "landscape" to theatre in a series of lectures written for her 1934 tour of the US; see Gertrude Stein, *Lectures in*

America (Boston, Beacon Press, 1985). See also Arnold Aronson discussing Stein's principles of landscape drama in *American Avant-Garde Theatre: A History* (London; Routledge, 2000).

2. Elinor Fuchs and Una Chaudhuri, eds, *Land/Scape/Theater* (Ann Arbor: University of Michigan Press, 2002), 3.
3. Elinor Fuchs, *The Death of Character* (Bloomington, IN: Indiana University Press, 1996), 96.
4. All references to *Marisol* are taken from José Rivera, *Marisol* (New York: Dramatists Play Service, 1999).
5. Fuchs, "Reading for Landscape: The Case of American Drama," in *Land/Scape/Theater*, 48.
6. See images from Andrei Tarkovski's *Stalker*, http://www.godisnotelsewhere.files.wordpress.com/2009/06 (accessed November 25, 2009).
7. See the CD album cover image for Henryk Górecki's *Symphony No. 3*, Warsaw Philharmonic Orchestra, conductor Kazimierz Kord, Phillips Digital Classics, 1994.
8. Hans-Thies Lehmann, *Postdramatic Theatre*, trans. Karen Jürs-Munby (New York: Routledge, 2006), 110.
9. Fuchs, "Reading for Landscape," in *Land/Scape/Theater*, 48.
10. Fuchs, *The Death of Character*, 93.
11. Scenery was designed by Mitch Orben, an undergraduate student in the BFA Design Program at the University of Central Florida. Lighting designer was Vandy Wood.
12. See photographs of Tsypin's sets in *George Tsypin Opera Factory: Building in the Black Void* with texts by Julie Taymor and Grigory Revzin (New York: Princeton Architectural Press, 2005).
13. Fuchs and Chaudhuri, *Land/Scape/Theater*, 6.
14. See images of Christo's environmental installations that he created in collaboration with Jeanne-Claude, specifically the wrapping of the Reichstag in Berlin, among others.
15. Lehmann, *Postdramatic Theatre*, 16.
16. See Aronson's description of Stein's landscape drama in *American Avant-Garde Theatre: A History*, 28.
17. Fuchs and Chaudhuri, *Land/Scape/Theater*, 2.
18. Sound designer was Eric Furbush, an undergraduate student in the BFA Design Program at the University of Central Florida.
19. Fuchs, *The Death of Character*, 93.

15
Voice and the Venus: Opening Up Voice and Speech with Post-Colonial Theories

Laura R. Dougherty

> To speak . . . it means above all to assume a culture, to
> support the weight of a civilization.[1]

As a voice and speech practitioner, I am constantly, viscerally aware of the reaches and effects of language, rhythm, and voice on audience and performers alike. These reaches are to be celebrated as well as scrutinized. As Frantz Fanon has repeatedly suggested, language, its appropriation and enforced performance, functions as part of a power dynamic. What we say, to whom, and in what structure is an active, embodied performance of regulating norms. It is this affective gravity of the effects of performed language that I focus on as a voice coach. I approach my work as a voice coach much like a dramaturge; I consider myself an advocate for the production as well as its audience and focus on how to best practice the production's score (the musicality and performance of language) to suit the director's vision. Considering voice and speech from a dramaturgical perspective also suggests mindful preparation regarding historical and philosophical contexts surrounding the production concept and content. By this I do not refer to a vocal dialect or regionalism of a given historic period, place, or genre, but rather to how the linguistic score of a performance works with and for production concept. It is from this perspective—that of voice and speech coach with a dramaturge's leaning—that I keep theory at play in my practice. I am specifically interested in how, when practiced together, theory and voice and speech mutually inform each other; for I think we in the theatre do not consider enough the great weight of the voice. Especially in our current climate, where accent and language are used as markers of citizenship and belonging, and are so often conflated with race, we cannot ignore the political and social gravity of the voice. Here I assert that the topography of language of each production needs to be carefully mapped and practiced accordingly. In my work with the practice of voice and speech, never has this assertion been a weightier endeavor than it was with *Venus*.

Venus

I worked as the voice coach for a production of Suzan-Lori Parks' *Venus*, guest directed by Laurie Carlos, at Arizona State University (ASU) in 2006 (see Figure 7). To work as a voice and text coach for a Parks piece is more akin to the work of conductor. (The play opens with an overture, after all.) The production team for *Venus* did not identify a specific need for a voice coach; due to my interests in Parks' work and voice and speech I approached the production team. Director Carlos gave me as much access to the cast and their voices as I was willing to take on. I worked in one-on-one sessions, led group work, sat in on rehearsals and run-throughs, and led warm-ups each night of the two-week run (I attended at least four rehearsals a week, working for four to five hours each night); I consider the level of my involvement to be the practice of a theoretical intervention in how we approach performance. Voice matters. How we engage with language matters. (Budget issues alone make

Figure 7:   *Venus*: "Venus" and "The Brother." Arizona State University. Photo by Tim Trumble Photography, Inc.

such lengthy voice and speech work on any given production a near impossibility, but I believe we need to carve out more time and attention to voice.) In my time with the actors, we spoke in sounds and repetitions; my notes to the actors were about riding out sustained vowel sounds, sliding higher up in pitch, or repeating a distinctly percussive consonant sound. The opportunity to talk about the text in a manner that distinguished its performance from its literal meaning opened up the musicality of the performance.

In style and structure, Parks employs her oft-noted repetition and revision and an almost (always) anti-story telling. Through these structural interventions, *Venus* unfolds to problematize the commodification and appropriation of the black female body while it works against (so closely approaching) reifying such colonial and performative histories as that of Saarjtie Baartman's life as the Hottentot Venus. This play can work to dismantle the performative power of appropriated stories and bodies; for not only is race at the center of this play, but how race is *told* and voiced is a key intervention in re-telling and re-staging the Venus. "The Hottentot Venus," Baartman, a Khoihoi woman, native to the Cape of Good Hope in South Africa, was brought to London in the early nineteenth century and shown in the freak-show circuit; the Venus moniker and subsequent exaggerated identity sensationalized the (purported, imagined, or suggested) size of her backside and genitals. Through the play, Parks riffs on strands of the Venus' story, reproducing her arrival in England, how she came to be put on stage, and then into the hands of a doctor who later preserved her remains. The structure of the play actively resists the comfort and simplicity of a particularly linear tale: beginning with an "Overture," the scenes are numbered in descending order from 31 to one. The play is constantly disrupting the progression of its story, peppered as it is with the inclusion of "Historical Extracts" and interrupted by a play-within-the-play. The "Historical Extracts" are historical footnotes performed by the Negro Resurrectionist, a one-time gravedigger/robber who functions as a narrator-of-sorts; and the play is "For the Love of the Venus" where a mother and "Bride-to-Be" reconstruct the bride as an African Hottentot Venus to garner interest and favor of her intended "Young Man." What becomes clear from this disruption of narrative is that there is no way of following this storyline; it has been erased and redrawn too many times to be read. What is left is to make sense of the constellation of extracts and reverberations of history. In structure, style, and content, the play is an act of de-colonizing the Venus' story, a production which is built upon the performance of an unperformable enactment. Baartman became the Venus in *how* she was consumed. If the Venus never actually looked like her billing, to reproduce her image reifies and re-inscribes the misreading of her body. This is the complexity of the play as well as its danger.

As with much of Parks' work, the metaphor of jazz resounds clearly with *Venus,* as the audience's ear needs to resist the urge to find a melody. From my perspective as a voice and speech practitioner, voice and language offer anchors to actors, the means and methodology for clarity, as well as a physical action to ground the emotional journey of a performance or to ignite such emotion in performer or audience. Similarly, I used theory to ground and support my ideas about my approach to voice and to this production's a-linear story. As a practitioner, I do not quote theory as an answer to a production question; such citations sound different in practice. Whether that problem be an actor tripping over a certain line or a question of rhythm in picking up lines between actors, there are practical solutions to these issues which can be grounded in theory. I have found that it is how critical theory helps me to approach the process before I walk into the rehearsal hall that gives me more tools to do my work and a better way to access those tools. I used critical theory—specifically post-colonial theories— as touchstones to ground the serious and complex work that language does in this production, as well as to reinforce the production's vision and help me to guide the actors to use language to better articulate that vision.

(Rests) and non-places

I believe the principle complexity of staging this play is how to tell the Venus' story without succumbing to the commodification of representation of the black female body—how to tell her story without engaging in the dangerous power dynamic of making spectacle out of that one woman's body. For the Venus was a colonized body. Can telling her story be an act of de-colonization? The approach Homi Bhabha uses to express the importance of the space of a post-colonial history or narrative helped me to focus on the need to create a space for the telling of this story. It was my charge to honor this needed space within the text's language. Bhabha writes,

> This cæsura in the narrative of modernity reveals something of what de Certeau has famously described as the non-place from which all historiographical operation starts, the lag which all histories must encounter in order to make a beginning. For the emergence of modernity—as an

ideology of *beginning, modernity as the new*—the template of this 'non-place' becomes the colonial space.[2]

The idea of a cæsura—a break, interruption, a breathing-place—was the key to understanding how to approach coaching Parks' language responsibly. Bhabha's suggestion of how colonized historicity exists within a non-place supported how I mapped out the performance of language with the actors. It was as if I could no longer view or hear the text without realizing how Parks' style works in and around non-places and cæsuras.

Parks' use of language is her now-trademarked dramatic blue-print. In notes that precede the text, she offers a heads up, of sorts. She explains her style:

> In *Venus* I'm continuing the use of my slightly unconventional theatrical elements. Here's a road map:
> · (*Rest*)
> Take a little time, a pause, a breather; make a transition.
> · A Spell
> An elongated and heightened (*Rest*). Denoted by repetition of figures' names with no dialogue. Has sort of an architectural look:
> **The Venus**
> **The Baron Docteur**
> **The Venus**
> **The Baron Docteur**
> This is a place where the figures experience their pure true simple state. While no action or stage business is necessary, directors should fill this moment as they best see fit.[3]

Parks interrupts linearity and rhythm; if a (*rest*) is a little time, then spells are heightened time. Syncopation in music does the same: silences denote presence. The melody does not repeat; we cannot expect the same refrain, as her style, self-admittedly influenced by jazz, employs repetition and revision. She doubles back. Time and rhythm are not even in jazz, nor in Parks' work. This deconstruction of time and rhythm played a focal role in the ASU production of *Venus*. A frequent directorial choice that I have seen in dealing with her (*rests*) and spells is to use them as one might a stage direction for a *pause*. Given the importance of the structure and architecture of her work in how she builds the text to deconstruct the story, I argue that these moments need to be different somehow, for they are an active intervention in the writing (and righting) of the history of this story. Carlos decided that the articulation of these (*rests*) were to be performed via the actors' breath. At each (*rest*)—at least half of the scenes have multiple successions of (*rests*)—every actor on stage would breathe audibly, a deep gasp for each scripted (*rest*). Much like a deep breathing exercise, one targeted at expanding into the diaphragm, but all done in unison and in quick bursts of inhalation, the (*rests*) were active moments outside of language but still about sound.

Carlos noted to me that she wanted each actor to be rooted to the stage in those moments—to have the opportunity to ground themselves individually and as an ensemble. What that collective breath did was to break from a usual pause. There was a visceral effect on the audience, too. There was urgent energy to that collective grasping at air, in that sudden expanding of core muscles in the body. The sound of that breath interrupted an aural score and was a discernible difference in what and how the audience heard. Still audible and vocal, that breath marked a place not usually mapped by language; it is not a sound that we hear or use in our daily lives. Interrupting the narrative or linear progression of language becomes an active and important intervention in resisting reifying the colonization implicit in the Venus' story.

Interruption in narratives was vital to how we attempted to retell the Venus' story. Those (*rests*) and spells worked as an aural reset—clearing the audience's register, in order to consistently shift attentions back to the unfolding of the story. The (*rests*) became vocal cues to the story's production; resisting a linear narrative, the spells were as needed as speech in order to fully score the gaps in the story. The Venus' story is, after all, about an appropriated body, and that body exists in the colonial space Bhabha explores. From the dramaturgical angle of voice coaching, I constantly questioned how the performed voices served the unfolding (and disrupting) of the play's story; in the case of the performed spells, breath worked in ways voice and silence couldn't have and created previously unchartered non-places in our vocal score.

The Overture (repped and revved)

Carlos took Parks at her word and used the Overture (the opening scene) to set the tone, an anti-melody to score the production. The Overture was an explosion of sound, layered voices, and language. As written, the Overture includes characters introducing themselves as well as other characters. The Venus is introduced by others before she calls out her own name. Shortly thereafter, the characters state that the Venus is dead and cancel the show for the evening. Parks begins the play where it ends; as soon as the Venus is introduced, the characters break the news of the Venus' death. "Tail end of our tale, for there must be end," riffs the Negro Resurrectionist, playing on the circularity of the narrative as well as punning on the Venus' posterior.[4] There is no action implied in this Overture; nothing *happens* through the text. As with its counterpart in opera, the Overture warms the audience's ear to each character's presence and voice. The suggestion is that the action, that which will *happen* in the play, is storytelling. Though the Venus does appear in the Overture, it is not she who tells her story. She is the object rather than the subject, as the story is never hers to tell.

In thinking about how to work with the actors to best fulfill Carlos' vision for this scene, I focused on how to create the fullest, most dynamic vocal score; theory underscores best the potential payoff in Carlos' plan. What is it to have a story told on one's behalf—to not own or perform that telling? Gayatri Spivak contends, "For the (gender-unspecified) 'true' subaltern group, whose identity is its difference, there is no unrepresentable subaltern subject that can know and speak itself; the intellectual's solution is not to abstain from representation. The problem is that the subject's itinerary has not been left traced so as to offer an object of seduction to the representing intellectual."[5] The subaltern (one without access to social mobility) Venus is spoken for throughout the play. It is the form and content of this Overture that both need to suggest to the audience that we (as audience of history as well as this production) can't get at the Venus; her body and story have been too greatly dissected. I worked with the actors to unearth as much sound and as much difference in those sounds as possible to conduct an aurally overwhelming vocal score, an almost cacophonous riff that the Venus would be helpless to counter.

The ASU production featured such repetition and revision of the dialogue in this first scene to make the reading of a linear narrative impossible. The ensemble was choreographed, both physically and vocally, in rounds of deconstructed text, with groups of characters beginning with different lines and repeating different verses. The scene completely interrupted the melody of story and became a means of establishing a foundation of soon-to-be repeated aural score between the actors and audience. The repetition of language was played in both full sentences (spelling and grammar hers)—"We know youre disuhpointed. We hate tuh let you down"[6]—as well as repeated singular words within lines. With the line "Gimmie gimmie back my buck!"[7] one actor might have only repeated the word "gimmie" without ever getting to the whole line. My notes to the cast would be about hitting different sounds in different moments, such as moving with dispatch to the hard "k" sound in "back" and "buck," or to call out on the resonant tone of the long "o" in "know." I frequently gave notes such as "your succession of "t"s was really crisp, keep playing with those while you and she are dancing down-center"; we choreographed sound and movement. The effect of the discord on stage was much like a reverberating echo. The audience might have only picked up certain words, perhaps even certain sounds, indistinguishable from linguistic contexts. Mirroring such linguistic deconstruction of this scene was the choreographed movement. Actors circled the stage, shuffle-stepped in place, danced with partners, ran in place—a physical chorus of seemingly unrelated movements which were not indicative of tasks or action as much as choreographed movement. The effect was a visual and aural collage stripping the story of the trappings of linear exposition. We created a no-place for our beginning; this is what I would work to hone, to find a way to conduct the sound to create a voiced cæsura of sorts for our anti-story.

The Mother-Showman vs neutrality

The play is laden with complicated power dynamics, most notably surrounding race and gender (embodied by the Venus herself). Approaching my work, I was ready to engage with these difficult, heavy interactions with the actors. The practice of voice and speech works to provide actors with stability and balance (emotionally and physically) in such situations; before I began the process I presumed that there would be moments where voices were strained, where speech was clumsy or difficult in, around, and because of these weighty dynamics. This turned out to be the case; though not at all where I had expected. My own personal preparation and rumination with the theory in large part pertained to the overall concept of the production, to the overarching themes of the play. Until, that is, I took up with the Mother-Showman. With this one young actor, *this* voice in *this* role—crossing genders and playing with power—there was dynamic exchange between voice and speech and the theory that had laid groundwork for my approach to the production. I worked most closely with the actor playing the character of the Mother-Showman.

The Mother-Showman produces the freak-show of which the Venus becomes. The Mother-Showman sells the Venus to the Baron Docteur, who then studies her, impregnates her (twice), and awaits her death so he might dissect her remains and publish his findings. Carlos cast a young, white man in the role of the Mother-Showman. I mention his race and age (range) specifically, because the power dynamics of race and gender function acutely in the Venus' story. The commodification of the Venus lies in the hands of the two characters: the Mother-Showman and the Baron Docteur, both played in our production by young, lanky, tall, white men. The actor playing the Venus was brought in from outside the university, an African-American woman in her late thirties. While not noted in the text, our Mother-Showman, played by a man, was much like a drag queen; she wore a long coat with swirling tails, visibly accentuated make-up, high-heeled shoes, was clearly a man who referred to herself as a woman, and moved with grand gesticulations as well as a pronounced strut.

The actor playing the Mother-Showman resisted the role at first. Carlos tried to set a specific series of gestures on the Mother-Showman's first lines. Her text itself is fairly enigmatic in its rhythm, more so than that of other characters. In the Mother-Showman's first interaction with the Venus (who, at this point, the Mother-Showman has purchased and owns), she directs the Venus to undress and bathe, planning on readying her for introduction to the awaiting public. The Venus asks for the man who had originally brought her to England, whom she believed to be her partner or producer. The Mother-Showman:

> Him? Girl, he skipped town.
> Yr lucky I was passing through
> good God girl he wasnt lying, you woulda starved to death or worse,
>   been throwed in jail for heh
> indecency. But its alright now, dear, Mother-Showmanll guard yr
>   Interests.
> Yr Secrets are safe with me.
> Scrub.
> SCRUB![8]

The rhythm of the text, the gestures Carlos choreographed, and the sinister actions seemed to make the actor gravely uncomfortable. His voice was strained; he forced sound from the back of his throat, working up to an unhealthy scream which he could not have sustained for the length of the rehearsal process, let alone the run of the production. (A rough, ugly, guttural cry that was nearly as painful to hear as I'm sure it was to create.) It was working on voice and speech that opened up the role to him and ultimately led his performance to be arguably the most successful in the production. Parks' rhythms can intimidate actors; I have seen a number of skilled performers chasing their roles throughout a performance, never quite in sync with the necessary rhythm. I believe that the

Mother-Showman's intimidation lay in how to perform power, which had everything to do with accent and its perceived implications in the US. This actor hailed from Mississippi, and in his daily life he worked to suppress his southern twang.[9] Read aurally as of lower economic and educated status, his regional dialect was one the actor had tried to erase from his speech. Lamentably, the practice of voice and speech tradition-ally encourages just that: the negation of regional, linguistic accents in favor of a presumed "neutrality" of speech, which is anything but neu-tral and can clearly be read as educated, rich, and white.

As much as I was steeped in the performative potential for language and the unique case for voice work, and as much as Carlos was bring-ing a complicated and layered history of black performance to how she staged and choreographed the production, I was prepared for under-graduate actors to need to be brought along on these journeys, and potentially to not be as invested as we were. The process became, for me as voice coach, about helping a young actor access *his* voice, and in so doing, to overcome stigma that has as much to do with class as with race and gender. The exclusion of accents, of dialects, of any voice which is other than the accepted, enforced "neutral," marks the stage as a colonized space. How we control, alter, and *correct* the voice in the theatre limits our scope as it limits access to the stage for the stories told, the performers, and the audiences. While the practice of voice and speech is often the limiting structure, it can be used to dismantle these same structures. This is the theoretical intervention that the practice of voice and speech has to offer.

In the Mother-Showman's case, it was just the sustention of sound and applicability of diphthongs that gave the actor more vocal space in which to move, and thus wield power over, the Venus. The word "fine" can be sustained, and the actor can slide down in the dipthong in pitch "fiii-uhn." The Mother-Showman's rhythm was so different from everyone else's that her scenes became about her. Her rhythm took over, and everyone else, especially the Venus, had to fill in around the fiery yet languid beat of her cadence. Adding range in pitch gave a certain sing-song quality that unlocked the actor's per-formance. To slide from high pitch to low in one word is a specific and noticeable choice, which can be felt in the difference between a short single pitch "Fine!" and a long slide from high to low on "fiiii—uhn!" Those slides helped the actor find the Mother-Showman's attitude, and the diva was born.

Dynamics in pitch gave the Mother-Showman even more room to play. "Him? Girl he skipped town." The word "Him" was high in pitch, sliding up on that short vowel, asking a question. On "Girl," the Mother-Showman spent some time on the "urrrl" leading the Venus along; she finished the phrase by elongating "town," the diphthong with sounded like "toww-uhhn." The score of line served to give the actor touchstones on which he knew he could vocally land, which afforded him the opportunity to layer the choreographed gestures on top of that vocal performance. That is, the score of the language was the music for the choreography of movement. In addition, the sustention of sound in the word "town" played too on the importance of locale (whose it was, and who couldn't leave it) for the Venus' story. Later in the line, the Mother-Showman had a guttural exhale on the "heh," which we juxtaposed next to the longest sustained sounds of the stanza on "indecency." I coached the actor to both hang on the first "n" for "innnnnn-decency" ("n"s are a rich, resonant, easily sustained consonant), and played too with adding more of the diphthong, "innnnn-dee-uh-sennseee." Without the southern drawl, such sustention of shorter vowel sounds might have been less accessible to the actor, or even sounded strange to the ear. However, with that southern twang, the Mother-Showman was able to hang on to, and spend more time on, each and every sound, resulting in a hyper-performative style that served that character's lascivious and greedy abuse of the Venus, which fueled the production's focus on the appropriation and sensationalizing of the Venus.

In my work with this young actor, it was in carefully mapping out the sounds that gave him the room to play within his voice and then develop his character. I find that how we get around such blocks as an actor shying away from her own speech patterns and rhythms is to find those sounds within the language to be performed that focus on possibility and opportunity in language. This is not just suggestive, not solely about an intellectual approach to voice, but about a mapping of sounds. This is also not to say that in this case the mere suggestion of sustainable consonants or diphthongal vowels negated the Mother-Showman's own feelings about his voice, or his regionalism. However, focusing on the opportunities, on chartable sounds in words, creates a space between the intellectual and emotional perception of language and its performance. I was haunted and fueled by Bhabha's suggestion of that breathing place, that cæsura. There is some interruption, some new space, created that can work to distance the actor from her perceptions. Working with the actor who played the Mother-Showman, I was able to talk about the language, the points on our vocal map, which proved an active, embodied means of performing language, one that, in this case, did work to vault him over his trepidations about his voice. For a play that is about misreading a body, working against how we misread voice proved apt, and proved important to performing our anti-storytelling, anti-melody re-staging of the Venus.

The tail end

The complexity of the play lies in the danger of subscribing to just what we are trying to address; the question in its staging became how do we (the production team) put the black body on stage when trying to decode how the black body has been exploited? My role was to use language to weather such subscription. It was also vital to resist a sentimentality that would only have inspired pity for the Venus; this play demands more for her story. Articulating the obfuscation of any linear truth to the Venus' history was played in the repetition and vision of visual images and aural scores. Language in this production served as the non-place where we could start to get at the retelling of the Venus' story. I hope how I coached my actors through the text helped to give them a foundation in which to work with the complexities of language and how we perform seemingly unperformable stories. I argue that we need to constantly struggle against perceived neutrality in voice; the traditions and practice of silencing voices, both historical and contemporary, are problematic and damaging. This is the intersection of theory and practice: in voice and speech we need to employ post-colonial theory (not exclusively, as performance theory, critical race theory, and gender theory—among others—are clearly so closely linked and equally applicable) to help navigate through this serious tension. My work on this production of *Venus* suggested and solidified the need for interruption, for *(rests)* in how we practitioners approach and perform language. There are gaps on our vocal maps; some are moments of necessary silence, while others are marked absences. We need to be cognizant of how we tell stories, how we use language, and with what assumptions. Including previously excluded histories on stage has to encompass including voices—accented, rough, and real—if the stage can become a de-colonized space.

Notes

1. Frantz Fanon, *Black Skin White Masks* (NY: Grove Press, 1967), 18.
2. Homi Bhabha, *The Location of Culture* (London: Routledge, 1994), 352.
3. Suzan-Lori Parks, *Venus* (NY: Theatre Communications Group, 1997), n.p.
4. Ibid., 8.

5. Gayatri Spivak, "Can the Subaltern Speak?," in *The Post-Colonial Studies Reader,* eds Bill Ashcroft, Gareth Griffiths, and Helen Tiffin (London: Routledge, 2006), 32.
6. Parks, 5.
7. Ibid.
8. Ibid., 30.
9. Using the word "twang," which is effective in communicating the dialect to which I am referring, is problematic in that it, as a term, is laden with the very associations that burdened this actor.

16

Theoretical Terrain and Performance Practice: An Actor's Journey into the Uncharted Territory of Landscape Theory

Brook Hanemann

> We must study the theorists of the past; Stanislavski, Delsarte, Lecoq . . . but they did yesterday. Who is doing tomorrow?[1]

Playing with theory is a practice most often relegated to scholars engaging in forensic examination, exacting post-mortems on systems of bygone eras. But how often do theatrical practitioners play with theory? Too often, we wait for systems to become well-established, mapped out—for the roads to be safely paved, *if* we play with them at all. But play is by nature a vital part of creative exploration, and a good place to start may well be at the beginning. As a scholar and practitioner keen on bridging those too often disparate territories, my interest lies in understanding and presenting a playwright's work in as fully realized a way as possible. To that end, I propose that we must bravely and shamelessly experiment with any established or bourgeoning theory deemed suitable for enlivening production practices, in the same brazen manner in which Charles L. Mee purports to ". . . take a Greek play, smash it to ruins, and then, atop the ruins, write a new play."[2] It is in this spirit that I undertook the radical task of playing with a theory by adapting it to my personal process as an actor, specifically by crafting my own modes of methodology in those instances when established modes failed me.

The following case study details my journey, as a performer, through the wilds of a relatively undomesticated theoretical paradigm—an experiment in the use of the nascent landscape theory to shape and inform character development. This is no dogmatic treatise, nor is it meant to be a how-to manual for performative application. It is instead a call to practitioners, so often segregated from scholars, to dare to PLAY with theory—a suggestion that theories may be broken apart, adapted, and absorbed. It is a charge that even the unanswered questions which arise from playing with theory may act as catalysts for deeper exploration and discovery.

Defining landscape theory

But what is landscape theory? It defies easy definition. The word landscape is believed to be a Dutch visual arts term coined in the late 1500s to describe the paintings of pastoral views. As the term was slowly assimilated into mainstream vernacular, it evolved to describe natural panoramas not linked to the visual arts[3] and encompassed a multifaceted and ever morphing philosophy or method of perception. Just as symbolism found its roots in Parisian painting and spread to poetry, literature, and theatre, landscape expanded from the narrow specificity of painting to broader utilization and influence across multiple disciplines ranging from dance, symphonics, performance art, and the spoken word. But pioneers in the theatrical employment of landscape theory—such as Gertrude Stein, who crafted conceptual translations of dramatic text through compositions that Jane Palatini Bowers refers to as *langscapes*,[4] applied the theory only in abstract performances.

I was curious to discover how one might use landscape theory to guide the performer of realistic or *selectively realistic* text, such as that of playwright Tennessee Williams. To do so, I needed less ethereal definitions/applications of the theory than existed. Stein, who took inspiration from the cubist movement, playfully deconstructed and reassembled language, arranging characters and patterning dialogue to signify physical landscapes. In her play *Four Saints in Three Acts*, she professed to have "made the saints the landscape."[5] In essence, the characters were created to embody a shared landscape via spatial arrangement, coupled with patterned linguistics. Stein's abstract methods, though intriguing, could not serve as a model for an engagement with landscape theory in combination with realistic text. I could take inspiration from Stein and her contemporaries, but I would have to deconstruct what I had found and develop a new methodology. I would have to *play*.

For the purpose of this study, I define and employ landscape theory as an approach to text, process, and production guided by the consideration of landscape as both an interactive participant and a character component. This process starts with a character's established interior terrain and broadens to encompass the living environment in which he finds himself. I found that the difference between landscape and the application of landscape theory in theatre is that while the former deals simply with a fixed geography, the latter urges psychophysical interplay between a character's native and physical landscape and that character's physicality, voice, and behavior. This goes well beyond a psychological study and delves into the physical terrain of the character's birth and upbringing. It speaks of the part that forests, flatlands, and rivers play in the development of a lifelong internal landscape that strongly influences a character's subsequent presence in any external environment. For example, a person born and raised in a sparsely populated, wide-open, rural area might be more expansive than one who grew up in a crowded, skyscraper-filled, urban setting. Landscape theory implies that a character's environment during his developmental years has a much more pervasive, influential, and active impact than is generally included in an actor's character study. Add to that, the theory's consideration of landscape as participant, and that landscape which was once fixed and static, can infuse dialect and become embodied and made manifest through use of gesture and physicality.

Case study: the *Tennessee Williams Project*

During the summer of 2007, I initiated a production that wove scenes and monologues from various Tennessee Williams plays together with biographical information about the prolific playwright. Performed on the steps of Williams' first home in Columbus, Mississippi, the mission of the project was two-fold. First, I wished to spread a greater awareness of the artist in his hometown and inspire appreciation of his work. The second, and less altruistic purpose for the production's conception, was my desire to create an experimental testing ground for my own application of landscape theory. I hoped to find a fresh approach to roles that have been performed now for the better half of a century, and felt that landscape theory might offer non-traditional methods for development. Billed as the *Tennessee Williams Project*, the production was, to my knowledge, the first performance of material from the Williams canon to be staged at the playwright's birth home. Though my project included scenes from *A Streetcar Named Desire*, *Cat on a Hot Tin Roof*, and monologues from *The Rose Tattoo*, this chapter chronicles my experimentation with only one of the three characters performed: Blanche Dubois from *A Streetcar Named Desire*. I wondered if, by finding her internal landscape beyond the traditional psychological and cultural study, I could add depth to the authenticity of my characterization. Specifically, I wanted to find inspiration for making physical, as well as vocal choices.

The physical, geographical landscapes of the Williams canon are rich, sensual, and very much alive. And while the term "landscape" generally evokes picturesque backdrops that do little more than set the scene for action, Williams' landscapes enter into the action. They instigate, imprison, motivate, and haunt. Through his use of plastic theatre[6] and poetic, selective realism, Williams broke from the confines of realistic theatrical conventions and crafted landscapes as alive and active as his iconic characters, who themselves seem to exude a richness that could be defined as landscape.

As a theatre practitioner and avid researcher of Williams and his work, I believed the importance of the playwright's landscapes to be self-evident, but questioned how these landscapes might move from the page to the stage in active collaboration with, and as influential parts of, human characters. Discovery of a new discourse involving the theoretical role of landscape in theatre inspired personal experimentation in my process as an actress. I was enlivened by the notion that landscape could transmute from a collective of given circumstances into an animated participant. But how could landscape participate exactly? Extant examples were scant. I had to hearken back to Mee's radical, creative directive and take it upon myself to forge a new methodology. I tackled my work through three separate modes, employing various compartmentalized and holistic experiments in the areas of vocal application, bodywork, and dramaturgical analysis. My efforts focused on approaching landscape as dialect coach, implementing framing as a model to guide body shaping, and the use of spatial dictation as inspiration for script and character analysis.

Building bridges: getting past the road blocks

By the time I set out to apply landscape theory to the performance of Williams' selectively realistic text, I still could only find evidence of abstract staging, such as the landscape driven multimedia compositions of musician, composer, and multimedia craftsman Robert Ashley. Ashley worked within physical landscapes chosen to inform, impact, and guide his work.[7] This is kindred to the manner in which Williams immersed himself in the landscape of his resident New Orleans to enliven *A Streetcar Named Desire*.[8] Ashley contends that landscape is more than just a backdrop. He urges transference of focus from landscape, which is perceived simply as locus, to landscape embraced as an entity of its own, one that affects other characters on a psychophysical level.[9] This concept became the guiding light for my trek into the unknown. I entered into the rehearsal process treating Williams' landscapes not as scenery, but as potential catalysts for character revelation and as scene partners, searching for instances where the landscapes influenced the emotional state of my characters and seeking ways for those emotive moments to manifest on stage through physical and vocal choices.

Landscape dramaturgy and spatial dictation

Author and practitioner Jon Jory emphasizes the crucial importance of dramaturgical excavation and the breaking open of gathered facts, which "helps you to explain behavior, stimulates you emotionally and allows you to deepen and make more dramatic key moments and scenes."[10] Although the cerebral, ethereal nature of a research approach does not always lend itself to easily discernible identification within performance, it can be argued that analysis can enhance a performance simply by inspiring and widening the artist's creative perception. Landscape dramaturgy, which I define here as the research of dramatic text using the concept of landscape as muse, provides a new filter for analysis. Simply gathering facts and images from a character's native landscape offers authentic images and information to call upon during times when that character refers to his or her own physical past. For example, having amassed a collection of photographs of the Laurel, Mississippi bus station, old seedy hotels, and the high school where Blanche would have taught, I could visualize those places easily while discussing them on stage as Blanche. Instead of employing such techniques as Constantin Stanislavski's *magic if*, or Lee Strasberg's *emotional recall*, which require disconnect from the character in favor of assimilation of actor experiences, I was able to stay focused on the character's landscapes.

Spatial dictation is a philosophy born of landscape dramaturgy which suggests that physical landscape determines the role of those within it. To that point, Ashley's quip that you "only know who you are depending on where you are"[11] is particularly perceptive and relevant. Spatial dictation of character is an everyday fact of life. When in front of a classroom, I play the role of professor; if I were to find myself behind bars, my role would shift to that of a prisoner. Landscape theory takes that two steps further. First, it can make that landscape a character of its own, prompting interaction just as if it were made of flesh and bone. Second, it suggests that my native environment also has influence when I am in any space. Because I am from a small southern, American town, my way of walking in the world and experiencing my surroundings will naturally be different than that of someone born in a palace or a third-world country. Just as my personal landscapes determine the part I play and shape my behavior in real life, so should the dramatic landscapes of my character.

The landscape of pre-tragedy Belle Reve casts Blanche as an inno- cent. Williams, with his penchant for creating stories that chronicle the plight of the delicate and the ostracized, gave Blanche a treacherous road to travel. The privileged landscape of her youth grew perilous, and the roles pressed upon her became increasingly desperate. The suicide of Blanche's young husband at the Moon Lake Casino stripped her of the role of adoring wife. When death descended and Belle Reve became the Grim Reaper's headquarters, her role changed to caregiver and survivor. After her arrival in New Orleans, Blanche is relegated to playing the refugee. The loss of Belle Reve forced her from her ancestral home; her dalliance with a young student prompted her dismissal from the teach- ing profession; and her promiscuity drove her from the Flamingo Hotel, exiling her from the city of Laurel altogether. Unforgiving landscapes, of which she cannot help but become a manifestation, compel Blanche to seek shelter in the most unlikely of places. By the end of the play, she has not only been driven out of every physical haven she has ever known, she is literally driven out of her mind.

While we may presuppose that Blanche's roles are naturally dictated by her inescapable personal and externally changing landscapes, the con- cept of spatial dictation grows more intricate and stimulating when those landscapes converge and integrate into the present moment. Through landscape theory, we become aware of compound layers of interacting environments and are therefore able to act and react with them all. Because of her fractured mental state and weakness for heavy drinking, Blanche already exists in multiple landscapes simultaneously. While physically sitting on a New Orleans park bench talking to Mitch, she is at the same time wholly present at the lake where her young husband has just committed suicide. By using detailed visualization to create the unseen landscapes Blanche was experiencing, it was then possible to react to them as though they were as palpable to her as the physi- cal landscape she and Mitch shared. I then choreographed kinesthetic responses to the invisible world into which her madness had thrust her and allowed both landscapes to have psychophysical effects in tandem. A specific instance of this can be cited in scene ten.

Blanche, while physically in the Kowalski's New Orleans home, in her mind believes and *acts* as though she is in the friendly embrace of her childhood home, Belle Reve. She thinks that she is entertaining suitors on their way to a moonlight swim at the old rock quarry. Stanley's entrance effectively splits her reality, thrusting her into two diametrically opposed environments at the same time. In one landscape, space dictates that she is the celebrated object of affection of a throng of would-be suitors; in the other, she is an unwanted house guest in danger. By expanding awareness to include both landscapes, her movement and gesture must be expanded to include physical responses to both.

Playing with theory offered actualization of tangible direction in the generation of blocking, gesture, and focus. To engage the landscapes of physical place and internal place, it was necessary to layer reactions to the inhabitants of both. For example, the line "How is my sister?" was directed toward the brute in the kitchen. Before moving in his direction, a coy, apologetic bow was given to the Belle Reve suitors. The doorway between the kitchen and bedroom became the bridge between the two landscapes. The first landscape offered a place inhabited by men Blanche could run to for protection. Because that landscape was hallucination, Stanley was able to overtake her, but the interaction with the invisible landscape offered solid visualization and images to respond to. It offered a *place* to run for. Instead of self-generating, I relied on spatial dictation to guide my choices.

The phenomenon of dual-landscape stimulus is further evidenced in Williams' stage directions for the end of scene ten and in the final scene of the play where Blanche is pursued by psychiatric workers. Blanche intermittently experiences those increasingly hostile landscapes through two progressively distorted lenses: madness and intoxication. Williams pulls the audience into the altered landscape of Blanche's mind by calling for jungle noise sound cues.[12] In essence, he paints the picture of Blanche's alternate landscapes by representing them audibly. Blanche becomes a cornered wild animal in the jungle. Here, the layering of actual and perceived landscapes provides the opportunity to physically react to the landscape of the Kowalski home, as well as to the jungle in Blanche's private consciousness. Space dictated a dual role: that of rape victim and of trapped animal. I used this awareness to motivate physical and vocal responses to both the visible and invisible threats by seeing and reacting to the jungle threat and to Stanley in pursuit, fighting for escape and running for shelter in two frightening landscapes.

Vocal application: the land is in the speech

"Each region has a distinctive tradition. One can hear the contours of the landscape shape the tonality and spirit of the music. The memory of the people is echoed in the music."[13]

As I began to craft Blanche's voice and speech patterns, I used interaction with landscape to help achieve authenticity in the dialect, spirit, and cadence of her oral communication. The International Phonetic Alphabet (IPA) arms the dialect hunter with tools for transforming vowels and consonants to arrive at a character's native way of speaking. How might we use the concept of landscape to achieve greater depth? Music theorist P. J. Curtis believes that if one wishes to access the soul of a land, one must listen to its music. He suggests that the landscape of a region permeates the music, as well as the speech of its inhabitants.[14] If one can find the soul of a land by listening to its music, I propose that that one can find the soul of the music or the dialect of a region by studying its landscape.

To illustrate this point, imagine the wild and open landscape of Southwestern Ireland. Gently sloping hills of emerald green stretch as far as the eye can see. The land's moist climate and ocean breezes contribute to a sky often blanketed in thick, fast-moving silver clouds. But every so often the sun pierces through in brilliant traveling shafts and the light dances over the hills and lakes, highlighting the peaks and valleys of the terrain. These dips and climbs are at the very heart of the Southwestern Irish dialect. The landscape offers a sensual and visceral key to Irish speech; the rhythm and the flow of the language mirror the land itself. Conversely, one searching for a key to the hard-edged New York dialect might look for inspiration to the city's endless blocks of imposing and crowded skyscrapers jutting aggressively into the sky.

In her book *Freeing the Natural Voice,* Kristin Linklater states that "Many accents owe their definitive regionality to a configuration of mouth muscles which trap the voice in one particular place."[15] One may further argue that these regional placements are directly linked to the speaker's indigenous terrain since landscape images offer fertile ground for the crafting of a character's voice. Having the luxury of living near Blanche's ancestral home, I immersed myself into her environment with the intention of gathering character enhancing clues from her native land. The first inescapable truth that Blanche's landscape divulged, without subtlety, is that Mississippi is inordinately hot. As one will discover, natives often omit "ing" endings and frequently use non-rhotic speech, where the letter R is rarely spoken if not directly followed by a vowel. While research may give a performer a superficial understanding of these facts, a day in the sweltering Mississippi sun gives these patterns greater resonance. It can be argued, perhaps cheekily, that these people were simply too *hot* to finish their words. The regional voice has been robbed of some of its consonants by a scorching climate, while its smooth elongated vowels find echo in the languid roll of southern breezes and muddy rivers.

Just as physical landscapes inspired Ashley and Williams, I immersed myself in the landscape of Blanche's youth, taking cues from her childhood environment to craft a natural voice with layers of complications reflecting her sprawling, genteel surroundings. I used non-rhotic speech as a sensory reaction to the heat and based the tempo of her natural voice on Mississippi river currents. Like the powerful waterways, her speech was rapid and fluid, stopping for no one.

In my journey through Blanche's native land, I found miles of fertile and flowery terrain in stark juxtaposition to the decay and ruins of deteriorating structures of once glorious estates. This dichotomy offered a framework for adding texture and levels to Blanche's voice. By deliberately altering pitch, tone, and rhythm, I created two contrasting voices. The first, lyrically rich, light, and airy in tone, belonged to those sections of text where Blanche remained lost in the memory of the refined, privileged landscape of Belle Reve. The second, less decorous voice, was deeper in tone and centered from the diaphragm. This voice emerged in response to the street/survival level earthiness of her New Orleans surroundings. I crafted my character's delivery by inviting specific qualities from her native landscape to interact—dictating tone, tempo, and the coloring of her speech.

The influence of landscape on Blanche's voice grew more complicated and exciting when I considered the fact that Blanche was simultaneously immersed within numerous parallel landscapes which were at violent odds with each other. Populous, urban New Orleans contrasted greatly with her uncrowded, rural upbringing, just as the convivial, childhood plantation environment of her youth differed from the cramped, two-room Kowalski house where Blanche felt unwanted and was ashamed. Such alien elements contributed to the warring landscapes of her past and her present. As Blanche fell victim to the extreme tension and strain caused by these incompatible landscapes, a third voice, more forceful and desperate in tone, emerged in times of great crisis. These voices, one for each of her landscapes, intertwined, submerged, and resurfaced according to circumstance. Although this three-voice construct may seem disharmonious or even schizophrenic, it allowed me the unexpected benefit of achieving a visceral understanding of Blanche's mental discord and the insight to discover landscape as sensory stimulus. This discovery of, and interaction with, a multi-layered landscape found echo in the discovery made previously in the exploration of spatial dictation.

Framing the body

The application of landscape theory to *A Streetcar Named Desire* not only provided rich layers in the area of voice, but it also furthered the development of Blanche's physicality. Linking Blanche bodily to landscape is textually supported. This is readily apparent in the scene where Blanche first meets her would-be suitor, Mitch. Blanche refers to herself in landscape vernacular, explaining that her first name is French for "white" and that her last name, Dubois, is French for "woods." She suggests that Mitch might remember the name by thinking of an orchard in spring, thus representing herself as an idyllic landscape, a pristine and youthful still life suitable for framing. The act of calculated framing became the basis for my physical portrayal of Blanche.

Una Chaudhuri writes that landscape is the "framing or staging, of geography,"[16] noting that the practice of framing was rooted not in theatre, but in the visual arts, particularly painting. Visual and performance artists have utilized framing for centuries. Similarly, everyday people are constantly in the process of choosing what to display and/or conceal. Typically, we show what is most attractive and painstakingly hide what we perceive to be flawed. Actors make sure to show their good side just as painters and photographers crop and frame their images to show only what they wish their audience to see.

Here, I played with a new approach to landscape interaction by electing to treat Blanche as though she were creating or framing landscapes of herself, ever aware of the viewer's gaze. The architecture of her body at rest or in motion to even the most subtle tilt of her head was designed so that the observer would just *happen* to see her best view. I altered the degree of deliberation according to the fluctuation of her needs and who was in the room at the time. For instance, during her scenes with Mitch, she constantly shifted herself so she would appear most alluring from Mitch's viewpoint. This practice was largely abandoned when she was alone with her sister Stella. As a general rule, articulated body framing occurred when Blanche was in the presence of a man. I allowed her to suddenly drop this framing when she was alone and gradually stripped her of her framing in public as her mental state grew more agitated and alcohol or psychosis caused her grasp of reality to slip.

The call of the wild

While on a recent retreat in Southwestern Ireland to study under the late philosopher John O'Donohue, I overheard a fellow traveler say she would be "unpacking from this trip for a very long time." I find that sentiment an apt response to my own trek through the wilds of land-scape theory application. As I reflect on what I learned from playing with theory, I find evidence of tangible growth in the character devel-opment of Blanche Dubois. An interactive partnership with landscape inspired very specific voice and body modifications. Landscape entered and divided Blanche's speech, and dictated body posturing, possessing her and ultimately causing her to create a landscape of herself. Tenuous as my methods may have been, I gained from the experiment.

It would be naïve to suggest that the trails I attempted to blaze would lead another to the same territories of discovery. I do, however, have a fervent belief that theory-play offers a provocative paradigm shift from traditional methodology. There is much to be discovered in terms of praxis and development of theory discourse. Perhaps the most valuable conclusion would be to simply offer a broad call to practitioners, one that urges creative interplay within theoretical constructs. Just as the-atrical text remains dead until given life on the stage, theory remains bereft of resonance unless creatively explored. We must not let the messy work of exploration deter us from taking the journey. Like Mee, we must explode what has been established and make it our own. We know what has come before, now what can we create for the future? Fear of the unknown must be replaced with enthusiastic curiosity, which finds voice in a familiar cry. It's one of Williams' favorite directives to move forward, "En Avant!"

Notes

1. Daniel Stein, "Physical Theatre" (lecture presented at the Accademia dell'Arte Summer Symposium, Tuscany, Italy, June 27–July 4, 2010).
2. Charles L. Mee, "I Like to Take a Greek Play," *Theatre Journal* 59 (October 2007), 361–3.
3. Una Chaudhuri, "Land/Scape/Theory," in *Land/Scape/Theater*, eds Elinor Fuchs and Una Chaudhuri (Ann Arbor: University of Michigan Press, 2002), 15.
4. Ibid., 131.
5. Gertrude Stein, *Selected Writings of Gertrude Stein* (New York: Random House, 1946), 510.
6. In his production notes for *The Glass Menagerie*, Tennessee Williams calls for the unconventional use of theatrical techniques in order to create a closer approximation of truth. He suggests that organic, poetic approaches could lead to a more successful and vivid expression of things than the use of straight realism. Tennessee Williams, *The Glass Menagerie* (New York: Chelsea House, 1945), 7.
7. Arthur J. Sabatini, "The Sonic Landscapes of Robert Ashley," in *Land/Scape/Theater*, 330.

8. Williams, in his collection of *Notebooks*, cites his love for New Orleans, saying "Here surely is the place I was made for if any place in this funny old world" (ed. Margaret Bradham Thornton [New Haven: Yale University Press, 2006], 131). Williams returned to the city many times and actually lived there when he began work on *Streetcar Named Desire*.
9. Sabatini, 327.
10. Jon Jory, *Tips: Ideas for Actors* (New Hampshire: Smith and Krauss, 2000), 2.
11. Sabatini, 327.
12. Tennessee Williams, *A Streetcar Named Desire* (New York: New Directions, 1947), 186, 194.
13. John O' Donohue, *Beauty: The Invisible Embrace* (New York: HarperCollins, 2004).
14. P. J. Curtis, "Irish Music" (lecture presented at the Contented Heart Retreat with John O' Donohue, Ballyvaughan, Ireland, May 1–11, 2007).
15. Kristin Linklater, *Freeing the Natural Voice* (New York: Drama Book, 1976), 145.
16. Una Chaudhuri, 15.

17
Under the Influence

Alissa Mello

As a performer and theatre maker, applying theory, and, more recently, theorizing my practice have played a key though not always explicit role in informing my work. Yet, as a relatively intuitive artist, "Theory" and "Theorizing" remain a bit intimidating, and playing with theory within my creative process seems antithetical. The dialogue between theory/theorizing and practice[1] is challenged by inherent differences between abstract contemplation about something and the physical doing/experiencing of something. And yet new insight and practical applications emerge in the struggle to negotiate this gap. Removing the capital "T" from Theory, as Hollis W. Huston[2] suggests, allows me to consider theory as simply a "proposition"[3] about something or a set of ideas based on a method of logic, observation, or the gathering of information. Given this understanding, I am interested in how theory can be used as a creative tool throughout a production process. As my own theatre project develops, I have the sense that I am simultaneously playing with, and being played by, theory.

This case study is a two-fold reflection on theory and theorizing, as well as literary analysis and criticism within my 2010 project with Inkfish,[4] *Three Good Wives*.[5] This production is also the practice component for my doctoral research—a qualitative, inductive investigation of workshop techniques developed and used by two contemporary European puppet-theatre makers. For the purposes of this case study, I consider work-in-progress moments on *Three Good Wives* from its conception to the beginning of my collaboration with the designer, Michael Kelly, and composer, Joemca. This case study looks at the use value of creating an ideological "grab bag" of theory, analysis, criticism, stories, and experiences from which to define and create characters, and develop a thematic core for each of the production's three scenes. Moreover, it considers how theory/theorizing is affecting, guiding, and influencing creative development and decision making, as well as the evolution of workshop techniques within my own practice. While writing this case study, the theoretical dialectic around puppet-theatre production and audience reception revealed a productive tension that exists in the creation and perceptions of life and agency in a performing object, and ultimately shaped my production process. Documenting my practice as research demonstrates how I intentionally bring together different theories and practices, consciously theorize about the practice of others, and then experiment with those practices in the development of our new puppet show.

Case study

The characters and thematic threads of the scenes for *Three Good Wives* will be developed using a grab bag of theory, as well as feminist literary criticism, folklore traditions, alternative histories, contemporary cultural criticism, art criticism, anthropology, and verbatim material gathered from online social media, news articles, and books. A "grab bag" is often defined as "an assortment of miscellaneous items."[6] I use it here to evoke a sense of gathering an assortment of ideas or propositions which one allows to influence, associatively or accidentally, one's thoughts about a particular problem, or in this case, character or theme. Ideas in a grab bag are not necessarily used together in an obvious or customary way. Although I am not literally placing concepts in a bag and blindly drawing on them as in chance models, there is a similar sense of randomness as I allow my investigations to sway the character and scene development. For the purposes of the case study, I will focus on my use of feminist literary criticism drawing on the work of Keri Elizabeth Ames, Marylin A. Katz, and Nancy Felson-Rubin; art criticism focusing on Giancarlo Fiorenza's interpretation of Giovanni Stradano's 1561–2 painting of Penelope; and Homer's *The Odyssey* to develop the character of and scene with Penelope.[7] Each criticism points to a contemporary feminist reading of Penelope which counters the notion of the passively waiting, simplistic "good" wife. Writing at this early stage is both challenging and a bit frightening. I know that much will change over the course of the project; new ideas will emerge and themes will shift. What I think now may or may not be radically adjusted during the next phases of development. However, documentation is a mechanism to capture what might otherwise be forgotten for future reflection and understanding about the creative process and uses of theory. Before investigating the function of theory in my current creative process, let me briefly illustrate the history of the project.

Where it began

The development of this project is more a product of intuition than methodical planning. The initial inspiration is a specific feminist re-imagining, or proposition, about Penelope by Margaret Atwood in her book *The Penelopiade: The Myth of Penelope and Odysseus*.[8] *Three Good Wives* however evolved into an original puppet-theatre piece that explores contemporary military wives' stories through three mytho-historic female characters: Penelope from Homer's *The Odyssey*, Scheherazade from *The Arabian Nights*, and Mandodari from the *Ramayana* to investigate the themes of revenge, war, regret, waiting, and healing. It will be developed using an experimental, non-narrative structure to create a meditation or visual poem. The research and gathering occurs in bursts of activity between which I work on numerous projects. As I collected information for my grab bag, a conscious and unconscious dialogue took place between the various ideas, research in the studio for my dissertation, my own experiences, news, and global affairs. From this, I crafted a thematic narrative accompanied by possible images. At one moment and without actively working on the production, I decided that to create a full evening production, a story about Penelope would not be sufficient to address the various and complex issues affecting women today as a result of our ongoing wars. The decision to add two additional mytho-historic characters was prompted by my own questions about one's duty to country during periods of war or violence, and relationships between storytelling and healing. Because of these questions, I felt that I needed at least two other characters, and the following women emerged as possibilities: Mandodari from the *Ramayana* and Sheherazade from *The Arabian Nights*. Mandodari appeared while reading Paula Richman's *Many Ramayanas*. I have had an ongoing interest in the story since doing research about the puppets used in the annual performance during Ram Lila at Ramnagar in India. Sheherazade emerged as a potential character while I was studying ethnography and performance in the Middle East at New York University and reading Susan Slymovichs' *The Performance of Human Rights in Morocco*. Each of these female characters creates an opportunity for striking visual images that address contemporary women's issues around waiting, war, duty, and healing.

Concepts are easy . . . what about the play?

So here I am—three mytho-historic characters and a vague notion about weaving these with contemporary women's stories. Where does it go from here? The grab bag of existing bodies of theoretical material, literary and art criticism about each of the characters, coupled with the original stories, informed our creative process and produced additional images to play with in preparation for going into rehearsal. I and, once in rehearsal, we are hybridizing theory and idea, using them as tools to develop character and narrative. This gives me an opportunity to consider ideas individually and together that I previously might not have if left to my own devices. For the character of Penelope, there are three key themes that have emerged from my research: fidelity and knowing, memory, and recognition. Each was researched from a feminist perspective. These themes inform my own conflicted portrait of Penelope and notions of contemporary women waiting for family to return from war.

The moment we have chosen to locate our scene is at midnight when Penelope is waiting with her maids for the return of Odysseus, and is secretly unweaving the burial shroud she is making for Odysseus' father, Laertes. Her deception is used to forestall the suitors' demands that she marry one of them. The scene will explore the fear, desire, hope, anxiety, and fantasy associated with waiting for, and the return of, a husband from war. On the one hand, we will position Penelope as a good and faithful wife; on the other, we are exploring her fantasies of potential infidelity in a cabaret song and dance number with two-dimensional suitor puppets, and the placement of her ambivalence about Odysseus' return possibly in dialogue with the Greek poet Sappho who would possess one of the maids in order to speak.[9] We will use this eclectic collection of references to develop the play text in collaboration with the performers and a playwright during rehearsal. Penelope's character will also be informed by contemporary women's experiences of waiting for loved ones in a time of war as found in news stories, on websites dedicated to wives and partners of military personnel, on television, and in fiction and non-fiction books. Through our re-imagining of Penelope's character, drawn from feminist character analysis and contemporary accounts, we aspire to tell a story exploring the challenges, hopes, fears, and fantasies of women waiting for someone's return from war today.

Penelope is most often associated with faithfulness, particularly in contrast to Helen of Troy and Clytemnestra. When describing Stradano's 1561 to 1562 painting of Penelope, Fiorenza notes "instead of illustrating any one particular episode from *The Odyssey*, Stradano visualizes Penelope's industry to underscore her virtue and fidelity, her most renowned traits."[10] In her article "The Oxymoron of Fidelity in Homer's *Odyssey* and Joyce's *Ulysses*," Ames argues that one of Penelope's trials is an unfaithful husband.[11] Atwood proposes that Penelope was aware Odysseus was "playing the field" on his long journey home. Our interpretation leads to the possibility that although Penelope is not unfaithful, she is fully conscious that she could have been, suggesting a tension between her public and private selves. As Felson-Rubin proposes in her book *Regarding Penelope: From Character to Poetics*,[12] throughout *The Odyssey*, Penelope is simultaneously an object of the male gaze and a subject acting from her own desires. In other words, the good faithful wife is perhaps the public self behind which is a subject who may have very different and unarticulated desires, wants, needs, and fears.

Another core debate that has influenced our understanding of Penelope revolves around her recognition of Odysseus. Did she or did she not recognize Odysseus upon his return? If yes, when did she recognize him, and why did she test his identity with the marital bed test?[13] It is often supposed that Penelope does not fully recognize or know it is Odysseus until the marriage bed test. Katz, in *Penelope's Renown: Meaning and Indeterminacy in The Odyssey*, however, argues that the trial of the marriage bed is not as much about her recognizing Odysseus, as it is about Penelope forcing Odysseus to reinstate himself and his being in relation to her. As I think about this in relation to contemporary women, and men, currently waiting for people to return from war, I cannot help but wonder how separation affects each individual and what a process of reinstating one's self in relation to another means. What does the need for active proclamation about one's status in relation to another say about an individual's fears, concerns, or even ambivalence about a relationship between two individuals? Penelope's apparent ambivalence is countered by what Felson-Rubin suggests is Odysseus' own knowledge or belief about his wife. Felson-Rubin states that Odysseus "alone apprehends her [Penelope's] strength and thrives on her wiliness" and that it is he who longs for the "like-mindedness . . . of a man and his wife 'being like minded in their thoughts.'"[14] Though Odysseus may pine for return, our scene will explore Penelope and contemporary women through this tension between public status, the notion of the good wife particularly in relation to contemporary military families, and a private conflicted state.

Throughout *The Odyssey*, Penelope, in addition to historically representing the good and faithful wife, is also referred to at different moments

by a variety of character types: mother, enchantress, weaver, siren, heroine, adulteress, and equal. In acknowledging these different attributes,
feminist critics broaden our notion of Penelope beyond a simple, waiting, good wife. Felson-Rubin suggests that Penelope has numerous plot
potentialities: courtship and marriage, dalliance and infidelity, disdain
and bride of death, patience and cunning. Katz proposes that a key to
Penelope's character is her "constancy and cleverness."[15] Each of these
propositions lends itself to a complex reading of Penelope as a character
that extends her archetype and opens a new space for Penelope as a character. She is a faithful wife, patiently awaiting her husband's return, who
uses deception to fend off a group of suitors after her wealth and power.
But she is also a complex matrix of potential other narratives.

Practicing play and playing with practice

So far, this case study has described how I have been using a grab bag
of ideas to develop one of the three characters in our production. This
grab bag has been a means to problematize and enrich the character
development and dramaturgy. Yet while this has been a particularly
constructive use of theory and critical analyses in the early, formation
stage, I anticipate there will be numerous changes as our show moves
into the next phase. These changes will be a direct result of the collaboration and interaction between the other artists as we engage with
each other, the propositions that I share with the creative team based
on my research and theoretical engagements, and their own research,
personalities as performers, ideas, and world views.

The influences of theory—and theorizing—in and on my creative
process are not limited to the character and dramaturgical questions
above. They also extend to methods of production and rehearsal techniques that we will implement. These influences, both overt and covert,
emerge from my current doctoral research and theoretical framing of
other artists' practices. Much of my fieldwork at this stage has been with
Stuffed Puppet, a performer-led, adult puppet-theatre company founded
in 1978 by actor and puppeteer Neville Tranter. Tranter's productions
are solo performances played by him and numerous puppet characters.
I was a participant-observer at three weeks of rehearsals for a production,[16] and a participant in one workshop. In addition, I conducted
numerous interviews and conversations with Tranter and his collaborators. My observations raised numerous questions about character development, interaction between live actors and puppets, collaboration, and
rehearsal; and my theorizing about Tranter's practice is having an effect

on how I am thinking now about character and on how Inkfish will rehearse for *Three Good Wives*. The immediate questions for me are: what is meant by equal status between ontologically different characters? How do the differences affect performance and character interaction? What possibilities does it open for character representation? And, how does one create it?

Here I will discuss just one aspect of Tranter's practice, which focuses on relationships between ontologically different characters, specifically between live human and puppet characters. In his work, Tranter strives for what he refers to as "equal status" between characters on stage. Although the concept of equal positioning between characters is certainly not new in theatre, creating it between ontologically different characters poses certain challenges to performance technique and opens an interesting space to play with representation on stage. By ontologically different performers, I am referring to the fact that by their very nature live actors and puppets are different. One is a living being, while the other is a constructed performing object, which is often manipulated to appear alive. In other words, it is the difference between being (live human actor) and symbolic representation (puppet). In rehearsal for *Three Good Wives*, questions that emerge from Tranter's methodology and technique will result in a practical investigation about reception of live and puppet characters and what performers need to do on stage to create equal status between them.

According to Tranter, "equal status is something that takes place on the stage between two believable characters."[17] But what is a "believable character"? And how does one create a "believable character" with an object or puppet performer or even with a live actor performing with and in the same world as a puppet? To a certain extent, believability in either performer is an agreement between performers and audience participants. As Jena Osman states in her article "The Puppet Theatre is the Epic Theatre":

> While the puppet theater has great powers of enchantment, it is impossible for the spectator to forget for long that s/he is agreeing to be put under a spell, that s/he is agreeing to grant humanity to an object. The pact is always in view, the device always laid bare.[18]

Believability then is not simply in the object but rather in the audience participant's[19] recognition of the object, its physical life, and, if used, its vocal meaning of words, tone, and tempo of utterance and their agreement to accept and co-create the life of a character.

Numerous scholars have theorized the concept of co-creating the life of a puppet.[20] This act of co-creation involves investment from the audience participant and the performing artist. The puppeteer—puppet—audience participant dynamic has also been discussed by numerous scholars[21] but most often in relation to the "life" of a puppet. I am suggesting that it is both the perception of life of the puppet and an inner emotional state. These perceptions, of course, overlap, are intertwined, and are far from clear-cut distinctions. To the audience participant, life of a puppet character is, I suggest, an interpreted state of being in which the puppet character is perceived as a recognizable, psychological subject. In other words, the puppet has an inner emotional life and presence that is performed on stage. However, puppets do not literally have an inner emotional life; they can only represent or symbolize the intention of emotion and presence through design and construction, gesture, tempo, and tone (if a voice or other audio component is used). Each of these elements and attributes is constructed and performed by the live performer. What is read as an inner emotional life of a puppet is a collaboration between the puppeteer, puppet, and audience participant. In other words, the audience participant co-creates and completes the inner life of the puppet through their active participation, interpretation of events, and recognition of gesture, tone, and atmosphere on stage. This co-creation shifts a puppet from a mere object to a character with the possibility of interaction with others.[22]

How then does one create equal status between live and puppet characters? Creating this perception between characters is a key consideration in Tranter's workshops. Additionally, equal status between two different ontological types of performers is important because it expands the palette of possible interaction between characters—live human and puppet—and the role of the puppeteer on stage. The more common relationship between puppets and puppeteers on stage is one in which a puppeteer, though visible, typically recedes into the background. Tranter goes on to describe a physical scenario of what equal status might look like:

> A good example: the first meeting of Romeo and Juliet at the banquet. The choreography is generally a direct line towards each other and on the same level, the body language of the two the same. If you did this movement as an exercise with two balls in your hands meeting each other, then the balls would also have equal status.[23]

Interestingly, his example uses ontologically alike performers. Though the principles of using direct lines in space, similar body language, and level apply, what happens to each character when the interaction is between a live performer and a puppet? How must a live actor's performance technique accommodate the representational performance style of a puppet? How does creating believability between the two affect dramaturgy, design, and rehearsal?

Additionally, reconsidering these questions about believability and equal status between live and puppet characters informs my decisions about each character. Who will be represented by a live actor? Who will be represented by a puppet? In what ways will these choices affect character interaction? For example, in the *Three Good Wives'* scene with Penelope, we have decided that Penelope will be a puppet. One live performer will double as narrator and will voice the puppet. In the scene, Penelope will be with two maids who will also function as her manipulators. Penelope will be the dominant character and voice, yet she will also be subject to the manipulation of others—society, waiting, war, etc. What will the various combinations of representation on stage mean in light of the propositions that are and will be used to develop each of the three mytho-historic characters? Will Penelope, as a puppet, be stronger or weaker as a character or an archetype? Does making her a puppet open the possibility for the character to exist between strength and weakness, to be ambivalent and conflicted? Or is it a question of representation and levels of identification—meaning that, as a puppet that is co-created by the audience spectators, she is not just an object or body on stage but also a character that has the potential to allow a particular kind of personal identification and empathy with the core themes of war and waiting? Although many of these questions are unanswered at this stage in the production, they will lead the way in our practical exploration to further our collaborative play and experimentation during design, construction, and rehearsal. One benefit of utilizing theory in performance making is that it generates abstract questions that must be explored and answered practically/physically, thus enriching the work. Just as Ames, Katz, Felson-Rubin, and my own interpretations suggest alternate propositions about Penelope's character, Tranter's methodology suggests practical ways to explore these propositions in rehearsal.

This case study foregrounds ways that I have been playing with, and am being played by, theory and theorizing, and how a grab bag of theory, criticism, verbatim, experience, and ideas have influenced the early development of our production. Our grab bag is a means to generate ideas from outside my own frame of reference and experience to develop, explore, and problematize the characters, themes, and dramaturgy in our show. This model has also functioned as a way of introducing and exploring propositions that are counter to my own knowledge base and assumptions, and thus widens and deepens the possibilities for character and theme development. In addition, I have discussed how a series of questions that emerged from an exploration of another artist's work has influenced my thinking not only about the field of puppet theatre but also about relationships between live actors and puppets on stage. My consideration and interpretation of specific theory and practice has in turn affected the character development and dramaturgy, and is beginning to affect the design and rehearsal structures of this production. While much of this exploration to date has been mine, each of these theoretical propositions and methodologies is and will be shared with the creative team through discussion and will therefore inform our collaborative work in the rehearsal studio as we build our production. While I have the sense, as mentioned above, of both playing with and being played by theory, this reflection also suggests a way in which I am under its influence.[24] Being "under the influence" connotes a state of being altered by externalities. I have learned over the course of looking at the work of others, and theorizing about it in practice and performance, that the practice of making theatre is rather a balance—consciously or not—of controlled and uncontrolled influences and ideas that come together at a particular time and place. This balance is influenced by each collaborator's own set of knowledge and project specific research. In this case, I find that I am covertly influenced beyond my overt intention to learn from others, explore their work, and play with theory/theorizing and ideas. I am indeed "under the influence."

Notes

1. The word practice is tricky because it is used to refer to both training and art making. I believe that practice in the sense of art making is closer to theory making than practice in the sense of training. In my case study, I am using practice in the sense of art making. I discuss theorizing in the sense of speculating on or about something. It is a way of reflecting on, exploring, and interrogating one's own and other artists' practice to develop a personal methodology for practice.
2. Huston has taught at Washington University and the University of Delaware. His publications include *The Actor's Instrument: Body Theory, Stage* (1992) and he is a contributor in *Acting (Re) Considered* edited by Phillip Zarrilli.
3. Hollis W. Huston, "The Gest of the Breath," *Theatre Journal*, 36.2 (1984), 12.
4. For more information please go to www.inkfishart.com.
5. *Three Good Wives* was developed in association with Little Angel Theatre, with support from the Centre for Excellence in Training for Theatre and The Puppet Centre Trust in London, and The Jerome Foundation. The production premiered in March 2010.

6. *The New Oxford American Dictionary Second Edition*, ed. Erin McKean (New York: Oxford University Press, 2005), 730.

7. Penelope references the faithful wife of Odysseus in Homer's *The Odyssey*.

8. Margaret Atwood, *The Penelopiad: The Myth of Penelope and Odysseus* (Edinburgh: Canongate, 2005).

9. After this case was written, the scene ideas were explored in rehearsal but were not used in the final production. Instead the scene evolved into a nightmare of the puppet Penelope, where she devolved into insect-like behavior and attacked her maids.

10. Giancarlo Fiorenza, "Penelope's Web: Francesco Primaticcio's Epic Revision at Fontainebleau," *Renaissance Quarterly*, 59.3 (2008), 795–827.

11. Keri Elizabeth Ames, "The Oxymoron of Fidelity in Homer's *Odyssey* and Joyce's *Ulysses*," *Joyce Studies Annual*, 14 (2004), 132–74.

12. Nancy Felson-Rubin, *Regarding Penelope: From Character to Poetics* (Princeton: Princeton University Press, 1994).

13. In *The Odyssey*, Penelope tests Odysseus after the battle with the suitors by suggesting that she will have the marital bed moved out of the marital chamber. This moment in the story has been used to argue a number of possibilities and conjectures about Penelope's motivation ranging from her verifying Odysseus' identity to teasing him. Each proposition points to a very different kind of person.

14. Ibid.

15. Marylin A. Katz, *Penelope's Renown: Meaning and Indeterminacy in the "Odyssey"* (Princeton: Princeton University Press, 1991).

16. The production is Stuffed Puppet Theatre's 2008 *Cuniculus*.

17. Neville Tranter, personal email communication, April 30, 2009.

18. Ingrid Schaffner and Carin Kuoni, *The Puppet Show* (Philadelphia: Institute of Contemporary Art, University of Pennsylvania, 2008).

19. I am using the phrase audience participant as framed by Anne Bogart in her recent book *And then, you act: making art in an unpredictable world* (London: Routledge, 2007) to call attention to the idea of an active rather than a passive spectator.

20. Scholars who have theorized the concept of co-creation include Petr Bogatreyev in his article "The Interconnection of Two Similar Semiotic Systems: The Puppet Theater and the Theater of Living Actors," and Jiri Veltrusky in his article "Puppetry and Acting." Both can be found in *Semiotica: The Semiotic Study of Puppets, Masks, and Performing Objects*, 47 (1983), and most recently John Bell in his introduction to his book *American Puppet Modernism: Essays on the Material World in Performance* (New York: Palgrave Macmillan, 2008).

21. Key scholars and writings include John Bell's *American Puppet Modernism: Essays on the Material World in Performance*. 1st edn (New York: Palgrave Macmillan, 2008); Thomas A. Green and W. J. Pepicello's article "Semiotic Interrelationships in the Puppet Play," *Semiotica: The Semiotic Study of Puppets, Masks, and Performing Objects*, 47 (1983); Steve Tillis' *Toward an Aesthetics of the Puppet: Puppetry as a Theatrical Art. Contributions in Drama and Theatre Studies*, 0163-3821; no. 47, (New York; London: Greenwood, 1992); and Jiri Veltrusky's article "Puppetry and Acting," *Semiotica: The Semiotic Study of Puppets, Masks, and Performing Objects*, 47 (1983).

22. Here I am concerned with a particular use of performing objects and puppets as characters. There are numerous examples of theatre work in which the artist(s) is not interested in creating characters but rather an abstract visual experience.
23. Neville Tranter, personal email communication, April 30, 2009.
24. Acknowledgments: I would like to thank Neville Tranter and Stuffed Puppet Theatre for sharing their art, technique, and thoughts about puppet theatre. For their insight, support, and thoughtful comments, I would like to thank Matthew Cohen, Michael Kelly, Frances Mello, Robin Ruby, Rachael Weisman, and Claudia Vorwaller. The research with Stuffed Puppet Theatre is partially funded by grants from The Central Research Fund at the University of London and The Helen Shackleton Fund. Additional research was conducted at and partially funded by Institut International de la Marionnette. Our production was supported by a residency with The Centre for Excellence in Training for Theatre, The Puppet Centre Trust, Royal Holloway, and by a travel and study grant from The Jerome Foundation.

18
Modulating Theory: Breaking New Ground in Musical Theatre Study

John Bell

Which comes first, the words or the music?

Theory is a set of principles used to shape method. As disciplines evolve, theory follows suit—quickly disposing of and/or transforming accepted notions of practice. In the study of musical theatre performance, past and existing theory has focused on the literary principles of a song's lyrics—rhyme, alliteration, meter, etc., as a key to shaping the methods by which actors and directors develop captivating performances. In recent years, as a new generation of musical theatre composers has emerged, attention to the musical principles of a song—melody, harmony, rhythm, etc.—as an increasingly useful tool in developing the singing actor's craft.

This relatively recent shift in the consideration of theory and practice for musical theatre performance took time to evolve. Formal study of musical theatre performance didn't really begin to take shape until the 1970s. Early performance-oriented musical theatre degree programs primarily endeavored to combine the resources of existing acting, dance, and music departments into a coherent course of study producing triple threat actor/singer/dancers.

One of the key developments of musical theatre training programs was the recognition of the need to offer acting courses specifically addressing the musical theatre repertoire. As new courses in musical theatre performance emerged, teachers began to ask important questions about, and experiment with, new ways to best train singing actors. Early progenitors conjectured that effective song acting was best achieved by focusing, as non-musical acting study does, on literary elements. This meant focusing on the work of the lyricist and attempting to make the study of song as similar to the study of monologue as possible. It was the logical first step in the evolution of performance theory for musical theatre training.

This approach, espoused by renowned singing and dramatic coaches such as David Craig[1] and H. Wesley Balk,[2] gives primacy to the written word as a first point of entry into song interpretation—an approach that is commensurate with the standard emphasis on script analysis used in the study of plays. By treating song lyrics as if they have as much literary value as a monologue or a scene, these master teachers elevated musical theatre's standing and cultivated a generation of performers and teachers who believe that an effective song lyric can reveal as much character and story as an effective play.

In treating song lyrics as monologues, early models encouraged performers to imbue songs with naturalism, delivering the lyric as if it were a realistic passage of conversational prose. Once rehearsed as a piece of spoken, literary text, the student was asked to speak the text while the music was played as underscoring. The theory behind this approach suggests that by treating the text as a monologue set to musical underscoring, the actor will gain new insights into how and why the character might eventually *need to sing* the thoughts. Consequently, the final stage in this theoretical construct asked the actor to sing the song as written. These early, text-based theorists helped musical theatre performers understand that careful analysis of textual elements—rhyme, alliteration, vocabulary, and form—provides insight into character motivation and intention in the same way that a non-singing actor mines dramatic value from the scansion of verse, or by scoring a scene into identifiable beats.

Many benefits were borne of these early theories. First and foremost, these approaches awakened singing actors to the notion that merely singing well would not suffice for the demands of the modern musical. Coaches like Craig and Balk realized that as musical theatre became more realistic, audiences expected deep emotional truth and active dramatic structures, qualities that go far beyond beautiful singing—a trait that has been traditionally paramount in opera.

Moreover, these early performance theories also deepened performers' awareness of the art and craft of lyric writing. By focusing attention on the minute components of the lyricist's craft, performers noted the dramatic construct of a song: a clever rhyme scheme becomes a clue to character intellect; punctuation becomes cues for intention and phrasing; and vocal quality and breath phrasing reveal objective and tactic. In short, these early approaches legitimized musical theatre performance and, by extension, musical theatre in general. But as with most theories in a new field of study, these early theories have limitations, which, once revealed, warrant a new set of theoretical explorations in order to move the art form forward. Focusing attention primarily on the lyricists' contribution to a song reveals two areas where the established theories on methodology remain inadequate in meeting the evolving demands of musical theatre performance.

The first of these is the acute sense that song lyrics, typically written in verse, do not translate efficiently into prose. Song lyrics, constrained by rhyme schemes and dictated by rhythm and tempo, become artificial when forced into prose-like elocution. In encouraging singing actors to treat a verse-like form—such as a lyric—prosaically, the actor is often forced to contradict or deny the natural qualities of lyrics.

The second risk that these early theories pose is in backgrounding, or ignoring altogether, the contributions of the composer as a full partner in the dramatic expression. This risk grows more disconcerting as the list of significant musical dramatists has grown throughout the twentieth and twenty-first centuries. While not exhaustive, legendary writers such as Jerome Kern, Richard Rodgers, Leonard Bernstein, and Stephen Sondheim, along with newcomers such as Craig Carnelia, Stephen Schwartz, Adam Guettel, and Jason Robert Brown, have illuminated just how significant the contributions of the composer can be, serving as an equal partner in the storytelling.

So, although flawed, early approaches played an important role in the evolution of the field and the vacuums they exposed contributed to the organic evolution of new approaches. One of the most important new approaches is the emergence of an emphasis on a song's musical principles as a primary influence in the shifting terrain of musical theatre training.

Foregrounding the composer

The principles of music serve as the composer's language. The building blocks that comprise melody, rhythm, and harmony prove just as potent for the composer as words do for the playwright and lyricist. In fact, pitches, chords, and musical motives serve the composer (musical dramatist) much the same way that words, sentences, and paragraphs serve the playwright. In this way, music provides a non-literary subtext, revealing underlying meanings of literary construction. Just as early approaches to musical theatre performance opted to parallel non-musical analysis as a means to dramatic validity, new approaches suggest a similar alignment in application to music. Joseph P. Swain's

The Broadway Musical: A Critical and Musical Survey[3] was one of the first scholarly books to provide in-depth exploration of how a composer utilizes musical ideas to characterize situation. *Music Theory for Musical Theatre*,[4] which I co-authored with Steven Chicurel, explores in more precise detail how musical ideas are used by composers to tell dramatic stories. These theoretical texts suggest that careful attention to the way that musical elements contextualize situation and character creates an additional layer of subtext which adds to the tools that dramatic personnel can use to interpret musically driven, dramatic moments. As the musical has grown more sophisticated, it is no longer enough for tunesmiths to hang marketable, stand-alone songs on the flimsy architecture of a trivial libretto. Musical theatre aficionados have come to expect sophisticated musical storytelling in the hands of true musical dramatists. And in this way, true musical dramatists writing for the musical theatre are connecting with the art form of opera, the musical's earliest ancestor, which, in general, has always placed emphasis on the music and the virtuosity of the human voice. Complex storytelling and textured acting were mostly subservient to the musical score. Therefore, the conductor has traditionally been considered opera's most important production team member, receiving primacy over even the stage director. In opera, it is not uncommon for a stage director to be asked to alter blocking, reconsider characterization, and/or adjust dramatic pace upon the request (or demand!) of the maestro seeking to ensure optimal musical delivery. So, as musical theatre performance theory shifts and begins to highlight the composer's contributions, it also assumes an increased role for the musical director/conductor.

Theory in action

Since application of any emerging theory is best illustrated in production contexts, for the purposes of this chapter, I examine a production of James Lapine and Stephen Sondheim's 1987 musical *Into the Woods*, for which I served as the musical director and conductor, to postulate how actors', directors', and musical directors' knowledge of and attention to musical properties provide resources for achieving heightened dramatic expression. This case study will also detail tensions that developed as a result of these new resources and how they were applied.

Sondheim's score for *Into the Woods* is incredibly textured and dense. Captured in the music are direct representations of emotional states, revelation, character arc, and transformation, as well as potent themes such as community responsibility and the importance of parenting. Specifically, I wondered if exploration of the music in the rehearsal process could prove useful to actors and directors in enriching characterizations and dramatic moments. The psychological layers inherent in the story are key to the musical's emotional power. How would an examination of Sondheim's score reveal important cues about the musical's dramatic depth?

With *Into the Woods*, Lapine and Sondheim have created a quest musical, intertwining multiple fairy-tale characters around one fictional couple—a baker and his wife—and their quest to have a child. Each character ventures into the woods to pursue a wish and, along the way, confronts their own human frailties and sense of social responsibility. It is an adult exploration of adult issues through the perspectives of simplistic and iconic character types. For this case study, I examine three songs wherein musical ideas were notably and specifically used as a tool in the rehearsal process: "I Know Things Now," sung by Little Red Riding Hood; "Giants in the Sky," sung by Jack; and "No One is Alone," a quartet sung by Jack, Little Red, Cinderella, and the Baker.

Since the show is a quest musical, Sondheim gave each of the main characters a song that allowed them to reflect upon their adventures and share what they learned along the way. While Sondheim has been criticized for the overt didacticism in these songs, most critics note that his real achievement is the rich subtext found in the music.

In "I Know Things Now," Little Red Riding Hood sings of the terror of being swallowed whole by the Wolf, and the eventual liberation of having been cut, alive, from his belly. Emotionally, the journey is one of danger, excitement, relief, and revelation—a life journey encapsulated in a mere three minutes. She sings of being drawn down the wolf's "slimy path" and learning "secrets that I never want to know" and waiting "in the dark" and being "brought into the light" before positing that she has learned "many valuable things" that she hadn't known before, such as that "scary is exciting" and "nice is different than good."[5]

Musically, Sondheim depicts this life-altering experience through keen use of musical key. To characterize the swallowing, Sondheim supports the lyric with a vacillating passage of harmonic shifts, which tend to deny key stability. This creates a distorted and disturbing sense of *disorientation* as the melodic line intensifies. This use of chromatic shifts is a simple way of providing active and emotional context to her retelling of the violent act. In similar fashion, Sondheim then provides a clear tonal center, anchoring her reflection in a strong, stable major key. As she sings of now knowing many valuable things as a result of her experience, the music is firmly rooted in the key of C major, one of the most accessible and open keys in Western music.

These ideas, discussed in rehearsal between the actor, the musical director, and the stage director, helped to intensify the performance. For instance, after considering the musical subtext, the actor's performance became much more animated, especially in the use of gesture, facial expression, and diction. Her performance became an active reliving of the character's experience, rather than a commentative retelling of the story. The director also revised and simplified the original staging, which was overly active and forced the actress to cover as much stage territory as possible. The director discovered that so much movement simply got in the way—the song itself was active enough. As the staging was simplified, it allowed the actress to transfer much of the expression to gesture and diction. This made sense since the patter song nature of the lyric was frenetic enough to convey the action, so long as the actress was able to deliver the text precisely and with clear intention. As musical director, I shaped the dynamics and musical phrasing of both singer and orchestra to help support the actor, character, and situation. In short, the changes made by the performer, director, and musical director transformed an overly physical and busy patter song into a powerful expression of action and discovery. The performance fulfilled the song's purpose, illuminating the character's arc and advancing the plot.

Jack, like Little Red, also undergoes a major change after climbing the beanstalk, where he encounters an angry giant and his wife, and then scrambles down the plant with their stolen gold. His adrenalin-laced adventure is filled with ambiguity. While he sings of the wonder of "big, tall, terrible, awesome, scary" giants in the sky, he also considers the new discovery of "the roof, the house and the world" he never "thought to explore." In contemplating the new found wisdom of these two worlds— that of the sky and his mother's house, he admits that he wishes he could "live in between." Sondheim captures the nervous energy and action of his trek up and down the stalk through driving, less-harmonic articulations that accentuate the danger and risk as Jack sings "the fun is done, you steal what you can and run," only then to move to a return to the open and non-dissonant harmony of the song's major key. This return to the familiar is a powerful recovery for Jack and, as composed by Sondheim, it is a lush and voluptuous musical moment that brings him home on the lyric "the roof, the house and your mother at the door."[6] His ambiguity is a symbol of his journey from boyhood to manhood. As he yearns for adventure, he's still tied to his emotional attachments of home and family. And like Little Red, the rest of his story, contingent upon his return to the kingdom in the sky, is only possible because of the palpable reality of this event—a reality the audience experiences first-hand, due in part to the depth of Sondheim's musical writing.

In rehearsal, the specific study of musical principles impacted different choices the singer made in terms of vocal dynamics, building and receding in volume and urgency as he moves from safety into danger and back again. Choices regarding vocal quality also came into play. In the soothing portions of the song, the actors played with warmer vocal qualities and softer articulation. In passages of danger and threat, the actor used more specific and forceful diction, particularly in the emphasis of hard, plosive consonants, to echo the staccato articulation in the orchestration. This alternation of force and tenderness specified the actor's performance and resulted in a full rendering of the song's dramatic potential. For instance, the lyric "the fun is done, you steal what you can and run" was delivered with explosive emphasis on the pinched and punched delivery of "fun" and "done," as well as a stinging sense of what it means to steal. Then, as the singer comes to the lyric "the roof, the house and your mother at the door," the vowels were stretched and elongated to give the line a lush, legato quality that communicated comfort and resolution. This investigation of the language of music and its power to inform and enrich interpretation is a perfect example of this new theory in action.

Music as subtext

Sondheim uses musical subtext to highlight and strengthen key themes and to help build dramatic structure toward climax and denouement. In the Act II quartet "No One is Alone," the four main characters, orphaned and alone, are faced with the reality that survival will depend upon their willingness to establish new familial bonds. Each character—the Baker, Cinderella, Jack, and Little Red—has lost either a parent, grandparent, or spouse. The lyrics communicate the theme of parents and children in somewhat oblique ways: "Sometimes people leave you, halfway through the wood." The song suggests that fathers and mothers make mistakes "holding to their own, thinking they're alone." It also cautions that simple assignments of evil are a fool's errand, admonishing that "witches can be right, giants can be good."[7]

To support these important themes, Sondheim makes a conscious choice to add a musical motive, a motive he called the "bean theme,"[8] to the accompaniment. In the show, the bean motive is used anytime the magic beans are referenced. This motive also becomes a key phrase in the relationship between Rapunzel and her mother, the Witch. Rapunzel sings the theme on open ah vowels throughout the story. The Witch then uses this motive as she sings "Stay with me the world is dark and wild"[9] in her Act I ballad "Stay with Me."

"No One is Alone" is sung just as the story is building to the climactic killing of the Giant's wife. As Jack, Little Red, the Baker, and Cinderella lament their loneliness and pledge their commitment to one another, Sondheim inverts the musical motive and adds it to the accompaniment on the lyric "sometimes people leave you."[10] It's a simple choice used to powerful effect. The addition of this one, almost subconscious, musical texture reveals the full depth of the musical's overarching theme. Discussion of this one moment among the actors, stage director, musical director, and orchestra members proved revelatory in terms of moving the dramatic moment beyond mere emotionality. My ability, as the musical director, to share a key but inconspicuous musical idea with the actors and other members of the production team, helped to expand everyone's understanding of the song's title. Through consideration of Sondheim's choice, all involved began to sense the larger purpose of the song in the structure of the overall story. Not only does the title mean that no one is alone in the sense that the four characters must now band together in order to help one another survive, but also that no one is alone and that the actions of each individual now impact the other members of the community. From this perspective, the song transforms into an implied anthem that champions the individual's responsibility to the communal good. Beyond being merely a sad and pretty ballad, the song serves as a call to action for a new order in the characters' changing world. Given that understanding, the actors' performance was far more nuanced, textured, and interesting.

Indeed, the value of considering the musical subtext is that no one in the dramatic enterprise acts alone. The storytelling impulse starts with the writer (or writers, in the case of the musical theatre's book writer, lyricist, and composer) and his or her creation is then handed off to the actors and directors who, plumbing the depth of the text, work to create the verisimilitude that facilitates dramatic catharsis. The musical director's knowledge of music theory, and his or her ability to analyze keenly the musical properties provided by the composer, elevate his or her contributions to the collaboration and add new layers of language—tools if you will—to the interpretative process.

Foregrounding the work of the composer puts the spotlight on conscious decisions made by musical dramatists. Many theatre composers would agree with Sondheim when he says that attention to the musical details can inform the process and the final product:

> [It] will help not only the musical director, but the director, I hope, and maybe even the actors, to understand the process of the composition of the show. . . . To know is very important. Then they know that things are not arbitrary in the show, and I'm going to guess that it helps them unify the show in terms of acting styles, in terms of scenic approach, whatever. If they know the music is conceived, not 'bitsy-piecy,' but that it has some kind of over-arching notion—or set of notions—maybe that will reflect itself in the work they do. I really believe that.[11]

Swain reinforces this notion when he states, "To understand how music performs as a significant dramatic element . . . a musical analysis is needed that connects the songs in their detail with the dramatic elements of plot, character and action."[12] Swain advances from an analytical standpoint that it is incumbent upon musical theatre practitioners (actors, directors, musical directors) to explore a song's musical properties to best understand how to fully present the composer's dramatic intentions, thus ensuring that the score serves the story.

In a series of interviews with successful musical theatre directors, Lawrence Thelan's book *The Show Makers: Great Directors of the American Musical Theatre* reveals that many directors do not know how to read music and most do not feel it is an important skill to possess;[13] they assert that the musical director's role is to assist in that capacity. While one might choose to debate the point, it begs a simple question: why wouldn't a dramatic artist working in musical theatre—actors, directors, choreographers, stage manager, etc.—not want to understand the musical language of the art form?

Our rehearsal process for *Into the Woods* foregrounded tensions that can arise when new theories/approaches intersect with existing methodology. At one point during the rehearsal of Little Red Riding Hood's "I Know Things Now," the actress was frustrated that the initial staging provided by the director was hindering her ability to maintain the breath control needed for the song. When she approach me, as the musical director, about suggestions on how best to regain breath control while remaining obedient to the director's staging, a discussion ensued on how the breathlessness was perhaps suggested in the accompaniment of the song, and how it might be utilized as part of the story she was telling. The director stumbled upon this conversation and grew concerned that I, the musical director, was giving the actor acting notes, and a mild confrontation ensued. However, discussion of the musical properties inherent in the song proved to be the watershed element that helped reconcile the misunderstanding. Ideas shared about the musical qualities gave both the actor and director new ideas, such as an enhanced awareness that the patter quality of the song was very active and might allow the actor and the director to simplify the blocking and let the lyrics do more of the "action" work. This then sparked ideas for the director on how he might revise the blocking. Ultimately, the ideas resulted in an exciting and open conversation, which allowed all three collaborators to contribute to finding a solution that served the actor, the director, and, ultimately, the story.

In this way, musical subtext, as a new theoretical component of musical theatre practice, opens new pathways for performer/director communication. When consideration is given to the composer's contribution to the story, actors, directors, conductors, and choreographers can plumb new layers of character intention, emotional shading, plot development, and physical expression. And, knowledge of these layers, when coupled with the familiar approaches of literary analysis, expands upon the potential richness of the musical theatre expression, an expression born of the notion that a song expresses what words alone cannot.

Notes

1. David Craig, *A Performer Prepares: A Guide to Song Preparation for Actors, Singers and Dancers* (New York: Applause Books, 1993).
2. Wesley H. Balk, *Performing Power: A New Approach for the Singer-Actor* (Minneapolis: University of Minnesota Press, 1986).
3. Joseph P. Swain, *The Broadway Musical: A Critical and Musical Survey* (Oxford: Oxford University Press, 1990).
4. John Bell and Steven Chicurel, *Music Theory for Musical Theatre* (Lanham, MD: Scarecrow Press, 2008).
5. James Lapine and Stephen Sondheim, *Into the Woods* (New York: TCG, 1987), 35.
6. Ibid., 43–4.
7. Ibid., 128–31.
8. Mark Eden Horowitz, *Sondheim on Music: Minor Details and Major Decisions* (Lanham, MD: Scarecrow Press, 2003), 85.
9. Lapine and Sondheim, *Into the Woods*, 60.
10. Ibid., 128.
11. Horowitz, *Sondheim on Music*, 84–5.
12. Swain, *The Broadway Musical*, 4.
13. Lawrence Thelan, *The Show Makers: Great Directors of the American Musical Theatre* (New York: Routledge, 2000), 61.

19

Tongues of Stone: Making Space Speak . . . Again and Again

Carol Brown and Dorita Hannah

Introduction

> Word and idea are not born of scientific or logical thinking but of creative language, which means of innumerable languages—for this act of 'conception' has taken place over and over again.

> Let my playing be my learning, and my learning be my playing.[1]

For Johannes Huizinga, all culture "bears the character of play,"[2] suggesting that the play-element is both a delight and a burden. Performance, like play, is comprised of a complex set of systems that embrace aesthetic displays, daily encounters, intellectual endeavors, institutionalization, and warfare. The play of performance, therefore, operates between the poles of entertainment and acts that are deadly serious. As Jon McKenzie states, we "perform or else."[3]

To play with theory is therefore to have something at stake: to be both light of being and heavy with purpose. The player entertains, contests, and stakes out a ground upon which rules are established, modified, and broken, often with grave consequences. As choreographer (Carol Brown) and designer (Dorita Hannah), we are players within the creation of our own productions, which play with, and on, theory through practice.

Practice-as-research provides a means for embodied investigations that both support and defy linear theoretical suppositions. In transposing thinking to making—not only from text to action, but beyond physical workshops or classroom explorations onto the public stage—the process moves from *in-vitro* (the theoretical laboratory) to *in-vivo* (live performance encounters). However, such references to scientific research models have their limitations, because performance is a slippery field that defies rational hypotheses and measurable outcomes. Ours is therefore a more playfully poetic approach, which seeks to resist a reductive logic aimed at easily explaining how practice is informed by theory and theory is informed by practice. As professional performance makers working between academia and the arts industries, our creative productions as embodied theory (a-thinking-through-making) challenge the binary between theory and practice. Susan Melrose describes this practice as "multi-dimensional theorizing":

> might it be possible to argue that some expert practitioners *already theorize* in multi-dimensional, multi-schematic and multi-participant modes, rather than in writing-dominant mode, just as it can be argued that some writers theorize in writing, but not others?[4]

The theoretical approaches we adopt are manifold and difficult to pick apart, and to do so would be to untangle threads that are necessarily embedded as creative knots, which morph throughout our process. The projects presented here are part of an ongoing research objective to provide alternative means of perceiving space for performance—through performance. Our aim is to challenge the embodied viewing of the audience itself by shifting borders between performer and spectator; between body and building; between fictive and real worlds; between the imagination and material perception. Such troubling of expectations elasticizes the spatio-temporal realm created by the performance event. In summoning phantoms from myth, media, and history, and incorporating these characters within moments of a lived experience, we hope to expose this simultaneous presencing of otherness as a continual, but often invisible condition, which exists beyond the performance event itself. In this way, the mixed-mode theorization that occurs through performance making is made visible, driven by a political-philosophical imperative, as much as a creative and professional imperative.

While our over-arching project is to rediscover space through dance and, reciprocally, to re-engage with movement through architecture, *Tongues of Stone* provides us with a means of giving voice to the unspeakable. In responding to political events through performance as a site of recovery, each performance iteration reconfigures the project and our theoretical concerns—taking place over and over again.

Since 2002, we have conceived and developed *dance-architectures* as spaces of encounter which aim to shift an understanding of our disciplinary fields from being object-centred (the making of a dance or a building) to being subject-centred (about relationships and inter-connections between people). Our *dance-architectures* explore what happens when the slow time of the built environment intersects with the varying temporalities of historical, aesthetic, and embodied daily events. In producing dynamic exchanges between bodies and places, we endeavor *to make space speak* and, thereby, shift spectators' expectations about how and where they might come to experience a dance or a building.

Our collaborations on site-responsive works fold audiences into the live performance while attending to the fractured narratives of place, memory, and mythology. The process has developed through a body of work that is profoundly informed by catastrophic events on the world stage. It seeks to make connections between the lived-present and long-buried traumatic pasts and, like Antonin Artaud, "to make space speak" in the face of the unspeakable.[5]

As a project, our research has undergone a number of iterations, each influenced by the specifics of site, the stories it harbors, and the collaborating dancers' embodied histories. Following a series of workshops, our first production in the cycle was *Her Topia*, commissioned by the Isadora and Raymond Duncan Dance Research Centre in Athens, Greece (October 2005); which then developed into the solo *Aarero Stone*, premiered at the New Zealand International Arts Festival in Wellington (March 2006); and was reshaped for the Australian city of Perth with STRUT dance company (September 2009 and March 2010) toward a full ensemble production in March 2011.

Through its various iterations, *Tongues of Stone* maintains its underlying themes and structure, while shifting radically from ensemble work to solos, from installation to theatrical performance, from professional performance to community participation; from stage-scape to landscape and city-scape; from mourning to rage.

Architect Bernard Tschumi has proclaimed, "*Events 'take place.' And again. And again.*"[6] Yet with every re-taking of place, something is learned or lost, and as with Friedrich Nietzsche's concept of the Eternal Return, difference, rather than sameness, is revealed. This text reviews our performance-as-research project by structuring it around events that have taken place over the last eight years, their provocations, and the processes they gave birth to.

Each section is concerned with an **ENTANGLED THRESHOLD OF ENCOUNTER**

between personal events and political forces

between historical events and embodied processes
between interior and exterior
between mythology and everyday life
between the palpably present and the distant
between the material and the virtual
between inhabiting architecture and its inhabitation of us
between the local and the global
between a hard and soft city
between theoretical reflections and incarnated practices

In structuring our research this way, we hope to reveal the impossibility of documenting a performance without revealing how it is always already ruptured by a host of past bodies and processes. Often, performance will try to suture these absences with the promise of live presence as a bare encounter, a being-in-the-moment. Yet, as Jacques Derrida explains, any system of marks cannot fully deliver a present that is not in some ways ruptured by both a past and a future.[7] By resisting the demand for completion and highlighting these thresholds of encounter as in-between states, we hope to reveal how iterations of performance recuperate and re-incorporate that which is never fully absent. Furthermore, we are interested in the inventions that arise from the surfacing of specters of the disappeared, the dispossessed, and the absented. Derrida proposes the *specter* as the repeat, the return, the revenant, "that which comes back." Our work therefore concerns many returns, and with each return there are shifts: shifts in thought, character, movement, and aesthetic play.

Black Window/Black Wi(n)dow

. . . between personal events and political forces

Tongues of Stone, as ongoing performance-as-research, was initially provoked by the 2002 Moscow Theatre Siege, when terror literally took to the stage and bodies were co-opted as potent explosive weapons. On October 23, 2002, the Dubrovka Theatre in Moscow was seized by Chechen rebels who infiltrated during the musical performance of *Nord-Ost*, interrupting and transforming the show into a prolonged international spectacle of terror that ended after three days with Russia's Spetsnaz soldiers storming the building, having filled it with a narcotic gas that killed over 170 people.

We were particularly affected by the spectral figure of the *Black Widows*, female suicide bombers—shrouded in black and strapped with bomb belts—who were co-opted as potent weapons by the Chechen rebels. Representing the ultimate spatial limit of self-annihilation, these figures are present in the media images of the seemingly benign auditorium released immediately after the tragedy. As the dark forms slumped in the seats, their haunting presence deliberately provides a cautionary tale from the Russian authorities that prevented their detonation (while sacrificing over 120 audience members, absent in the image). The banality and passivity of the architecture are haunted by the specter of explosive violence.[8]

Researching this synthesis of war and theatre in images of women, we sought to look behind these images, to think with them to explore the recurring mythologizing of Woman as martyr, murderess, and mourner across cultures.

> The absence of women in our persistent myths informs our response to the absence we call death, the signifier of absolute alterity. Repeatedly assigning women to this position of absence in our central narratives we make an association between the dread of death and the dread of women that is still routine in contemporary life.[9]

The Black Widows are primarily utilized for the powerful psychic charge elicited by the spectacle of a destructive sacrificial woman. It is this mythological figure, conflated in the seemingly inscrutable object of the darkly veiled Middle Eastern female body, which affected us, particularly Dorita, who is of Lebanese origin.

> What does it take for a woman to turn her body into a precision bomb?
> What kind of transformations must she undergo?
> When her body becomes an incendiary device—exploding, annihilating—what mourning then this bodiless death?
> This exploded absence?
> Her grave as gravity denied.

Black Widow/Black Wi(n)dow emerged as a precursor to *Tongues of Stone* through a series of interdisciplinary workshops in which we asked of our collaborating artists and researchers how, as artists, do we deal with these complex *"constructions of terror"* and their representation within a mediatized spectacle? Four workshops—Schloss Brollin, Germany June 2002; Centre for Performance Research, Aberystwyth, Wales 2004; Faultlines, Wanganui and Wellington November/December

2004; and Choreodrome, The Place Theatre, London July 2005—provided the foundation for a collaborative process that *invited listening to these images* as a critical and creative strategy for encounter, whilst simultaneously exploring performance composition that began with the question of the body's disappearance and de-materialization.

Listening to the image

. . . between historical events and embodied processes

Prepare a bare studio with photographic images of recent traumatic events carefully placed around the edges of the floor
Invite the performers to enter silently and to find an image they are willing to spend time with
Listen to the Image
Pay attention to it with your ears and heart
Ask what is behind the image?
When you are ready create a movement on the floor embodying your response

"Listening to the Image" is a strategy for making connections between contemporary performance practices and the social, cultural, and political events that inform our lives. This workshop considered that to listen is not to hear but to concentrate, to pay attention to something, and take it into account. To act with our ears and our hearts. To make sense of a world that seems to have lost its senses. To be touched by an image becomes a form of resistance to the disembodying effects of the media spectacle and opens a potential space through sense-based dialogues with the Other.[10]

Gravity as grave denied
Begin lying on your back on the floor
Close your eyes
Surrender to gravity
Feel your breath moving within your still and silent body touching air and skin
Witness the movement of your thinking whilst staying completely still
Establish a sense of complete stillness (this may take five minutes or more)

Open your eyes
Move your eyes seeing from within your corpselike pose
Where does mouring overtake us?

. . . between interior and exterior

The presence of the Chechen "black widow" conveys the ultimate abject figure: she is the mythical mother in mourning, her "black wrath" provoking action, transforming sorrow to fury and fury to murder.[11] As a veiled and armed insurgent, she forms a powerful trope for the limit reached by the melancholic shrouded stage of the twentieth century, which resisted definition and containment. Her explosive materiality as spatial abjection, returns not only the avenging characters of Hecuba, Medea, and Clytemnestra to the stage, but also embodies the blood sacrifice of the ancient theatre.

Performing myth

. . . between mythology and everyday life

Somatic-based tasks developed during our *Black Widow/Black Wi(n)dow* workshops were structured around a metamorphic score based on the elements of *stone, flesh, dust,* and *phantom.* As an emergent dramaturgy, these elements framed sensations for the choreographic score and became the substratum for a critical mythologizing.

Myths as stories told in public carry a sense of constancy and an air of wisdom. But they also have a seductive charm. Female mythical figures in particular risk essentializing the feminine, as they form touchstones through which archetypal imagery becomes entwined with the environment. At their heart is a view of history turned into nature.[12]

Drucilla Cornell (1991) defends the allegory of the feminine through myth arguing with Roland Barthes that "the best weapon against myth is perhaps to mythify it in its turn, and to produce an *artificial myth*: and this reconstituted myth will in fact be a mythology."[13] Cornell sees dialogues with mythical structures and figures as a form of coexistence, through which we can mark the specificity of feminine sexual difference.

Working with myths of metamorphoses as a primordial structure, we glimpse partial states between organic and artificial life: stone becoming flesh; flesh becoming stone; stone becoming dust; dust becoming phantom; phantom becoming flesh. If choreography and design set up an oscillating rhythm between these states as acts of becoming, mythology provides the synthesizing dramaturgical layer for gathering these sequences into constellations of meaning.

A critical mythologizing through performance becomes a way of retelling the self in an age of exploded limits for the (im)materiality of corporeality. The transglobal nature of myths of metamorphosis and their *making strange* allows us to connect across species (human becoming insect/bird/animal), times (past and present), distances (the proximate and the distant), and ecologies (mineral, animal, and vegetable). As embodied states, myths of metamorphic transformation allow us to shift between figurative and non-figurative states, literal and non-literal meanings. They allow us to make connections between different dimensions, stories, and habitations, sticking the local into a global cosmology, physicalizing change, and speaking to a potential space of heterogeneity:

> Perhaps she was thinking of a completely other history: a history of paradoxical laws and non-dialectical discontinuities, a history of absolutely heterogeneous pockets, irreducible particularities, of unheard of and incalculable sexual differences.[14]

As a practice of space, this critical embodiment of mythology aims to destabilize relationships between figure and ground, body and place, inside and outside. We step back from the stories literalness to explore paradoxical states, discontinuities, and peculiarities. As the performers inhabit costumes informed by these stories—an over-sized dress; a semi-transparent veil; a yellow raincoat; a slip—they learn to dance, otherwise incorporating and metabolizing imagery informed by these myths, but without literally representing them, negotiating narrative as space, as well as time. This dramaturgical layer provides a soft scaffold to move space into another register.

. . . between the palpably present and the distant

Myths recur again and again, not only within cultures, but between cultures. The ancient Greek legend of Niobe tells the story of a woman who is literally turned to stone with grief after the gods vengefully slaughter her 14 children as punishment for her boasting of a fertile superiority.[15] Merging forever with the land as a weeping rock, Niobe slowly wears away, her petrified body transforming into particles inevitably dispersed upon the air. This ancient myth of female metamorphosis is echoed in a Maori *pakiwaitara* in which an ancestress is transformed into a stone formation also destined to erode over time, and it is said that when the rock disappears she will finally be at peace.[16]

> Her tongue
> Solidified in her stone mouth.
> Her feet could not move, her hands
> Could not move: they were stone,
> Her veins were stone veins.
> Her bowels, her womb, all stone
> Packed in stone.
> And yet
> This stone woman wept.[17]

Such myths, which carry across vast distances, multiple epochs, and diverse cultures, have provided us with the basis for exploring performance space as the realm of dreams, reality, death, and dispersion: four distinct spatial states that interconnect and interweave through performance. These spatial states were presented as part of a Show and Tell event for Creative New Zealand as conceptual drawings of a veiled figure constructed of ice and stones that dissolves into a landscape.

Phantom, flesh, stone, and dust

. . . between the material and the virtual

The picture-frame stage is approached as a site-specific locale for the enactment of epic events. Its fourth wall is explored, exploded, and realigned to reveal a space of phantoms (virtuality), of reality (matter), of death (crypt), and of dispersion (dust). These liminal states form mutable thresholds, connected by an itinerary of loss and recovery.

The first space is PHANTOM SPACE, the stage as a dark void; liquid immersed and atmospheric, out of which images and dreams awake . . . the black window of theatrical re-production.

FLESH SPACE is that of confrontation where the stage and auditorium are revealed as site-specific zones, exposing the theatrical apparatus and the performing body. It is the space of matter; of palpable flesh, its annihilation and corruption.

STONE SPACE belongs to sorrow, loss, and lamentation. It is the world of gravity, the crypt, and the underworld. . . . Persephone lost below, Lot's wife abandoned, Niobe turned to stone. . . . Hinenuitepo crushing Maui between her monumental thighs.

The last space is that of DUST and dissolution. A scattering of atomized matter . . . beyond the borders . . . a place of atonement . . . emptying out the 'empty space' of the stage . . . dancing on particles.

This spatial sequence forms a scenographic dramaturgy for three distinct but related performance projects in Athens, Wellington, and Perth.

Her Topia, Athens 2005

. . . between inhabiting architecture and its inhabitation of us

Her Topia (Athens, October 2005) took on Isadora Duncan's notion of dance as an expression of freedom and asked: what is it to dance free dom at a time when wars are being waged in its name?

The project, a commission by the British Council for the Isadora and Raymond Duncan Centre for Dance Research in Athens, investigated what happens when the slow performance of ancient rock and architecture coheres with the fluctuating temporalities of observing and dancing bodies.[18] Stones became linking elements across time, holding memory in their inscrutable objectality.[19] Body-site relationships were explored and established through connections between Isadora and mortal women from Greek mythology such as Arachne and Niobe who, defying the gods, were punished by them through tragic events and brutal metamorphoses. (This equated with moral judgment on the tragedies that befell Isadora Duncan—considered too thoroughly modern in her ways—who lost her children to drowning and was strangled by her own red scarf caught in the wheel of a sports car). Ariadne is acknowledged as the first architect, providing the thread to negotiate the labyrinth. This is seen in the use of the red stitch, a recurring trope in costumes and setting, operating as performative seam, ephemeral architecture, and way-finding mechanism. The ubiquitous dance studio mirror becomes a means of invoking and replicating a virtual other through smaller reflective units that reconfigure bodies and space.

Over a two-week period in autumn 2005, we developed research initiated in *Black Widow/Black Wi(n)dow* to explore the building, its adjoining site, and the surrounding neighborhood with 14 contemporary Greek, Japanese, and French dancers. Our initial research, which drew on specific images of terror as catalysts for improvised responses, had shifted toward a more oblique strategy. In developing our research, we focused upon the three figures whose stories of metamorphic transformation dealt in different ways with the trauma of loss (Niobe) or losing (Arachne), and the possibilities of repair (Ariadne). Alongside these stories, we introduced the objects whose properties resonated with significance in these narratives of transformation—stones, red thread, and mirrors—as well as costumes that made reference to veiled women, the freeing of the feminine form in the self-mythologizing of Isadora Duncan, and dresses of different scales that either freed the dancer or severely encumbered her movements through excessive weight and volume.

Combining ancient, modern, and contemporary images, stitched into a fluctuating temporal continuum, we conceived a *dance-architecture* event. The audience moved between interior and exterior spaces as the dancers' bodies were fragmented, multiplied, and dematerialized in an orchestration of sound, light, video, mirrors, and movement that eventually projected the performance out into the cityscape of Athens (see Figures 8 and 9). Rather than a utopian site, the Duncans' temple was rendered a *heterotopia*—a place of "other" spaces.[20] As such, it proposed a performative monumentality, where dance as movement veiled in immobility reveals architecture as stasis veiled in movement.[21]

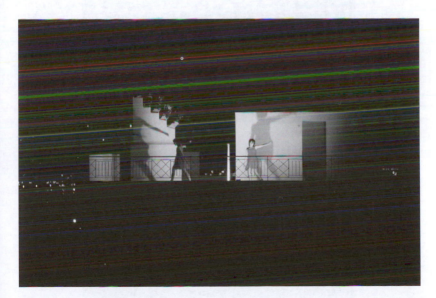

Figure 8:   Her Topia: A Dance-Architecture Event. Duncan Dance Research Center. Photo by Fotis Traganoudakis.

Become a bodily archive for the re-enactment of Duncan's
Revolutionary Dance
Carry and pass stones in a grid formation
De-form your silhouette by extruding lines, creating folds and
concavities whilst dressed in a sheath
Hold a mirror to your audience
Create a spatial dissection of body and site using a mirrored surface
Dance ecstatically for the duration of a song
Pile up rocks on a table
Make a river of stones to balance upon
Sew a monstrous dress and move across the table in it
Call across the rooftops
Balance, hold, and rest rocks on the crevices of your body

Figure 9:   Her Topia: A Dance-Architecture Event. Duncan Dance Research Center.
Photo by Fotis Traganoudakis.

Aarero Stone, Wellington 2006

. . . between the local and the global

Her Topia, an ensemble work within the city of Athens, was followed by *Aarero Stone*, a solo in a performance landscape sited within the Soundings Theatre, Te Papa Tongarewa Museum of New Zealand in Wellington. Unlike its precursor, the primary landscape is the stage itself, which precedes the production as an active space. The stage house was treated as a site-specific space for performance, exposing the walls and technology and referencing the timber paneling of the auditorium. Exposed as a machine for transformation, the stage is folded in with the new design interventions, composed of monumental forms, inspired by memorial architecture including Wellington's polished granite Tomb for the Unknown Warrior. Black reflective elements intersect with a paneled slab wall indented with a dark tomb, below which lies a shallow pool and above which floats an angled mirror. The floor is a cartographer's grid of silver crosses. A promontory form on the forestage juts out into the auditorium and a vessel of white stones intersects with and overhangs the pool. Stage house and architectonic setting merge into a single performance landscape, stitched together by the red dash of a horizon line (see Figure 10).

Referring to the project as "a lament for the living inscribed with love" we asked the question, "how do we care for the strangely familiar and mourn the distant dead?" *Aarero* translates as *tongue* in Maori and, as hard talk; the stone tongue is the speaking landscape. Talking in forgotten languages with their remote rites, *Aarero Stone* performed an archeology of buried voices. Loosening the tongue of frozen speech, geology became mythology: Sibyl's voice endured as her body disappeared within a cave; Niobe turned to stone in mourning for her dead children; the women of Belstone were petrified as punishment for dancing on the Sabbath. Rather than a place of too few lovers, we found the lovers were many, distant, and near. The solo concluded with the soloist (in this case, Carol the choreographer) moving in the water, her image suspended, doubled, and dissolving in the overhanging black mirror.

Tongues of Stone, Perth 2011

. . . between a hard and soft city

These seemingly sleepy, old-fashioned things. . .
the debris of shipwrecked histories still today raise up the ruins of an unknown, strange city. They burst forth within the modernist,

Figure 10:   Aarero Stone: Two Solos in a Performance Landscape. New Zealand International Arts Festival. Photo by Robert Catto.

massive, homogeneous city like slips of the tongue from an unknown, perhaps unconscious language. They surprise.[22]

With the invitation to work with STRUT dance company in Western Australia, we took this concept of the stone tongue developed in solo performance for *Aarero Stone*, and translated it for the specific conditions—physical, geological, and cultural—of the city of Perth. Material was developed through two research and development work-shops (2009 and 2010) for a performance in 2011.[23] We began our research from the premise that underlying the contemporary city of Perth—built on sand, stone, and histories shaped by the surrounding mining industry—run rivers of song, blood, and memories. As a multi-site performance event, *Tongues* mines these sedimented stories: expressed and embodied through moments of theatrical transformation.

> Was there a river Here
> In tongues of this land[24]

Perth, formerly composed of wetlands that ran from the river westward to the sea, once provided fluid gathering grounds for the Noongar people. However, with the coming of other peoples, the land was reclaimed and sedimented into the sand, stone, and concrete of a modern metropolis, covering over diverse and numerous histories. In paying attention to the resonances of these histories, *Tongues of Stone* reconceives the city as flows and counter-flows, energized by currents, undercurrents, and counter-currents.

As a public dance event staged within Perth's urban environment *Tongues of Stone* was created for a diverse mobile audience who will either happen upon performance moments, embedded in the folds of the city, or follow an itinerary guided by a soundscape and the fleeting appearance of performers.[25] Sound and choreography led the public from the underground station (once Lake Kingsford) to the Convention Centre blocking the link to the Swan River, connecting ancient wetlands to the major waterway of this settler city.

By drawing on maps, metamorphoses, and memories, as well as ancient and contemporary texts, the city becomes a museum of gestures as the STRUT performers harvest dance movements from their own histories as well as the embodied memories of Perth inhabitants. These are translated into site-specific performance propositions as to how body, building, and site cohere through movement, sound, garment, and object. A further Ovidian myth of revenge and transformation provided the underlying narrative to shape the dramaturgy. Procne searches for her sister, Philomela, who was raped and made dumb by her husband Tereus. Bride and widow cohere as blinded and gagged figures, which appear and disappear on platforms, in laneways, and at windows. Philomela's trailing red gown becomes a way-finding clue as it snakes toward the river. The lamentation of earlier productions turns to rage as furies, veiled by their hair, storm the streets like avenging crows (see Figure 11). Poetic and disciplinary messages are revealed in the architecture and written onto headscarves that bleed when washed by a chorus of waterbearers who carry buckets through the streets. Transformational moments unfold from the cracks and crevices of forgotten sites, temporarily theatricalizing the city into a three-dimensional matrix of multiple events (see Figure 12).

Figure 11:   Tongues of Stone: Research and Development Workshops. Strut Dance Company. Photo by Sarah Burrell.

Figure 12:   Tongues of Stone: Research and Development Workshops. Strut Dance Company. Photo by Sarah Burrell.

The city that lies beneath.
Draw a map to describe your journey here.
Place yourself inside this map.
Imagine that it stretches sagitally in front of your torso (like a
table).
Incorporate the tracings of this journey into upper and lower body
movements that scribe space simultaneously on two planes.

Subdivide the map into four quadrants.
Each quadrant corresponds to a different moment of rapture,
number these 1–4

Write three sentences summarizing your personal history of Perth
Reduce this to three words

Write a story into the city with your body and rub it out again

Mark your bodily outline on the street with dust

With buckets of water in a chorus carry, hold, place, squat over,
pour out, leak
Run from one end of the street to the other with a bucket of water
in each hand

Polyrhythmic City
Listen to your pulse, listen to your breathing
Make a movement gesture on two different beats of your pulse
counted to nine
Make a syllable sound on two alternating beats of this nine-count pulse
Intersect the vocal and movement material within small ensembles
of five dancers

Site moving in a state of internalized rapture in a non-place
Sing a poem with gathering energies of a river

Invite a stranger to dance with you
Imitate the movement of birds

The city we imagine is the soft city of illusion, myth, aspiration,
and nightmare.

It is as real, maybe more real, than the hard city one can locate on maps in statistics and in monographs on architecture.
This is your city and its language is the language you've always known.
Allow the city to go soft, to await the imprint of your identity.
See how it invites you to remake it, to consolidate it into a shape you can inhabit.

Practices of encounter
Your body is a polyrhythmic tool for negotiating the urbanscape.
Traverse the city by shadowing the movements of strangers you encounter.
Use mimesis and imitation to fall into step with the rhythms of others.

Ask a stranger to teach you a dance they know.
Ask a passerby what they would like to see here?

Place gathers meaning through repetition
We make a place for ourselves through the iterative processes of our joint works
By these means personal rituals of making become public events

. . . between the distant and the near

If my own body is the one I have and the history of the ones I've lost, then the present is where I meet some fragment of the past.[26] Thoughts of death make a good dance partner. In this meeting however, we are not fated to simply repeat the same old dance; we can *be* out of step in these encounters, and out of time. For the invention of an *other* inscription requires a displacement of bodies and places that is quite different from what is known.[27] Our performance inventions are ciphers, coded ways of activating and interrupting the civic space. So that what is proposed is not so much an "alternative place" as an *altering space*.[28]

. . . between theoretical reflections and incarnated practices

Notes

1. Johannes Huizinga, *Homo Ludens: A Study of the Play-Element in Culture* (New York: Roy, 1950), 28.
2. Ibid., ix.

3. Jon McKenzie, *Perform or Else* (London and New York: Routledge Press, 2001).
4. Susan Melrose, ". . . just intuitive . . ." Keynote presentation, AHRC Research Centre for Cross-Cultural Music and Dance Performance, SOAS, 23 April 2005. http://eprints.mdx.ac.uk/3072/1/ (accessed September 28, 2010).
5. Antonin Artaud, *Theatre and its Double, trans. Mary Caroline Richards* (New York: Grove Press, 1958), 98.
6. Bernard Tschumi, *Architecture and Disjunction* (Cambridge: MIT Press, 1996), 160.
7. Jacques Derrida, "Signature Event Context," in Barry Stocker, ed., *Jacques Derrida: Basic Writings*, trans. Alan Bass (London and New York: Routledge, 2007), 105–34.
8. These photographs are two of many that can be found on the internet. Staged for the camera by the Russian authorities, which emptied the auditorium of the dead bodies of its citizens, the explosive body simultaneously represents a threat and a cautionary tale.
9. Peggy Phelan, "Trisha Brown's Orfeo: Two Takes on Double Endings," in André Lepecki, ed., *Of the Presence of the Body: Essays on Dance and Performance Theory* (Connecticut: Wesleyan University Press, 2004), 15.
10. In *I Love to You: Sketch of a Possible Felicity in History* (trans. Alison Martin, [London and New York: Routledge, 1996]), Luce Irigaray calls for a recovery of the sensibility of touch through her theory of sexuate subjectivity, an ethical project toward enabling the different sexes to live with each other.
11. Nicole Loraux, *Mothers in Mourning* (Ithaca: Cornell University Press, 1988), 43.
12. Marina Warner, *Managing Monsters: Six Myths of Our Time* (UK: Vintage, 1994).
13. Roland Barthes, *Mythologies*, trans. Annette Lavers (New York: Noonday Press, 1972) 135. See also Drucilla Cornell, *Beyond Accommodation: Ethical Feminism, Deconstruction and the Law* (New York and London: Routledge, 1991), 165.
14. Jacques Derrida and Christie McDonald, "Choreographies," *Diacritics* 12 (Summer, 1982, 66–76), 68.
15. Niobe, Queen of Thebes, mocked the goddess Leto, who had only twins—Apollo and Artemis. In retaliation, the goddess sent her two offspring to brutally slay Niobe's 14 children.
16. Discussions with Charles Koroneho.
17. Ted Hughes, *Tales from Ovid* (London: Faber and Faber, 1997), 223.
18. As Americans in self-imposed exile in Athens "Clan" Duncan constructed a hilltop sanctuary for dancing and living on the outskirts of the city and facing the Parthenon. Modeled on the Temple of Agamemnon, their rough stone structure was an attempt to create a utopian elsewhere, drawing on mythology and history, while oblivious to the political, cultural, and economic realities of the place it occupied. In 1980 the ruined structure, now surrounded by apartment buildings in the suburb of Byron, was transformed into the Isadora and Raymond Duncan Dance Research Centre. Although by no means an architectural masterpiece, it represents the first attempt to build a space specifically for modern dance and is today a working centre for contemporary choreographic research in the Duncans' name.

19. This refers to Henri Lefebvre's notion of objectality as a brutal and resistant force in *The Production of Space*, trans. Donald Nicholson-Smith (Oxford: Blackwell, 1991), 57.

20. Michel Foucault established the notion of heterotopia as a site that is both mythic and real in contrast to the fundamentally unreal spaces of projected utopias. This is outlined and discussed in his essay "Of Other Spaces" reproduced in *Rethinking Architecture: Reader in Cultural Theory*, ed. Neil Leach (London: Routledge, 1997), 350–5.

21. This is a reworking of Sandra Horton Fraleigh's contention that "dance is movement veiled in immobility." See Sandra Horton Fraleigh, *Dance and the Lived Body: A Descriptive Aesthetics* (Pittsburgh: University of Pittsburgh Press), 93.

22. Michel de Certeau and Luce Giard, Luce, "Ghosts in the City" from *The Practice of Everyday Life*, trans. Steven Rendell (Berkeley: University of California Press, 1984), 133.

23. Since this book has gone to press, *Tongues of Stone* performed in Perth, 2011.

24. Unpublished poem by Perth-based artist Audrey Fernandes-Satar.

25. The audience who book for the event will be issued mp3 players and earphones in order to listen to a soundscape composed by Russell Scoones, created harvesting sounds from the city.

26. Peggy Phelan, *Unmarked* (London and New York: Routledge, 1993).

27. Derrida and McDonald, "Choreographies."

28. Doina Petrescu, *Altering Practices: Feminist Politics and Poetics of Space* (London and New York: Routledge, 2007).

20
Seven Introductions: A Dialogue

Michael Rohd and Shannon Scrofano

INTRO #1: Enter *BUILT*
Michael Rohd (MR), Creator/Director *BUILT*; Sojourn Theatre Founding Artistic Director

You're in the South Waterfront District on Portland, Oregon's Riverfront—a new high-rise, green, urban community development filled with condos, empty retail stores, and holes in the earth surrounded by cranes.

You arrive at the Discovery Center, a large concrete warehouse with a large orange asterisk on the front wall next to giant letters that read YOU ARE HERE.

You have found your destination. The site of Sojourn Theatre's production of *BUILT*.

You walk into the building. It is a cross between an Ikea store and a realty office. High ceilings, neutral colors, so much space. On your left, a front desk. Behind the front desk is a woman with a list. She asks if you have a reservation. You say yes.

She gives you no program, no ticket. She sends you to a man who stands at a table filled with what he tells you are game boards. One foot-long and three inches-wide pieces of foam core divided into seven squares. Each has a color. Yours is blue. You know this because you are given a small round sticker and asked to place it on your shirt. You are told this is important.

The man hands you off to another woman who walks you 25 feet further into the building. On the way, you look down corridors and catch glimpses of fully furnished kitchens at the other end of the building. Each corridor is filled with models and displays and video monitors. You arrive at a larger table and are told to put your game board down.

You do. You realize that there are other people with other game boards and other hosts scattered around this large table and that all the people seem to be in various stages of some sort of game . . . which your host now teaches you. You complete the task.

He introduces you to someone else. You leave your board at the large table. The new host guides you further into the building, toward the kitchens. The music is getting louder. As you walk, someone passes by with a tray of cookies, and you are offered one. You smell fresh baking throughout the building.

You arrive at one of three kitchens stretched along this side of the building. There is more food on an island counter. You are introduced to someone new. She tells you that until the show starts, this kitchen is your home. She tells you that there are activities in this kitchen. She tells you there is a video you can watch. She tells you that you can wander the building, so long as you return to her and this kitchen when an announcement is made. She says—

Welcome.

INTRO #2: What we reach for
In 2007, when we began work on BUILT, a project that explored the changing nature of cities and exploding population growth in the United States through the lens of the question "Where will we live?," we knew we wanted to push the dialogical nature of our work forward not through post event conversations or proven engagement strategies . . . we wanted to develop new approaches via participation within the dramaturgy of our event. We wanted an audience to experience spectacle and exchange—to be witnesses and participants, to occupy spaces of imagination and reflection. We wanted to make an experience we had neither built nor seen before.

Shannon Scrofano (SS), Designer/Media Artist *BUILT*; Sojourn Theatre Company Member
In a time-based event, with a limited number of occurrences, constructed for a finite number of viewer-participants, we reach for a convergence that can only be contained in that unique moment, in that specific

space, with that particular quorum. The reach is the act of the maker, generator, and facilitator of such a convergence.

We reach toward invitation, toward contract of event. Sometimes we call it performance; sometimes we call it dialogue or participation; sometimes a journey, an engagement, a conversation, an experiment, an exchange, a show. We bat around the language with each new project to help us find our way as practitioners, and to help build access and expectation for those who will join us in each event. The alignment of language is also a means by which to engage, both intra- and inter-disciplinarily with other artists past and present, and with theory that carves the way, trips us up, affirms our inquiries.

In both culminating event and dynamics of process, we reach for moments of collective action. For me, the impossible act of collaboration is a chief motive in art practice. I am lured by the abandonment of ownership in creative processes, of giving away ideas to belief in a greater whole, not knowing whether a contribution may land in a place of intelligent violence or fearful consensus, of community-building or mediated empathy, and accepting all those possibilities and more.

We reach toward who and what is in the room. Collaboration in its fullest sense is inseparable from assets—human, physical, memorial. It requires performer, viewer-participant, architecture, contract, host, map, time; all these elements are democratic collaborators. In the honest incorporation of each to its fullest extent, as valuable natural resources, we attempt to create prescience and immediacy of experience. Not an illusion of alchemy, but actual dependence on and commitment to the unique circumstances of every event in time and place, every constitution of audience. It proves a rather rewarding partnership to agree to be incomplete within one another's company and diversity, even if only for 75 minutes at a time.

We reach for relevance, which is not to be confused with familiarity in
   all instances.
We reach for new and hybrid forms.
We reach for permission or, failing that, forgiveness.
We reach toward place as honesty, toward performer as facilitator, toward
   conversation as panacea—which it isn't, but few things are closer.

(MR)
We reach.
But, how do we reach?

Mike Pearson, founder of seminal performance company Brith Gof and Professor of Performance Studies at University of Wales, writes: "Performance resides primarily within a set of contracts and transactional conventions between two orders of participant—watchers and watched; spectators and performers; witnesses and protagonists—and in three sets of relationship: performer to performer, performer to spectator and vice versa, spectator to spectator. Significantly, each and all of these contracts is available for re-assessment and renegotiation."[1]

The idea of contract is at the heart of the work we focus on with performers. Pearson writes of relationships, but in the moment, for the performer, a contract is action. It is what I need from you, and it is the way I invite you to interact with me. For any event that functions in direct proportion to the level of participation the event engenders, negotiation is indeed constant.

Pearson also writes that "Rules, albeit fluid, constantly renegotiated understandings, help to communicate intention. Rules decide what can, and cannot, be done. . . . They require self and group organization to maximize the effort. . . . Rules give direction and purpose to the release of energy. Once they are agreed, there can be planning, organization, strategy, to achieve the desired effect. . . . Rules can be communicated to watchers who can begin to understand and appreciate the activity. And there may be a sequence or pattern—"I do it, now you do it"—if not plot."[2]

There are two key principles at work here for us. One is the way that rules, or parameters, allow us to create a safe if not always comfortable space by articulating clear expectations, tasks, and boundaries. And two is the way that a task, or series of tasks, acts as a dramaturgy. If, as in *BUILT*, you start the event by playing a one-person version of a game that you later play with six other people, this simple progression offers a satisfying recurrence that story and psychological arc might offer in other events.

INTRO #3: What we don't know
(MR)
Many artists approach theatre as an encounter with a text that leads to interpretation. They believe that in the space between the existing dramaturgy on the page and their own response to that dramaturgy will arise an understanding of what that text needs to communicate to speak into the world today. This is described as articulating a vision. This vision

then guides a process focused on bringing other artists to that vision and, through a collective act of will and effort, expressing that vision on the stage for others to experience. In this model, the text is a question, and the production is a clear response to that question.

There is a pursuit to move from what is not known to what is known. It is the known that is then placed on a stage to be witnessed.

Shannon and I approach theatre as an encounter with a question, a site or a query, that leads to investigation. We believe that in the collaborative space between the starting impulse and the work that occurs in the room(s) breathes an opportunity to move our questions into the world today. We pursue vision not as a solid immovable expression, but as a route to a space for encounter, exchange, and dialogue. The pursuit becomes a process. The process becomes a collective act of will and effort with a specific intention—to infect our audience/participants with our curiosity, and to compel them to join the quest.

There is a pursuit to move from what is not known to what you don't know. It is the not known at the intersection of the personal and the political, with you the participant bringing the personal, that becomes the stuff of experience.

Interruption

What is site-specific work?

(SS)

Working site-specifically extends such experience to a living, physicalized manifestation of that exact personal and political intersection. The term site-specific is problematic as terminology, in no small part because of the extraordinary elasticity with which it is applied, but it persists as useful currency, describing a host of visual, installation, sonic, and performance events that have experienced a surge of attention both academically and in practice over the last 50 years, and in the course of that time a number of other terms have joined it to define and refine the nuances between various practices. For us, working site-specifically holds a depth of connotation and responsibility. It is about integrity of architecture and form, but it is also about authenticity of experience, knowing you are in a real place, public or private. It is about the structural, utilitarian, and social history of every site, within itself, and unto its larger, physical context, as part of a community. It is about occupation, both ours as guest/interventionist/collaborator, but also the quotidian realities of its functions and infrastructure, both existing and possible, and the patterns and intricacies of its habitants or visitors. All are requisite integrations in the making of a piece whose content and intent incorporate constructive, investigative reverence to site.

(MR)
Site-specific performance is a time-based theatrical event that includes performer, audience, and a dynamic partnership with, and use of, architecture/ site which is not traditionally a setting for performance.

INTRO #4: Theory as situation
(SS)
If critique functions to analyze work in hindsight, theory can be a means to situate work in process, to intersect our inquiries with the work of other artists or social researchers. Cross-disciplinarily, it offers illumination, access, situation. The words of contemporary architects, art historians, dialogical artists, interventionists, urban theorists, geographers, and curators build new castles on the wide foundations of Michel Foucault, Roland Barthes, Michel de Certeau, Guy DeBord, Gaston Bachelard, and more, whose respective imprints are perhaps impossible to overestimate. Contemporary theory rarely functions as prescription, either in intent or in receipt/translation to practitioner, but instead as context, as furtherer of deep inquiry, as tether to the relevance of performance work in a greater cultural dialogue.

Architect and theorist Markus Miessen asserts a need for practitioners "operating from outside existing disciplinary networks, leaving behind conventional expertise whilst inventing new species of knowledge-space,"[3] working toward what curator and artist Hans Ulrich Obrist identifies as "breaking the consensus machine."[4] In such an event, the "practitioner is presented as an enabler, a facilitator of interaction that stimulates alternative debates and speculations."[5] The intersection of disciplinary ideologies and methodologies is a superior soil in which to grow dialogue-based, site-specific performance events. Again, relevance should not be mistaken for familiarity, and yet there is immense complexity in what is brought, as outsider, to a situation. Theory can be a useful outsider, an established situation, or even a mobile hypothesis, and thus, its requisite consumption.

It's also responsible output. Is the performance act an expression of knowledge (separate from a communication-based dissemination of facts)? Of reasoning? What is the practice-reason relationship offered to the event, inclusive of the presence of its authors, a live process, a participating audience, and the intent for differentiated experience within each cycle of the experiment? Anna Pakes discusses "art's claim to knowledge" in her paper "Art as Action or Art as Object? The Embodiment of Knowledge in Practice as Research," as a part of her ongoing studies in practice as research (PaR). She engages with "the question of whether the practice itself or the reflection upon it embodies the knowledge artistic action produces," articulating that "the originality requirement—in the production of new works and/or new knowledge—pushes artistic practice beyond [the tasks and frameworks of the everyday]."[6] Performance events in particular, as results of "collective production and collective action" operate within "an intersubjective context in which it is crucial to have a creative sensitivity to others participating in the process, to the materials at hand and to the evolving situation which heavily influences the decisions and circumstances in such an event." The decisions necessarily "arise out of the circumstances of the moment and are governed by a different, more flexible kind of rationality, sensitive to contingencies."[7]

BUILT was an event full of alternative occupations of space, physically, navigationally, and through encounters of information. Very early in the event, small audience groups traversed the space with performer tour guides who may share a moment of awe at the new skyline, lambast affordability, and then invite you to cram into a shower stall for a real discussion of density. It is hardly the experience you would usually have in such a site, as a potential condo-buyer, and yet as an intervention it invites a complex examination of the politics of belonging and the many prices of being an urban pioneer. Architectural models, trophies of monumental real estate possibility became uncontainable, as media brought their cars, pets, and human inhabitants alive, alternately occupying their tiny idyllic worlds by walking down the street, flying kites, scaling towers, or getting sucked up into the sky. An earlier experience of kitchen counters, supporting everything from food to iPods to choreography, eventually translated to large flat-panel video counters, employed to draw a map of a new vision of the city, created live from viewer-participant ideas, a map that served as evidence of the unrepeatable and unique experience of that group of participants, experts and non, in a democratized space of opinion and reflection.

If practice, our practice, is by design forwarding new forms, re-contextualizing or even displacing expertise, constructing access over consensus, then we are, in a sense, also building our own theories.

They emerge largely intuitively and unarticulated, through the tangible projects and our acts of collaboration, and through a body of work invested in progressing relationships between performance and dialogue, interaction and physical space, democracy and witness.

INTRO #5: Theory as muscle
(MR)

When we received the invitation to write about our work in the context of a theory/practice relationship, Shannon and I were excited. As we worked on two projects with this invitation in mind, fully aware that each day's process existed in relation to this particular writing task ahead of us, we occasionally grew intimidated by the mandate to articulate the connection between idea and choice. We even, at times, became overwhelmed at the prospect of teasing out two distinct but seemingly inseparable strands: an often unexpressed but present intellectual logic that guides us and the creative impulse that puts intuition at the core of artistic voice. We arrived, finally, at a tension that allowed us to approach this chapter as a challenge with a starting place—the belief that, for us, theory is an integrated set of skills, a muscle that allows practice to be strong. Without it, craft and vision are half what they might be; but, make the work about the muscle, and that strength can turn the endeavor into an exercise, not a fully formed piece of creative energy.

We could find instances in the worlds of installation and conceptual and performance and social change art in which audiences are involved in the act of making. There is no lack of history, or documentation, on the notion of participation as a phenomenon that crosses discipline, intention, and form.

Harder to find was theory that directly addressed events where signification attempted to blend metaphor and public reality with a goal of bringing strangers together in space and time to collectively strategize, or where the ethical muscle of conscience was placed alongside the communal muscle of responsibility, and a hybridized moment of spectacle/dialogue existed within an aesthetic framework closer to experimental performance than to community-based story sharing.

So, we set out to make the work.
And then, after, amidst evaluating what we accomplished, we begin to see paths already forged that we are stumbling onto, and, perhaps, some paths that we have begun to clear.

INTRO #6: Dialogue about dialogue

Between 2003 and 2005 we created a piece about public education in Oregon that traveled with a series of town hall performance dialogues around the state of Oregon for nine months. We were invited to perform for the State Legislature at the Capitol and facilitate a dialogue about the matters we had researched.

In 2006, we were asked by the Office of The Mayor of Portland to create a theatre and dialogue project to aid the city's Vision Project, a public listening initiative designed to engage 100,000 Portlanders in the drafting of a new City Plan. We created an event that blended narrative with question-and-answer style sessions placing fictional Portlanders and real Portlanders in contexts of problem solving together. The Mayor's staff transcribed and heard every proposal.

(SS)
Site-specific work allows us—through performance, facilitation, and specific strategies of inquiry and engagement—to transform diverse sites and circumstances into conversation spaces of "vulnerable receptivity"[8] between actor-facilitator and viewer-participant, into what Michael calls "civic dialogue with performance interruptions." The event is convergent with art historian and critic Grant Kester's research and analysis of "dialogical art," in which "conversation becomes an integral part of the work itself . . . reframed as an active, generative process that can help us speak and imagine beyond the limits of fixed identities, official discourse, and the perceived inevitability of partisan conflict."[9]

(MR)
In *Pedagogy of the Oppressed*, Paolo Freire wrote, "Problem-posing education bases itself on creativity and stimulates true reflection and action upon reality. . . . [B]anking theory and practice, as immobilizing and fixating forces, fail to acknowledge men and women as historical beings; problem-posing theory and practice take the people's historicity as their starting point."[10]

Theatre is not education.
But for me, there is a transaction involved in theatre that bears a strong correlation to the practice of education as elucidated by Freire.
Knowledge. Action. Empathy.

(SS)
Kester posits a series of essential considerations in the incorporation of dialogue into art practice, questions we navigate in the process of

making work, even as we encounter them in his analysis. "How do we form collective or communal identities without scapegoating those who are excluded from them? Is it possible to develop a cross-cultural dialogue without sacrificing the unique identities of individual speakers? And what does it mean for the artist to surrender the security of self-expression for the risk of intersubjective engagement?"[11]

(MR)
I think I knew this before I read Freire's words.
Or, I felt it.
I operated as if I knew it.

And Augusto Boal—whose Theatre of the Oppressed exists in relation to, and in dialogue with, Freire's work—knew this idea in his bones before he read these words.

And my earlier work with a program I founded, called Hope Is Vital, bore a visibly strong relation to Boal's work, although I had never read Boal.
I know many artists and teachers with the same experience.

(SS)
These inquiries are at the heart of participation, place, and dialogue, and where responsibility and responsiveness fall in the making of an event that includes and requires viewer voice.

(MR)
Ideas and practice sometimes run like a current through people's minds across the globe. And then someone articulates an idea . . . and, suddenly, practice has context. There is affirmation. There is amplification. There is expansion. There is relationship.

Freire didn't invent dialogue. But he framed a way to consider how dialogue did and didn't manifest in relation to power. A core element of traditional Western Drama is the relationship of power, or status, to character, relationship, and narrative. Boal took Freire's proposal, wedded it to his understanding and critique of Aristotelian dramatic structure, and re-framed the performance process as a powerful tool for dialogue.

We can do this work without knowing who Freire or Boal are.

We can feed an audience while asking them to consider where they do and don't want to live.

We can invite an audience to write their hopes and we can speak back to them amidst song, dance, and complication.

We can ask 60 strangers to create a values census using technology that allows them to remain invisible, yet seen.

We can make a unique, playful space for meaningful dialogue. . . .

The question becomes, with Freire and Boal deep in my muscles, how much further have I been able to go?

It's hard to know. We want, or I want, to believe that I hold within myself the potential for original thought; for discovery; for imagining into the world that which didn't exist before I took on the task at hand. But as our bodies and minds remake themselves cell by cell, year after year, we are new—*and* we are what we have previously taken in. If my musculature gets built on the body of knowledge I have learned, then what comes after inevitably stands on the shoulders of what has come before. And the muscles of theory give my body, my self, the strength to create.

INTRO #7: Enter *BUILT*—introduction as conclusion
(SS)

Lateral concrete monolith, partial glass facade looks out, obstructed, onto an infant micro-tropolis. What was once a brown field at the river's edge, just south of downtown Portland, now gives literal rise to some of the tallest buildings in the region, modernist steel towers plated with floor to ceiling windows whose arteries are proud LEED—pioneers of innovative air and water systems. You're here to see a show, not buy a piece of the sky. Is this your vision of Portland future tense? Where would you choose to live? And with whom are you willing to share your sidewalks, your parks, your schools, your public living rooms? The building itself, a soon-to-be-former "sales and interpretation space" is, to some, beautiful. Open, airy, the concrete shell seems levitated by sunlight, pervasive white walls giving way to the raw ceiling—evidence of the building's former, less glamorous life as a storage facility.

The space is for us, as artists, "the chance to conceive the site as something more than a place,"[12] pushing the work's "relationship to the actuality of a location (as site) and the social conditions of the institutional frame (as site)"[13] per art historian Miwon Kwon's pioneering descriptions of site-specific or site-oriented work. In the case of *BUILT*, site is architecture, site is city, site is circumstance, "a means of encountering and creating other maps of the cultural space."[14]

You enter. You are a guest—you don't live here; no one does. It is a place not for living but for imagination of living. In real estate, this manifests in granite countertops, modern light fixtures, movies of sweeping vistas of river and skyline, and warm, welcoming, well-dressed staff. In performance, in *BUILT*, this manifests in the catalyzed conversations of city stakeholders in the fast-changing urban landscape that is Portland, toward Kwon's discursive site "delineated as a field of knowledge, intellectual exchange, or cultural debate."[15]

In the course of 75 minutes in the space, you will talk to your neighbors, master-plan cities from only scratch and priorities, be fed, ask questions, answer questions, have experiences that confirm your expectations and then defy them, and the confirmation-defiance relationship may well be opposite from the person standing next to you. You will witness a site physically explored to its edges, up-on-above-below-between-within, performers occupying other lives in one moment, and baring their own the next, before finding out about yours. You will hear single voices that don't always get proper shrift, and a chorus of voices who are just like you, in that they may have never set foot in this place before today.

Architect and educator Bernard Tschumi argues that architecture "cannot be dissociated from the events that 'happen' in it,"[16] going on to advocate "exploration of the disjunction between expected form and expected use,"[17] which is explicitly our task in the making of site-specific events, particularly for myself in a designer role.

We aren't making place in the way that an architect shapes the floor plan, or a mason lays the bricks, or even a multimedia exhibit company installs the interactive map and touch screens; we are re-making place, with and despite all its existing intentions, failures, and resources, every single time an event transpires. In each act of performance, we work toward intersecting, in live time, "sequences of transformation and sequences of spaces."[18] Immediate, dynamic site allows us to have context built into or carved out of a real place, with physical and human history in it, instead of from scratch, foregrounding function over decoration, nativism over manufacture.

In content, and by design, at the heart of *BUILT* is the city—invisible, radiant, instant, meta, creative, endless, shadow, generic, scattered, convertible, no-stop, post-bubble, topographical, unfinished, imaginative, portable, and a right.[19] A city is the physical, dynamic and continuous expression of consent and dissent. It is a conversation, structural and social. The performance event attempts all this: to host a sustained moment of co-existence, forced and voluntary, visualized out of scale of interpersonal experience, into a scale of intention and dialogue, beyond the sounds of the street, the concrete of the sidewalks, the traffic lights and crowding or emptiness, the people accidental, trapped and fluid within participation.

Welcome.

Notes

1. Mike Pearson and Michael Shanks, *Theatre/Archaelogy* (London: Routledge, 2001), 20.
2. Ibid., 19.
3. Shumon, Basar and Markus Miessen, *Did Someone Say Participate? An Atlas of Spatial Practice* (Cambridge: MIT Press, 2006), 24.
4. See Hans Ulrich Obrist quoted in ibid., 25.
5. Ibid., 25.
6. Anna Pakes, "Art as Action or Art as Object? The Embodiment of Knowledge in Practice as Research," *Working Papers in Art and Design* 3, 2004. Retrieved from URL http://sitem.herts.ac.uk/artdes_research/papers/wpades/vol3/apfull.html ISSN 1466-4917 (accessed May 21, 2011).
7. Ibid.
8. See Grant H. Kester, *Conversation Pieces: Community and Communication in Modern Art* (Berkeley: University of California Press, 2004), 13.
9. Ibid., 8.
10. Paul Freire, *Pedagogy of the Oppressed* (New York: Continuum, 2000), 83.
11. Kester, *Conversation Pieces*, 8. In the last half of this sentence Kester loosely pulls from Ken Hirschkop, *Mikhail Bakhtin: An Aesthetic for Democracy* (New York: Oxford University Press, 1999), 107.
12. Miwon Kwon, *One Place After Another: Site-Specific Art and Locational Identity* (Cambridge: MIT Press, 2004), 30.
13. Ibid., 26.
14. Fiona Wilkie, "Mapping the Terrain: A Survey of Site-Specific Performance in Britain," *New Theatre Quarterly*, 18.70 (May 2002), 144.
15. Kwon, *One Place After Another*, 26.
16. Bernard Tschumi, *Architecture and Disjunction* (Cambridge: MIT Press, 1996), 139.
17. Ibid., 147.
18. Ibid., 156.

19. This sentence includes a list of city descriptors made known by the work of many artists/architects/theorists who are not otherwise cited in this piece, but who, for the author (SS), both as a designer and in regards to the specific content of *BUILT* which was urbanism-centric, are extremely influential in their work, writings, and the visible exchanges and compromises between product and idea, which is what we attempt to dig up a bit in this chapter as well. Credited, in order, the city descriptors come from Italo Calvino, Le Corbusier, Archigram (although there are other uses of it as well), Paul Virilio, Charles Landry and Franco Bianchini, Gabriele Basilico, Ricky Burdett/Devan Sudjic, Rem Koolhaas, Robert Neuwirth, German Pavillion at the Venice Biennale 06, 11, Andrea Branzi, Momoyo Kajima and Yoshiharu Tsukamoto (Atelier Bow-Wow), Martin Aurand, Thomas Bender, Alan Blum, Vito Acconci, Henri Lefebvre.

Index